# Hayek's Living Legacy in Economics, Philosophy and Policy

NEW THINKING IN POLITICAL ECONOMY

**Series Editor:** Peter J. Boettke, *George Mason University, USA*

New Thinking in Political Economy aims to encourage scholarship in the intersection of the disciplines of politics, philosophy and economics. It has the ambitious purpose of reinvigorating political economy as a progressive force for understanding social and economic change.

The series is an important forum for the publication of new work analysing the social world from a multidisciplinary perspective. With increased specialization (and professionalization) within universities, interdisciplinary work has become increasingly uncommon. Indeed, during the 20th century, the process of disciplinary specialization reduced the intersection between economics, philosophy and politics and impoverished our understanding of society. Modern economics in particular has become increasingly mathematical and largely ignores the role of institutions and the contribution of moral philosophy and politics.

New Thinking in Political Economy will stimulate new work that combines technical knowledge provided by the 'dismal science' and the wisdom gleaned from the serious study of the 'worldly philosophy'. The series will reinvigorate our understanding of the social world by encouraging a multidisciplinary approach to the challenges confronting society in the new century.

For a full list of Edward Elgar published titles, including the titles in this series, visit our website at www.e-elgar.com.

# Hayek's Living Legacy in Economics, Philosophy and Policy

## 50 Years Beyond his Nobel Prize

*Edited by*

Alicja Sielska

*Assistant Professor, Institute of Economic Sciences, Faculty of Law, Administration and Economics, University of Wrocław, Poland; Researcher, University of New York, Prague, the Czech Republic and Senior Fellow, Ludwig von Mises Institute of Economic Education, Poland*

Joanna Turowska

*Fellow, Ludwig von Mises Institute of Economic Education, Poland*

Krzysztof Turowski

*Lecturer, Theoretical Computer Science Department, Jagiellonian University, Kraków, Poland and Fellow, Ludwig von Mises Institute of Economic Education, Poland*

NEW THINKING IN POLITICAL ECONOMY

Edward Elgar
PUBLISHING

Cheltenham, UK • Northampton, MA, USA

Cover image: 19740101_PD3340 (Friedrich von Hayek, Nobelpreisverleihung 1974) Votava / brandstaetter images / picturedesk.com.



Published by

Edward Elgar Publishing Limited
The Lypiatts
15 Lansdown Road
Cheltenham
Glos GL50 2JA
UK

Edward Elgar Publishing, Inc.
William Pratt House
9 Dewey Court
Northampton
Massachusetts 01060
USA

Authorised representative in the EU for GPSR queries only: Easy Access System Europe – Mustamäe tee 50, 10621 Tallinn, Estonia, gpsr.requests@easproject.com

A catalogue record for this book is available from the British Library

Library of Congress Control Number: 2026932088

This book is available electronically in the Elgaronline Economics subject collection
https://doi.org/10.4337/9781035394227

MIX
Paper | Supporting responsible forestry
FSC® C013604

ISBN 978 1 0353 9423 4 (cased)
ISBN 978 1 0353 9422 7 (eBook)
ISBN 978 1 0353 9421 0 (ePub)

Printed and bound by CPI Group (UK) Ltd, Croydon, CR0 4YY

# Contents

# List of contributors

**Mateusz Benedyk** is Assistant Professor at the Institute of Economic Sciences of the University of Wrocław.

**Eamonn Butler** is Director of the Adam Smith Institute.

**Per L. Bylund** is Associate Professor of Entrepreneurship and Johnny D. Pope Chair in the School of Entrepreneurship at Oklahoma State University.

**Kristoffer Mousten Hansen** is Research Fellow at the Institute for Economic Policy at Leipzig University.

**Mihaela Ifrim** is Professor at the Faculty of Economics of the Alexandru Ioan Cuza University, Iași.

**Aliaksandr Kavaliou** is Professor of Economics at the Belarusian National Technical University, Minsk.

**Hansjörg Klausinger** is Professor at the Vienna University of Economics and Business.

**Tomáš Krištofóry** is Researcher at the Institute of Economic Research, Slovak Academy of Sciences.

**Phillip W. Magness** is the David J. Theroux Chair in Political Economy the Independent Institute.

**Emilio Mazza** is Professor at IULM University of Milan.

**Alberto Mingardi** is Assistant Professor of History of Political Thought at the IULM University of Milan.

**Stefano Moroni** is Professor of Urban Policies and Planning at the Polytechnic University of Milan.

**Olga Peniaz** is Lecturer in Economic Sciences at the Catholic University of the West, Angers.

**Przemysław Rapka** is Assistant Professor at the Department of Economics of the University of Economics in Katowice.

**Alicja Sielska** is Assistant Professor in the Faculty of Law, Administration and Economics at the University of Wrocław, Researcher at the University of New York in Prague, and Senior Fellow at the Ludwig von Mises Institute of Economic Education.

**Josef Šíma** is Professor at the Department of International Business of the Metropolitan University Prague.

**Miłosz Ślepowroński** is PhD student at the Jagiellonian University in Kraków.

**Joanna Turowska** is Fellow at the Ludwig von Mises Institute of Economic Education.

**Krzysztof Turowski** is Lecturer in the Theoretical Computer Science Department at Jagiellonian University in Kraków and Fellow at the Ludwig von Mises Institute of Economic Education.

# Acknowledgments

We wish to extend our deepest gratitude to Alfred Wirth, Anne-Marie Sweeney and the Wirth Institute for Austrian and Central European Studies—in particular Alexander Carpenter and Sylvia Chrobak—for their generous sponsorship of the Wirth Institute event on Austrian Economics, marking the 50th anniversary of the Nobel Prize in Economic Sciences awarded to Friedrich August von Hayek. Their support made it possible to bring together scholars from around the world for a fruitful exchange of ideas, and we are sincerely appreciative of their contribution to the success of both the event and this publication.

# Introduction: F. A. Hayek and his living legacy, fifty years after the Nobel Prize

**Alicja Sielska, Joanna Turowska, and Krzysztof Turowski**

"... the Nobel Prize confers on an individual an authority which in economics no man ought to possess..."
(F. A. von Hayek 1874 – from a speech at the Nobel Banquet)

From the late 1920s to the early 1930s, the ideas of Austrian economists were marginalized within the economic community. The departure of its leading figures from Vienna in the 1930s, prompted by personal and subsequently political reasons, precipitated the virtual demise of this school of thought. Subsequent blows came when Paul Samuelson began introducing tools from the exact sciences into economics, while Milton Friedman championed his version of positive economics. During these difficult times for the Austrian School of Economics, the primary figures who carried the tradition forward were Israel Kirzner, Ludwig Lachmann, and Murray Rothbard, while Friedrich August von Hayek shifted his focus to other disciplines, including political philosophy, law, and psychology.

Fortunately, the 1970s welcomed a resurgence of interest in the Austrian ideas, coinciding with the collapse of the post-war Keynesian consensus. The 1974 Sveriges Riksbank Prize in Economic Sciences in Memory of Alfred Nobel was awarded to Hayek—alongside Gunnar Myrdal—for "pioneering work in the theory of money and economic fluctuations and for their penetrating analysis of the interdependence of economic, social and institutional phenomena."[1] Our teacher and late friend, Prof Witold Kwaśnicki, used to say that since the Nobel Prize was awarded to an Austrian economist, it became customary to remark that economics is the only field where the highest honor can be awarded simultaneously for entirely opposing views—it is no secret that both laureates were ideological adversaries who also held profound personal disagreements.

Hayek himself expressed doubts about the legitimacy of the Nobel Prize in Economics, and in the acceptance speech, he pointed out his opposition to creating it in the first place. He advanced two main arguments: first, that the prize tends to reward proponents of temporarily fashionable ideas, though he immediately added that his own recognition might serve as a counterexample. Second, he contended that the prize confers an unwarranted authority upon laureates in the eyes of non-specialists, that is, politicians, journalists, civil servants, and the general public, who may consequently perceive them as qualified to pronounce on all societal issues. Even worse, as Hayek pointed out, some laureates might even develop a sense of obligation to comment publicly on matters beyond their expertise. For this reason, he argued, they ought to swear a kind of Hippocratic Oath before the prize committee, pledging not to add their public authority to the claims beyond their sphere of competence.

The Nobel lecture contains only a handful of the many profound insights that one can find in Hayekian oeuvre. The year 2024 marked exactly fifty years since the Nobel Committee recognized Hayek's achievements and 125 years since the birth of one of the most famous Austrian economists. It is therefore an excellent opportunity not only to reflect on his legacy but, above all, to attempt to apply it to contemporary challenges. We believe that by shedding new light on Hayek's theories, we aim to demonstrate that he is not only relevant as a historical figure but that his insights continue to offer valuable applications today. If contemporary academics and intellectuals were to draw more inspiration from Hayek, they could greatly benefit from his deep understanding of markets, knowledge, and institutions. As we argue, his ideas touch on many critical points in modern research.

Hayek is widely known for his insights into business cycles and capital theory, his analysis of information's role in markets, his idea of spontaneous order, and his critique of central planning's limits represent major advances in economic thought. Moreover, his interdisciplinary research program—spanning economics, political philosophy, law, and psychology—integrated a broad set of fundamental issues about social organization and individual liberty.

The collection covers a broad range of topics related to Hayek's thought, with the intention of bringing diverse contemporary scholarship of the Austrian School and Hayek in particular to the forefront. Moreover, we wanted to make Hayek relevant for the twenty-first century in a two-fold fashion. On the one hand, we wanted to get a better understanding of Friedrich Hayek's thought itself, diving also into less explored dimensions of his thought, e.g. about his views on the role of religion in society, his critique of the welfare state, or his unique reading of David Hume. However, it often comes with an emphasis on considerations that could be relevant for today, for example about his insights on the role of intellectuals in the modern world. On the other hand, we wanted to engage with modern debates not only in Austrian economics, but also in other social sciences, for example by fruitfully employing his modes of analysis for the contemporary views on entrepreneurship, monetary theory, and macroeconomics. By drawing on diverse perspectives and intellectual connections (e.g. to evolutionary game theory), these essays contribute to a deeper understanding of Hayek's relevance for modern economic and social thought.

The book is divided into thirteen thematic chapters, each exploring different aspects of Hayek's ideas. Eamonn Butler examines *Law, Legislation and Liberty*, famous but complex work on legal and political theory, where Hayek argues that social, economic, and legal institutions evolve organically through cultural adaptation rather than deliberate design. He highlights the book's central theme of spontaneous order, where social rules and norms emerge over time, providing a framework for a stable, free, and prosperous society. However, he also critiques the structural flaws, noting the long gestation period of the book, its shifting priorities, and at times disjointed arguments. In *Why the Intellectuals Are Still Drawn to Socialism: Revisiting Hayek's Warning at 75 Years*, Phillip W. Magness explores F. A. Hayek's argument that socialism has historically been pursued by intellectuals rather than the working class. He argues that the prominence of Karl Marx in academia happened not due to the validity of his economic theories but rather to political and ideological forces, particularly the impact of the 1917 Bolshevik Revolution. He reiterates Hayek's warning about the susceptibility of intellectuals to fashionable yet flawed ideas, highlighting how they spread through ideological trends, rather than because of their empirical grounding.

Stefano Moroni also revisits the idea of spontaneous order, and argues that in Hayek we can actually find two distinct theories: the spontaneous evolution of social institutions and the spontaneous order of actions. He contends these ideas were often conflated, although the first describes how the evolution of social institutions involves a gradual, unintended process of rule formation through group selection, while the second captures how individuals coordinate within a market or society through abstract rules. In short, the evolution of institutions stores accumulated knowledge over generations; the spontaneous order of actions generates dynamic, real-time information, particularly in markets.

In subsequent chapters, Mihaela Ifrim, Josef Šíma, and Tomáš Krištofóry reexamine Hayek's perspectives on welfare state and religion, respectively. Even though concerned with such diverse topics, both contributions highlight his strong interest in social orders and their evolutionary and moral underpinnings, while at the same time acknowledging the limits of knowledge and its dispersed, decentralized character. Next, Emilio Mazza and Alberto Mingardi provide a thorough reconstruction of a lifelong intellectual influence that the famous Scottish philosopher David Hume had on Hayek's thinking about knowledge, law, and politics.

Later chapters provide a deep dive into the intricacies of Hayekian economic theory. Per Bylund investigates an often-overlooked aspect of Hayek's work: his implicit theory of entrepreneurship and its function in driving market efficiency and adaptation. He argues that his insights on market processes, competition, and knowledge implicitly acknowledge the entrepreneur's central role in economic coordination and innovation. Similarly, Przemysław Rapka provides a new analysis of Hayek's business cycle theory, particularly his underappreciated insights on investment dynamics. He argues that Hayek's approach explains why investment responses to interest rate changes are not immediate or uniform, shedding light on modern financial crises and central banking policies in a way not captured by mainstream macroeconomic models. The chapter by Kristoffer Mousten Hansen revisits the long-standing and still hotly debated issue in Austrian capital theory over the graphical representation of production structures. This chapter critically defends core Rothbardian insights about trapezoids while incorporating new developments in capital theory. In turn, Mateusz Benedyk outlines Hayekian criticism of stabilizing the level of nominal spending as a monetary policy rule as incompatible with his business cycle and monetary theory. Finally, Olga Peniaz and Aliaksandr Kavaliou's *Bitcoin in Light of the Austrian Theory of Money* applies Austrian monetary theory to the rise of Bitcoin, assessing its compatibility with Carl Menger's evolutionary theory of money, Ludwig von Mises' regression theorem, and Hayek's advocacy of currency competition potential as an alternative to centralized state fiat currency regimes.

The book closes with a chapter by Miłosz Ślepowroński. He compares Hayek's distinction between micro- and macrocosmic orders (localized personal relationships versus the extended order of markets) with contemporary evolutionary game theory, particularly the work of Ken Binmore. While both thinkers warn against applying small-group moral norms to the broader economy, Ślepowroński argues that in evolutionary research there is a more fluid interaction between egalitarian impulses and market mechanisms, complicating this strict separation envisioned by Hayek.

As evident in this short overview, this book presents a broad coverage of Hayek's intellectual legacy. Hayek himself considered it dangerous to treat Nobel laureates as authorities possessing remedies for all societal problems. Nevertheless, certain solutions proposed by the Austrian economist can be successfully applied to understand contemporary challenges—an insight we hope readers of this book will likewise recognize.

## NOTE

1. https://www.nobelprize.org/prizes/economic-sciences/1974/press-release/

# 1. Hayek's *Law, Legislation, and Liberty*—a great book, but not a good book

**Eamonn Butler**

## THE IMPORTANCE OF HAYEK'S THOUGHT

F. A. Hayek (1899–1992) was one of the most important social thinkers of the twentieth century. Though awarded the 1974 Nobel Prize in Economic Science for his economic writings, he was a polymath, raised in Vienna in a family of academics. His wide and deep understanding of economics, political theory, law, the history of ideas, evolution, human psychology, information science, and epistemology enabled him to bring all of these elements to his classical liberal approach to the study of social, political, and economic life. This breadth of understanding would show in many of his books, none more so than *The Fatal Conceit* (Hayek, 1988).

In the 1920s and 1930s, Hayek famously debated John Maynard Keynes, whose fame as an economist he nearly matched. His wartime book *The Road to Serfdom* (Hayek, 1944) gave an intellectual explanation of how easily the social democracy of a civilized country could slide into totalitarianism. Hayek's aim in it was to show how a naïve acceptance of the idea of social democracy can lead us, step by step, into a totalitarian nightmare. Social democracy was a popular idea at the time, being seen as a 'third way' between individualism and communism. But, Hayek explained, it still required an apparatus of compulsion to impose its vision. And unfortunately, that power of compulsion provides the very tool kit that less benign rulers need to entrench their tyranny.

Hugely successful, *The Road to Serfdom* influenced many prominent people, including notably the UK Prime Minister Winston Churchill and a young Battle of Britain pilot, Antony Fisher, who would go on to found a network of pro-freedom think tanks around the world. And later, Hayek's writings on business cycles, inflation, markets, and economic management would influence world leaders such as Ronald Reagan, Margaret Thatcher in the 1970s and 1980s, and more recently many others, from Mart Laar in Estonia to Javier Milei in Argentina.

Over the postwar decades, however, Hayek's mind was turning more and more to evolutionary explanations of social institutions—such as our ideas of justice, our laws, institutions, customs, manners, traditions, and economic structures—and how important this evolutionary process was to our lives. The early signs of this thinking can be found in *The Road to Serfdom*, but they come more clearly into existence in Hayek's much larger book, *The Constitution of Liberty* (Hayek, 1960), and culminate in *Law, Legislation and Liberty.*[1]

*The Constitution of Liberty* was informed by four decades of Hayek's thinking about the nature and origin of social, political, and economic institutions, and his personal experience of their fragility. Its first part, 'The Value of Freedom,' develops the philosophy underpinning and justifying a free society, and it delivers a robust critique of the main intellectual challenges to this view. The second part, 'Freedom and the Law,' gives an account of the growth and development of the rule of law, of the concept of justice, and of common law as the deep foundations and essential safeguards of a free society. The third part, 'Freedom in the Welfare State,' shows how much current public policy, particularly on welfare issues such as social security, housing, education, healthcare, and redistributive taxation, is at odds with the principles of liberty that Hayek had explained and developed in the earlier two parts. And he ventures some constitutional principles that he hopes might help protect the free society against such unprincipled assaults.

This structure, and the broad themes within it, anticipates the tripartite structure and themes of *Law, Legislation and Liberty*. Indeed, Hayek conceived *Law, Legislation and Liberty* as an elaboration of those emerging themes, filling some gaps and putting more detail on a number of its points.

This new book would expand 'Freedom and the Law,' developing the evolutionary explanation of our very deep notions of justice and would show how vital they are to the origin, development, and growth of successful societies. It would explain how these ideas are undermined by many contemporary political ideologies. Hayek intended that the new book would also take on those ideologies (as indeed it did, in *The Mirage of Social Justice* [Hayek, 1976]). And it would lay out in greater detail the constitutional principles and institutions that are necessary to ensure that the abstract and impersonal *rules of justice* were no longer conflated with the specific *commands* needed to organize the state.

*Law, Legislation and Liberty* (see Butler, 2025) highlights the dangers of imagining that we can replace our evolving social institutions wholesale by a social structure that might be more to our liking and that we might consider less 'chaotic' and more 'rational.' Drawing on Hayek's understanding of evolutionary theory, it explains that such social engineering can never match the 'wisdom' encapsulated in institutions that have evolved over centuries and millennia and is consequently doomed to the sort of failure he wrote of in *The Road to Serfdom.* As part of this, the book criticizes the very idea of social justice; it explains the widespread discontent people have against democracy today and proposes a new constitution designed to protect our evolved institutions and our personal freedom for the future.

Though Hayek was thinking about this new book from the early 1960s, ill health meant that it was the mid-1970s before the appearance of the first volume, *Rules and Order* (Hayek, 1973). This was followed at three-year intervals by the next two volumes, *The Mirage of Social Justice* (Hayek, 1976) and *The Political Order of a Free People* (Hayek, 1979).

## THE ORIGINS AND THEMES OF *LAW, LEGISLATION AND LIBERTY*

### The Gestation of the Book

From the 1950s, Hayek had been thinking about how social, legal, and economic ideas all fit together. In *The Sensory Order* (Hayek, 1952), he explained how the human mind is not something 'given' but adapts and evolves through experience. This is why our minds have evolved in ways that facilitate human interaction, communication, and indeed cultural evolution. He began to think that this last facility of cultural evolution might be the key principle by which to explain the development of human institutions such as law, morals, and markets.

As *The Constitution of Liberty* explained, this was an idea with a long history, particularly within classical liberal thinking, starting long before Charles Darwin developed his theory of evolution (Darwin, 1859). Traces are found in the work of the seventeenth-century liberal political philosopher John Locke (Locke, 1689), and it was further developed by the eighteenth-century scholars of the Scottish Enlightenment. The social scientist Adam Ferguson famously noted that "nations stumble upon establishments, which are indeed the result of human action, but not the execution of any human design" (Ferguson, 1767, 183). And the economist and moral philosopher Adam Smith wrote of the invisible hand that "promote[s] an end which was no part of his [agent's] intention" (Smith, 1776, II, 35).

Hayek called this idea of the unplanned evolution of our social institutions 'spontaneous order.' But having introduced the concept in *The Constitution of Liberty*, he came to believe that more work was needed to explain how it came about and worked. His ideas on this started to come together in 1962, after he read *Freedom and the Law*, a book by his friend the Italian lawyer and philosopher Bruno Leoni (Leoni, 1961). It explained the importance of common law—the sort of law that evolves through the decisions and precedents laid down by judges of disputes in the civil courts—for the growth and adaptability of society and the freedom of the individuals who comprise it. To Hayek, common law seemed to be a prime example of the evolution of social institutions; and our notion of justice, which common law judges aimed to serve and uphold, seemed to be the very foundation of it. He resolved to write a 'little pamphlet' on the subject.

Relocating from the University of Chicago to the University of Freiburg in 1962 gave Hayek access to an extensive library and a vibrant liberal academic body with whom to discuss his ideas. The 'little pamphlet' fast became a 'small book,' and then a much larger one, as Hayek worked up his ideas in articles, essays, and lectures, many of which appeared in *Studies in Philosophy, Politics and Economics* (Hayek, 1967). By 1968 he could report that he had the first of its three parts of the proposed book 'in semi-finished form' and rougher drafts of the rest. But the work slowed after another move to Salzburg, where he suffered debilitating illness (possibly due to undiagnosed heart attacks) and depression. He would not recover sufficiently to work on the book for some years.

Now, in his early 70s and in imperfect health, Hayek's priority became getting each of the three parts out as they were completed, rather than as a single large work. Accordingly, the first volume, *Rules and Order*, appeared in 1973. A year later, he was awarded the Nobel Prize in Economics, which boosted his morale but led to a time-consuming round of visits and lectures that again interrupted his writing. By then, he had also concluded that much more work was needed to challenge the increasingly popular idea of 'social justice.' This thought wrenched the book in a new direction and required major expansion and revision of the second volume, *The Mirage of Social Justice*, which appeared only in 1976. But then there were new distractions. Hayek's mounting concern with inflation made him prioritize his output on that (Hayek, 1972, 1978), and he was also working on his long-cherished but ultimately unsuccessful idea of staging a major international debate on the question of whether socialism had been a mistake.

So, it was 1979 before the appearance of the last volume, *The Political Order of a Free People*. It reads like a book that the author is rushing to finish; by this point, Hayek was thinking that this might be his last chance to create a systematic defense of individual freedom and of the evolution of law and culture on which it rests.

## The Themes in *Law, Legislation and Liberty*

When, in 1982, *Law, Legislation and Liberty* was finally re-published in a single volume, as its author originally intended, Hayek's 'Consolidated Preface' apologized for the many weaknesses in it that had resulted from its long and difficult gestation. The self-criticism was fully justified. *Law, Legislation and Liberty* is a great book, but as Hayek readily admitted, it is not a *good* book.

*Law, Legislation and Liberty* is a great book in the sense that it is monumental in scope and presents ideas that are remarkably original and of huge importance to our understanding of society and its development. It demonstrates with great thoroughness how our laws, morals, and institutions evolve. It reminds us that this cultural evolution necessarily works at the level of the individual, making it vital that we respect individuals' freedom to act—and so provide the diversity that any evolutionary process needs to work through. And yet, almost paradoxically, the preservation and prosperity of human society depend on individuals having evolved to behave in broadly predictable ways and respect broadly established values and principles.

Hayek calls these regularities of action *rules*. We might not be able to explain why we behave in these predictable ways, nor understand how the overall social order depends on and emerges from our doing so. But just as the rules of the most popular games endure through the generations because they produce good games that we want to play again, the regular patterns of our actions and interactions endure because they produce a society that survives and thrives.

In our rationalist age, we have come to believe that we can change the outcome of these evolved (and still evolving) processes and create a result that is more to our liking, or that we suppose will be more rational. But that vision is a mirage, says Hayek. It almost always produces unintended and disastrous results. We need constitutional safeguards to save us from this error, to protect the freedom on which our institutional evolution depends, and to deny politicians and planners the power to usurp it.

How these profound ideas are expressed in *Law, Legislation and Liberty* is less than perfect. In his long period of ill health, Hayek's ideas and priorities changed. He had become much more concerned about the rising clamor for 'social justice' (he always put the phrase in inverted commas), forcing him to rewrite large sections. He was also alarmed by the growing disillusionment with democracy and anxious to develop solutions to it. So the argument lurches in different directions, while the book contains the gaps, repetitions, and changes in pace that betray something written over a long period.

## Cultural Evolution

The unifying theme of *Law, Legislation and Liberty* is *cultural evolution*: the idea that our social structures are not the product of our deliberate creation, but have evolved with us, and have endured because they help us to flourish. That is why our conscious attempts to replace them with some new vision, such as social justice, are not only inadequate to the task, but also risk fracturing our complex social fabric and risk visiting disaster upon us. The fate of the free society rests on us preserving the conditions that allow our social structures to adapt and evolve, and on robustly protecting them from their destruction at the hands of social engineers, however well-intentioned.

The book acknowledges the tension that exists in all forms of evolutionary theory: in this case, the delicate balance between the progressive benefits that stem from the creative spontaneity of free individuals and the more solid base for human interactions that stems from the restrictive principles of law, justice, morality, tradition, and custom. Human freedom, says Hayek, depends on getting this balance right. If individuals' free, voluntary cooperation is to flourish and prosper, there has to be some mutual understanding that comes through shared and respected principles of justice and morality, and shared traditions, dispositions, manners, and habits. Most importantly, we need to accept what we should *not* do and how we should *not* behave toward others. And yet, for our social institutions to evolve and grow, individuals must be free enough to challenge these principles and thereby enable them to adapt to meet the needs and opportunities brought about by changing events and circumstances.

## Evolving Orders

*Law, Legislation and Liberty* explains in great detail how individuals' following of general *rules* of action builds into a functioning but unplanned overall *order*. Hayek begins by noting how very important to us such rules are. We have deep feelings about justice and injustice, enforced by laws, which discourage others from subjecting us to violence or intimidation. We observe manners that make it easier to get along with others. We share a cultural understanding. The culture, the manners, and the laws may vary from place to place, but we find some form of rule-guided social order everywhere. We would not last very long if we did not have them.

The market system is another *rule*-guided social *order*, one that has brought us astonishing material benefits. It has made us hundreds of times richer than our ancestors just a few hundred years ago. But it was not deliberately planned by us: it is so complex and non-intuitive that no human mind could have done that. On the contrary, the rules of the market *order* arose, grew, and persisted because they worked and helped us flourish. They *evolved*, and we evolved along with them. Our minds evolved to dispose us to follow and learn the behaviors that promoted these orders and to avoid the behaviors that disrupted them.

We have evolved, says Hayek, to be guided by and learn the *rules* of behavior that—in ways we hardly understand—produce various kinds of overall *order*. But evolution works through variation and selection. So, people have to be able to challenge those *rules* and do something different that they believe will bring benefits to themselves and others. If they are mistaken and their new practices prove unhelpful, their experiment will be abandoned. If they are right, their new ways will spread and the whole of society will benefit.

In his essay 'Notes on the Evolution of Systems of Rules of Conduct' in *Studies in Philosophy, Politics and Economics* (Hayek, 1967), Hayek gives us some examples that help illustrate his point. The complicated societies of social insects such as bees are one: different bees perform the various tasks needed to sustain the hive, and yet there is no conscious mind that is instructing and managing them. There are examples in human behavior too: when people take a shortcut across a field, for instance, they naturally take the easiest route. When a person walks across, they walk on the earth that has been compacted, and the grass trampled. As more people follow the same flattened route, they gradually wear away a path, which makes things even easier for all who follow. But it is nobody's *intention* to make a path; that result is simply the happy outcome of their regular behavior.

Another example, *language*, demonstrates how complex human social *orders* can become. Plainly, we benefit from being able to communicate with other human beings—warning them of danger, perhaps, or telling them where they might find food. A series of grunts and gestures might be sufficient for some such purposes; but by following *rules* of grammar, we can put much more complex ideas into sentences and share them with others who follow the same *rules*. The actual words and grammar may vary from one place to the next. But through sharing them, humans can communicate very sophisticated ideas that help them to thrive. We did not *intend* to create complex languages at any stage of this process; that was just the useful result of us acting in these regular ways. And, underscoring the point that complex orders are not the result of deliberate action, is the remarkable fact that often we follow the rules of grammar without fully understanding them or even being able to express them in words.

The evolution of the economic *order*—of property, markets, competition and the price system—is another example. It probably began when people started to have possessions of their own, and then started to barter their property (or their services) in exchange for someone else's that they valued more. Gradually, as the number of people doing this grew, individuals would learn how much of one good they could commonly exchange for another. Such was the origin of prices. But from there, the price system has developed to embrace hundreds of millions of products and services all over the globe. And the reason it has spread is that it is incredibly useful and beneficial to us.

No human mind could have designed something so vast, so fast, and so automatic. Rising prices indicate when something is scarce, and the prospect of making a profit prompts people to divert resources into producing it; while falling prices indicate that resources are better employed on something else.

The self-interest of producers means that they quickly and constantly adapt their production to changing circumstances. This in turn means that resources are steered automatically toward the uses that customers value most. Yet this hugely beneficial *order* grew out of aspects of our individual behavior: our move from communal ownership to personal property ownership and the respecting of certain rights associated with it, the development of peaceful exchange, the gradual emergence of prices, the respect of promises and contracts, and our following the evolving principles of fair competition.

Nobody *invented* this *order*. Nor could they. After all, it routinely processes vast amounts of highly valuable information—such as changes in the supply of or demand for resources, and variations in vast numbers of prices across the entire planet—of far greater complexity than any individual could ever grasp; and it does so far more comprehensively and quicker than any human computer could ever achieve. Yet many people still believe that our economic *order* is a human invention that we can deconstruct and redesign—along with many other parts of our social life. But we are deeply ignorant of how these evolved *rules* and *orders* work.

## Hayek's Vocabulary

When it came to explaining all this, Hayek faced two problems. First, he had to find new terms to describe his new, or at least little understood, concepts. Second, though he was writing in English, it was not his native language.

For example, he refers to the regularities in human behavior as *rules*; but that may suggest something consciously constructed, like the rules of a game. Indeed, as Hayek notes, what we commonly refer to as 'rules' are in fact the *commands* issued by the authorities responsible for some *organization* (such as a government agency) with the aim of realizing some specific, intentional purpose. They are, in his words, *concrete*: they tell specific individuals to do specific things at specific times in specific circumstances. And they can change quickly, on a whim or on the result of an election.

Hayek's *rules* are exactly the opposite. His *rules* grow and evolve, without any conscious direction. They are *general*, *abstract*, and relatively *permanent* in character. They apply to everyone, everywhere, in every circumstance, including unknown future circumstances. Though we may not know the exact situations that we might face in some different time or place, we have a general idea of how we should behave (and *not* behave) when they do.

Of course, sometimes the *rules* conflict and we are thrown into doubt. For example, strong moral sentiments might urge us to do things that are against the law, such as ending the life of a sick elderly relative in great pain. Or the law might allow some activities, such as abortion or capital punishment, that we think deeply immoral. It is then for the courts to judge (Hayek says 'discover') which *rules* of justice take precedence.

The overall result of us following these rules is what Hayek calls *spontaneous order.* Again, these words may be misinterpreted. Again, in English, 'spontaneous' suggests something done on sudden impulse, but still a conscious action—as in 'spontaneous applause.' But Hayek means only something unconscious and unplanned. Likewise, 'order' in German means little more than the disposition of people or things in relation to others, as in the natural arrangement of atoms in a crystal. But in English, the word 'order' may suggest something *deliberately* ordered or arranged—again, the opposite of what Hayek has in mind. It is not easy to find alternative terms for Hayek's *rules* and *spontaneous order* that are free from ambiguity. Perhaps *evolved* and *outcome* are better.

## OUTLINE OF *LAW, LEGISLATION AND LIBERTY*

### Rules and Order

Hayek starts *Law, Legislation and Liberty* by drawing attention to the difference between evolved *orders* and deliberate *organizations.* Human life is a mixture of both, of course: but the evolved institutions, and the *rules* that underpin them, are much more important than we commonly realize.

Hayek explains here how a functioning social *order* emerges spontaneously through individuals following these *rules*—acting in certain ways, and not others. Our welfare depends on us following these *rules*, even if we do not understand the overall effect of doing so, nor appreciate the contribution of any particular *rule* to the overall *order.* These behaviors evolve over time, through adaptation and testing that favors successful outcomes—not so much trial and error, but trial and the survival of success.

The *rules*, though, are mostly *negative* proscriptions telling us what *not* to do; in particular, guiding us away from *injustice.* That still leaves individuals with plenty of freedom to pursue their own aims within these limits and for individuals to propose amendments to the rules. That is important because those amendments might prove beneficial, and then they can spread (and if not, they will be selected out). By such piecemeal adaptations, we respond to changing circumstances and make progress.

Hayek argues that such a free, evolving society will be more efficient, prosperous, and just than any we could purposefully create. Our evolved social institutions encapsulate millennia of experience and trial-and-success improvement: a 'wisdom' that uses and processes vast amounts of knowledge, far more than any human mind could ever compute. To replace the evolved *rules*, those behavioral regularities that contain this wisdom would risk the whole delicate structure of the social *order* they bring about.

It is a matter of regret, then, that we continue to confuse the evolved principles of *law* with acts of *legislation*—the *commands* by which such deliberately designed *organizations* (such as government agencies and programs) are run. No wonder, then, that our political structures have become so unfit for purpose.

## The Mirage of Social Justice

In his second volume, Hayek explores some of the implications of his evolutionary view. Our worldwide *great society* (as he calls it) of today cannot possibly be run through specific *commands* telling each of us what to do. That is simply unfeasible in a world of billions of people, with even more billions of interactions between them. No human mind or agency could deal with all those possibilities. The only principle on which such a *great society* can operate is if its members each follow certain *general principles* or *rules* of behavior—regularities that are abstract, relatively permanent, and apply to everyone, everywhere. Unlike *commands*, these *rules* do not tell us what to do. Rather, they dispose us against doing what we should *not* do—stealing property, for example, or breaking promises. It is not so much a matter of *prescribing action* but *avoiding injustice*.

Having explained that background, Hayek then embarks on an extended critique of the idea of 'social justice.' It had not been part of his original intention to do so, but his substantial focus on it reflects his mounting concern at the time about the damage being done by the 'social justice' idea, which had grown significantly in popularity while *Law, Legislation and Liberty* was gestating.

To Hayek, 'social justice' is a term empty of meaning. The idea is impossible to pin down, because different people have different ideas about what it means. It may sound broadly attractive, but on what principles would it be based? Does it mean that people should be rewarded according to merit? If so, who is to determine what 'merit' is and who is to judge people on the basis of it? Or again, should people be rewarded according to their 'value to society?' But then, who could possibly judge the relative value, to society as a whole, of different people and occupations? As Hayek puts it: "When we ask what ought to be the relative remunerations of a nurse or a butcher, or a coal miner and a judge at a high court, of the deep sea diver or the cleaner of sewers, or the organizer of a new industry and a jockey, of the inspector of taxes and the inventor of a life-saving drug, of the jet pilot or the professor of mathematics, the appeal to 'social justice' does not give us the slightest help of deciding…" (Hayek, 1982, vol. 2, 77–78). In other words, there is no objective meaning of 'social justice,' and any meaning proposed by the authorities would inevitably provoke bitter dispute.

Moreover, trying to create a predetermined outcome like this would cut across the delicate and interconnected operations of markets and the information-signaling function of prices. That would destabilize the evolved social *order* that generates our efficiency and prosperity. And there is a moral difficulty too: treating people as mere components in a deliberately *organized* economic strategy would require *compulsion* to prevent individuals from acting on the basis of their own circumstances and instead forcing them to pursue the limited vision of the authorities.

But again, our authorities persistently confuse the conscious *organization* of social and economic life with its *evolution*. Even the 'rights' detailed in the United Nations Charter, explains Hayek, are a mixture of genuine principles of justice and the demands of *organization*-led thinking. But then, so much of human existence has been life in small groups that it is no surprise such thinking is so strong. But the needs of a *great society* are well beyond the *command* structures that might serve a small *organization*.

## The Political Order of a Free People

Hayek's analysis of the dereliction (and public distrust) into which our political systems have fallen, and his solutions to that, form the third volume of *Law, Legislation and Liberty*.

While democracy has profound benefits, there are severe dangers in *unrestrained* majority power. A majority with power can exploit minorities, trample over their rights, and become a tyranny itself. And politicians are easy prey to the demands of special interest groups—who know that the larger government expands, the larger are the potential favors it can dispense to them.

Such factors mean that our political systems have strayed very far from the original purposes for which they were established. The first parliaments were established precisely to protect us from exploitation by those with executive power. But now, the representative and executive functions have been conflated. Those who are supposed to uphold and nurture the rules of justice also issue the *commands* by which government is *organized*. But they use the word 'law' for both. The result is that politicians imagine that they can shape the rules of justice as easily, and with as much authority, as they shape the operation of a government agency.

How, then, might we restore and preserve a free, evolving social *order*, with all its benefits? We need a *constitution*, says Hayek, one that protects that *order* from the political desire to impose predetermined designs upon it. Previous efforts have failed because their authors have not understood the profound importance of separating these two separate functions.

Hayek's solution is bicameral government, with one house focused on maintaining *justice* and the *rule of law*—where everyone, including the government, is subject to general rules—and the other focused on the *organization* of government, but subject to the *law* and the rules of justice.

### Epilogue

*Law, Legislation and Liberty* closes with an Epilogue that summarizes its theme. There are, Hayek observes, "three sources of our human values" (1982, vol. 3, 153). Some behaviors are genetic, born into us. Some of our institutions are the results of our conscious design. But, larger and more important than these, he says, is *cultural evolution*—something neither innate nor designed.

There is a tension to this, as there is in all evolved processes. Cultural evolution allows us to adapt much faster than biological evolution. But at the same time, the rules it works through have to remain strong. Much more than in *The Constitution of Liberty*, Hayek stresses that our evolved notions of justice, our traditions and customs, and our morals and markets, deserve respect. Even so, we progress by allowing these *rules* to adapt to circumstance. But we should not imagine that we have the intellectual ability to reshape them, without risk, as we choose.

## THE RELEVANCE OF *LAW, LEGISLATION AND LIBERTY*

The key argument in *Law, Legislation and Liberty*, then, is that the cultural evolution of our values and institutions is far more important than we realize. Indeed, everyone who lives in the worldwide *great society* of today is dependent on its ability to maintain a functioning society that can adapt to future challenges. It rests on deep and shared notions of justice, moral norms, culture, and tradition. But the temptation of social engineering, the attempt to deliberately reshape society into something we (or political ideologues) prefer, remains great. The only hope for this adaptive system, and for our freedom within it, is to ensure we protect our profoundly held and shared principles of justice from the political authorities. If justice depends on the whims of the politicians of the moment, justice will soon cease to exist.

### The Corruption of Politics

These thoughts seem even more relevant today than when Hayek was writing them. He anticipated many contemporary trends; or at least, he recognized their early development in the politics of the 1970s.

With governments making their own rules and acquiring more and more power, few have resisted the temptation to use that power to steer public resources toward their own supporters (and often, toward themselves). That breach of trust with the public has led to disillusionment, not just with the politicians who happen to be in power at any one time, but with the political system in general. Citizens feel, increasingly, that their interests are not being represented. The echo chambers of social media and partisan news services have created a deepening polarization between different political ideologies. There is increasing partisanship, with politicians less willing to negotiate or compromise with their opponents. As a result, electors have been giving increased support to extremist parties and causes, and to populist and nationalist politicians whom they believe are more likely to share their mistrust of the political system than those politicians who have risen to power within it.

### Hayek's Argument Today

Today's technological, legislative, and other developments further increase people's mistrust of governments and pose threats to our individual liberty. The expansion of police and security powers, the increased use of surveillance, and the ability to track citizens—for example, through their phone and credit card usage, their email and browsing history, or their medical and tax records—give the authorities a set of powerful tools that, in unscrupulous hands, could be used as a weapon against opponents. Meanwhile, the complexity of modern legislation has obscured the principles on which laws should rest and has left wide authority in the hands of civil servants, government agencies, and regulators, whose decisions have the power of law but who are not subject to any appeal or public recall.

This is a dire situation, even more so than when Hayek was writing. It is a good reason why we should strive to understand the argument he puts forward in *Law, Legislation and Liberty.* However difficult and flawed the book may be, it is of vital importance to anyone who is concerned about the present and future state of politics and of individual freedom.

## NOTE

1. For a detailed exposition of *Law, Legislation and Liberty* see Butler (2025).

## REFERENCES

Butler E. (2025). *Hayek's Law, Legislation and Liberty.* London: Institute of Economic Affairs.

Darwin C. (1859). *The Origin of Species.* London: John Murray.

Ferguson A. (1767). *An Essay on the History of Civil Society.* Dublin: Boulter Grierson.

Hayek F. von (1944). *The Road to Serfdom.* London: Routledge and Chicago: University of Chicago Press.

Hayek F. von (1952). *The Sensory Order: An Inquiry into the Foundations of Theoretical Psychology*. London: Routledge and Chicago: University of Chicago Press.
Hayek F. von (1960). *The Constitution of Liberty*. London: Routledge and Chicago: University of Chicago Press.
Hayek F. von (1967). *Studies in Philosophy, Politics and Economics*. London: Routledge and Chicago: University of Chicago Press.
Hayek F. von (1972). *A Tiger by the Tail: The Keynesian Legacy of Inflation*. London: Institute of Economic Affairs.
Hayek F. von (1973). *Rules and Order*. London: Routledge and Chicago: University of Chicago Press.
Hayek F. von (1976). *The Mirage of Social Justice*. London: Routledge and Chicago: University of Chicago Press.
Hayek F. von (1978). *Denationalization of Money*. London: Institute of Economic Affairs.
Hayek F. von (1979). *The Political Order of a Free People*. London: Routledge and Chicago: University of Chicago Press.
Hayek F. von (1982). *Law, Legislation and Liberty*, vols. 1–3. London: Routledge & Kegan Paul.
Hayek F. von (1988). *The Fatal Conceit: The Errors of Socialism*. London: Routledge and Chicago: University of Chicago Press.
Leoni B. (1961). *Freedom and the Law*. New York: Van Nostrand.
Locke J. (1689). *Two Treatises of Civil Government*. London: George Routledge and Sons.
Smith A. (1776). *An Inquiry into the Nature and Causes of the Wealth of Nations*. London: W. Strahan and T. Cadell.

# 2. Why the intellectuals are still drawn to socialism: revisiting Hayek's warning at 75 years

**Phillip W. Magness**

In his classic essay "Intellectuals and Socialism," F. A. Hayek observed that "Socialism has never and nowhere been at first a working-class movement... It is a construction of theorists, deriving from certain tendencies of abstract thought with which for a long time only the intellectuals were familiar; and it required long efforts by the intellectuals before the working classes could be persuaded to adopt it as their program" (Hayek 1949, p. 417).

His words reflected a time when socialist thought, and particularly Marxism, was a rising geopolitical force. The settlement of the Second World War extended the Soviet empire's control across eastern Europe, and in 1949, the same year of Hayek's essay, China fell to the Marxist movement of Mao Zedong. Like the Bolshevik Revolution a quarter of a century earlier, these events did not emerge from mass popular uprisings but rather from the force of conquest by violent and fanatical Marxist activists. And therein lies the fundamental contradiction of Marxist theory, as diagnosed in Hayek's essay.

According to its self-portrayal, Marxist political action derives its authority from a numerical majority. The laboring classes, or proletariat, outnumber the owners of capital, who in turn are said to dispossess them of the products of their labor. The task of the Marxist theoretician, then, is to awaken the exploited masses such that they rise up, seize the means of production, and usher in a socialist era. In fact, Marx deemed this outcome an inevitable arc of historical progression, shaped and defined by an eternal contest to control material resources. The socialist theoretician therefore only needs to awaken the masses into collective revolutionary action – a course that is further guaranteed by alleged contradictions in the capitalist system it seeks to replace.

And so would the socialist era commence, except that the Marxist Revolution never quite plays out on the terms that Marx predicted. Hayek diagnosed another route of transmission, more readily observable in the events of his time. Socialism took root not among the masses but among certain intellectuals, or as Hayek described them, secondhand dealers in ideas. The moniker was meant as a pejorative, as these intellectuals displayed very little in the way of intellect. An intellectual, in this sense, exhibited neither originality of thought nor subject matter expertise. "[H]e need not possess special knowledge of anything in particular, nor need he even be particularly intelligent" as he performed his function, the intermediary transmission of certain fashionable ideas (Hayek 1949, p. 418).

In no small irony, the socialist intellectuals of Hayek's time displayed little in common with the laboring masses they appointed themselves to represent. On the contrary, they tended to come from the very same "bourgeois" backgrounds that formed the object of their rage. They were often born into material comfort and enjoyed the benefits of university education. To the extent that they "labored" at all, it took the form of endeavors of the mind rather than the body: professorial instruction, journalism, novel writing, and the ubiquitous activism of abstract "organizing." Marxists rationalized this visible contradiction in their theory by developing the concept of vanguardism, wherein a small and specially suited socialist intellectual class serves the necessary function of awakening the masses and alerting them to their own condition of exploitation.[1] But even then, the mass revolutions never developed.

In 1965 the political scientist Mancur Olson explained this conundrum of socialist organizing. Free-ridership undermined Marx's entire theory of revolution, for "a worker who thought he would benefit from a 'proletarian' government would not find it rational to risk his life and resources to start a revolution against the bourgeois government." Assuming the revolution succeeded, he "would get the benefits of the class action whether he participated or not" (Olson 1965, p. 106). Therefore, the expected position of the proletariat is to not participate at all in a game where the personal risks are extremely high and the personal rewards are diffuse and theoretical.

Olson therefore concludes that "[i]t is natural then that the 'Marxian' revolutions that have taken place have been brought about by small conspiratorial elites that took advantage of weak governments during periods of social disorganization" (Olson 1965, p. 106). Existing socialist regimes emerge not from worker movements or numerical majorities, but from the actions of secondhand dealers in ideas.

As we take a further step in this inquiry into socialist intellectuals, let us turn to a specific secondhand dealer in ideas, and one who enjoys immense intellectual favor today. Let us turn to Karl Marx.

Some might dispute my characterization of Marx as a mere secondhand dealer. It is true that he enjoys a reputation as a bold and original thinker. Elements of this reputation date to the historical Karl Marx and his followers from his lifetime. Engels famously analogized his contributions to the social sciences to those of Darwin in the natural sciences (Engels 1883). Marx's esteem for his own ideas was only matched in intensity by his derisive scorn toward other contemporaries who failed to accord him recognition for his alleged genius. Yet in Marx's own lifetime, he was a non-entity outside of the far-left labor movement he inhabited.

The Marxist historian Philip Foner made this discovery by accident when he commenced work on a book about Marx's funeral in 1883: "I discovered in the course of my research that there were many countries in which Marx's death was not even noticed, and that newspapers of many cities where some notice was taken of the event, carried not even a brief obituary note." Foner continued with astonishment over the "flagrant" omission of any notice in leading magazines, including outlets that otherwise covered socialist political theorizing (Foner 1973, pp. 18–19).

In a revelation that many today will find surprising, this status is confirmed among Marx's contemporaries. Arthur Balfour, the future British Prime Minister and a voracious consumer of books, remarked in 1885 that "Marx is but little read in this country," while "Mr. [Henry] George has been read a great deal" (Balfour 1885, p. 344). His sentiments were shared by Henry Hyndman, a British socialist who befriended Marx at the end of his life. As Hyndman recounted, "In 1880 it is scarcely too much to say that Marx was practically unknown to the English public" despite his residing in London for most of his adult life (Hyndman 1911, p. 272). For many years, Marx lived in the same neighborhood as John Stuart Mill. He wrote on similar topics as Mill and attempted to engage Mill as an interlocutor. Yet as far as we know, Mill's voluminous writings and papers contain not a single reference to Marx by name. They evince no awareness of a German neighbor who produced lengthy treatises on closely related subjects. To the extent that the living Karl Marx qualified as an intellectual, he was also an obscure one, known only to other socialists on the extreme periphery of the political realm.

I nonetheless maintain that Marx was an intellectual in the secondhand dealer sense, owing to the content of his works. Marx's most famous contributions consist of (1) the theory of surplus value, from which he derives the mechanism of exploitation in his economic analysis and thus the agent of his own revolutionary system, and (2) his materialist conception of historical progression. No less than Engels designated these two concepts as Marx's most important and original contributions to philosophical thought. But neither idea is original to Marx. Historical materialism, the more esoteric of the two, has clear antecedents in both the eighteenth-century French socialist Henri de Saint-Simon and the Hegelian intellectual scene where Marx completed his university studies. The more defined doctrine of surplus value appears in numerous writings a decade or more before Marx's *Capital*. He may not have been aware of some of these iterations. The American proslavery sociologist George Fitzhugh developed a nearly identical indictment of industrial capitalism on surplus value grounds in the 1850s (Fitzhugh 1857). Another surplus value theoretician, the Prussian socialist Johann Karl Rodbertus, was brought to Marx's attention by Engels in an 1851 letter (Engels 1851; see also Rodbertus-Jagetzow 1850). When Marx adopted a strikingly similar concept as his own almost a decade later, Rodbertus and his followers charged the London-based expatriate with plagiarism. It was but the most famous of many plagiarism allegations that plagued Marx in his lifetime and beyond. The anarchist followers of French theorist Victor Considerant, for example, hounded the Marxists with charges that the *Communist Manifesto* of 1848 employed a structure and form of argumentation that resembled a Considerant pamphlet published a few years prior (Ramus et al. 1906).

Without rendering a verdict on these charges, it is sufficient to note that even the most "original" examples of Marx's ideas had many close cousins in their vicinity. Marx realized as much in his own writings while touting its originality – and heaping vicious scorn on other socialist competitors over the tiniest of differences in their thought. Marx's notorious style of argumentation and his habit of exaggerating the originality of his theories are revelatory. They both attest to an insecurity about the novelty of his own contributions – the hallmark of a secondhand dealer.

Of equal significance, a wider nineteenth-century socialist intellectual scene, albeit one that still inhabited the periphery of political discussion, becomes apparent when considering the similarities between Marx and his competitors. So why, then, is Marx the dominant figure of socialist theorizing today? Why do we no longer speak of Rodbertian socialism? Why are Proudhon and Lassalle relegated to niche investigations into the history of thought, as opposed to the intellectual fathers of active political traditions today?[2]

The answer cannot possibly come from Marx's track record in the intervening century and a half.

In 1991, with the collapse of the Soviet Union, the conclusive defeat of Marxism was widely proclaimed. Marx's theories left a catastrophic toll – over 100 million dead, massive impoverishment worldwide, dozens of authoritarian political regimes, an even greater number of attempted coups and violent insurrections, and an uninterrupted legacy of economic dysfunction. Even the intellectual admirers of these regimes began to concede their mistakes or reinvent themselves as heirs of an allegedly alternative Marxist tradition that was untainted by the Gulags, purges, famines, and killing fields.

We recently marked the 30th anniversary of that event, and while Marxism's failures are still impossible to deny, the intellectual classes have re-embraced Marx the man – even attempting to separate him from his system's deadly legacy. In 2018 on the 200th anniversary of Marx's birth, intellectual elites showered him with praise. Headlines in the *Financial Times* declared that

"Karl Marx is More Relevant than Ever." The *New York Times* said "Happy Birthday, Karl Marx. You were right!" (Tooze 2018; Barker 2018).

The statistics from academia paint an even more dismal picture:

- A 2007 study of university faculty found that one fifth of social science professors openly described themselves as Marxists. This number has undoubtedly gone up in 15 years as faculty ranks have shifted further leftward (Gross and Simmons 2007; Magness and Waugh 2022).
- The Scholarometer bibliometric tool, a browser plugin that calculates comparative citation indexes from the Google Scholar search engine, consistently ranks Karl Marx around the 99th percentile for all-time citation influence among scholars, past and present (Green 2016).[3]
- As of 2020, Marx's *Communist Manifesto* consistently ranks as the most frequently assigned reading by a philosopher on university course syllabi, with only Plato's *Republic* coming close to matching him.[4]
- A 2022 analysis using the Google Trends tool to measure search patterns for historical and current economic writers found that Marx ranked 3rd overall in terms of trend frequency, behind only Plato and Aristotle. Among prominent modern economists, Marx's Google Trends score was roughly four times that of Adam Smith and six times that of John Maynard Keynes (Coupé 2022).

Marx's influence today is not just confined to Marxist economics, which remains relatively obscure in economics departments. It has spawned dozens of Marxist schools of thought in history, philosophy, sociology, literature, art, architecture, and anything with the name "studies" attached to it. Marxist-inspired movements now include the academic mainstream of literary criticism, legal analysis, postcolonial studies, art, music, and the vast array of methodological approaches operating under the moniker of "Critical Theory."

My purpose, then, is to ask why Karl Marx's reputation is so resilient among the intellectuals – and why Marx even has a reputation at all.

In Marx's own lifetime, he was never anything more than a fringe figure confined to radical labor activist circles. For the three decades that followed Marx's death in 1883, his principles were almost universally rejected by economists. The Marginal Revolution of 1871 rendered Marx's *Das Kapital* obsolete only four years after it was published.

Marx built his entire system upon the labor theory of value. His economic framework depended on accepting that economic value arises from labor performed. The capitalist in Marx's system then appropriates the surplus value of the laborer as his own – a process that Marx deems exploitative. Eventually, a labor uprising emerges in the form of a proletarian revolution to seize the means of production from the owners of capital. All rests on the aforementioned doctrine of surplus value.

Except surplus value is a myth. As Carl Menger and William Stanley Jevons demonstrated in 1871, value does not arise from labor performed – it is necessarily subjective, arising from individual preferences (Jevons 1871; Menger 2007). And individuals value goods at the margin. When mainstream economics first seriously engaged Marx, it happened two years after his death. In 1885, marginalist economist Philip Wicksteed published a devastating critique of Marx's system for being based on an erroneous theory of value (Wicksteed 1885).

The hits on Marx's doctrines kept piling on from there. When Alfred Marshall published his landmark *Principles of Economics* – the first true economics textbook – in 1890, he dismissed Marx's system. It "argue[d] in a complete circle" from an erroneous theory of value, hiding its sleight of hand by keeping it "shrouded in mysterious Hegelian phrases" (Marshall 1890, pp. 619–620). Eugen von Böhm-Bawerk wrote a book-length rebuttal of Marx in 1898 that contemporaries regarded as an authoritative refutation of *Capital's* internal inconsistencies (Böhm-Bawerk 1949).

In 1907 the *Economic Journal* was asked to review a new translation of the second volume of Marx's *Das Kapital.* Reviewer C. Violet Butler quipped about its obsolescence by likening it to Don Quixote's imagined monsters: "Who should tilt at such a windmill?" (Butler 1907, p. 560). In 1922 economist Thomas Nixon Carver, who taught Harvard University's only specialized class on socialist economics, offered a damning assessment of Marx's low stature in the eyes of other scholars:

> No economist today accepts a single one of the dogmas of Marx. His materialistic interpretation of history is rejected even by most socialists; his labor theory of value is antiquated and inadequate. His theory of surplus value is childish. His theory of commercial crises is still held by a few vociferous but uninformed people in spite of the fact that it is a logical absurdity. His theory of the concentration of capital, to the effect that capital tends to be concentrated more and more into the hands of fewer and fewer persons simply does not work out in fact. His doctrine that all social evolution comes through class struggle contradicts the observed fact that most of the significant reforms come, not through class struggle, but through the efforts of well-meaning people who have nothing whatever to gain by the reforms they are putting through. (Carver 1922, pp. 363–364)

Francis Y. Edgeworth, founding editor of the *Economic Journal,* expressed sympathy with the position that "the theories of Marx are beneath the notice of a scientific writer" while lamenting that the economist's province required him to refute such fallacies (Edgeworth 1921, p. 71).

John Maynard Keynes reached a similar conclusion in 1925, dismissing Marx's *Capital* as "an obsolete economic textbook … without interest or application for the modern world" (Keynes 1931, p. 257). Ludwig von Mises called the same book "essentially a garbled rehash of…[David] Ricardo" (Mises 1957, pp. 124–125). So did Paul Samuelson, no friend of laissez-faire purism. In his 1962 American Economic Association presidential address, he stated that "From the viewpoint of pure economic theory, Karl Marx can be regarded as a minor post-Ricardian" (Samuelson 1962, p. 12).

The message had been clear since the turn of the last century: economists had seriously considered Marx's arguments in the decades that followed his death, and they soundly rejected them.

Even those who tried to make Marx's system work eventually came to concede its internal inconsistencies. Marx's arithmetic for converting the value of labor into prices had a self-contradiction: it assumed that input values derive from labor performed, and yet inputs are purchased at market prices. In 1907, mathematician Ladislaus Bortkiewicz attempted to solve this "transformation problem" in an obscure unpublished analysis before hitting a mathematical dead end. When Marxist central planners rediscovered it in the 1940s, they quickly realized the implications for the classical version of Marx's system (Bortkiewicz 1949). The math would never add up, and to get around this problem they would need to invent new and non-literal reinterpretations of Marx's writings.

While economists rejected Marx, most other academic disciplines simply ignored him. In 1909, Harvard University assembled what became known as "Dr. Eliot's Five Foot Shelf" – a compendium of the Western intellectual canon up until that point in history, covering philosophy, literature, religion, science, art, politics, and economics. The collection prominently featured an entire volume on Adam Smith, as well as other economic writers such as John Stuart Mill. But Karl Marx was nowhere to be found – rejected by his peers, and too obscure to warrant inclusion in the collection.

A survey of top academic journals in economics, law, politics, literature, philosophy, sociology, and education similarly reveals Marx's obscurity before the early twentieth century. His only real citations appeared in economics journals, which were busy debating and dissecting his system. In all of the other fields, Marx seldom accrues more than a handful of references (Magness and Makovi 2023, Table 1, p. 1514).

Today in 2024, the pattern has completely reversed. Marxism remains a rejected doctrine in the economics discipline, seldom appearing outside of a passing reference to his place in the history of economic thought.[5] In sociology, philosophy, political theory, and law, Marx is now everywhere. Literature now has entire subfields dedicated to Marxist analysis. And education theory has been overwhelmed by the Critical Pedagogy movement of Marxist revolutionary writer Paulo Freire – one of the most commonly assigned texts today in schools of education.[6]

In the past century, Marx has moved from obscure obsolescence into the intellectual mainstream. But why?

The answer I propose traces to one specific event: the violent seizure of the Russian government in a coup d'etat in 1917 by a small band of Marxist intellectuals. This event led to the creation of the Soviet Union and subsequent propagandizing of Marxist doctrine across the intellectual world. I am not the first to suggest this explanation. Frederick Charles Copleston noticed it in his landmark history of philosophy, suggesting that Marx owed his reputation not to the merits of his ideas but to the political violence of his progeny (Copleston 2003, p. 306). So did Loren Lomasky, who writes that without the Soviet Union Marx's "visible presence … today would probably be roughly the same number of textbook footnotes enjoyed by other defunct nineteenth-century economists of similar stature – Nassau Senior, for example" (Lomasky 1989, p. 131).

But what I can offer for this explanation is empirical demonstration.

To see how, we turn to bibliometrics, or citation analysis over time. One such tool is found in Google's Ngram project – a massive and ongoing effort to scan and digitize the texts of the world's great libraries. Ngram allows us to track the prevalence of words and phrases in published works over time, dating back centuries and encompassing millions of books. It also allows us to see how often certain authors are cited – authors including Adam Smith, Aristotle, John Locke, David Hume, and of course Karl Marx.

Using the Ngram database, I worked with economist Michael Makovi to assemble yearly Ngram citation records for over 225 intellectual figures covering the period between antiquity and the late nineteenth century, when Marx died (see Magness and Makovi 2023). Our series includes both prominent writers from science, social science, and the humanities, and the comparatively obscure: socialist writers such as Johann Karl Rodbertus, Ferdinand Lassalle, and – before 1917 – Karl Marx.

Our hypothesis is straightforward: the Soviet Union rescued Marx from relative obscurity in 1917 and thrust him into the intellectual mainstream. If this is the case, we should expect Marx's citations to parallel other relatively obscure socialists between his death in 1883 and 1916. After 1917, they should skyrocket – even overtaking prominent figures such as Adam Smith, which is where Marx's citation patterns stand today.

To test our theory, we employed a form of analysis known as the Synthetic Control Method. In layman's terms, the Synthetic Control allows us to construct a counterfactual citation pattern for Karl Marx to test an alternative world in which the events of 1917 never happened. It does so by matching Marx's pre-1917 citations to other authors in the database who closely paralleled his works, including in their own relative obscurity. These authors are selected by computer algorithm based on their own citation patterns, to reduce the chance of bias or human error. Together, they allow us to generate a "synthetic" Karl Marx after 1917 – a composite of other authors who were not similarly elevated by the Soviet Union.

Our results are robust and clear (see Figure 2.1). In addition to seizing power, Lenin and the Bolsheviks ignited a philosophical elevation of Karl Marx into the intellectual mainstream. Just over a decade after 1917, Marx's citations increased sharply – approximately three-fold. And that pattern has only continued. By contrast, the synthetic counterfactual Karl Marx lingers in comparative obscurity as do its composite authors such as Ferdinand Lassalle and Johann Karl Rodbertus.

To ensure that our results were not a chance coincidence, we tested them exhaustively for robustness – by examining alternative treatment dates besides 1917, by looking at Marx's citation patterns in other languages such as German, and by restricting our pool of authors to socialist, non-socialist, English, German, and other subsets. In each case, the main finding holds up: 1917 was a transformative year in the intellectual reputation of Karl Marx (Magness and Makovi 2024).

How did these events play out? At first it was likely curiosity, as newspapers around the world picked up Marx's works in an attempt to understand the quirky dead philosopher whose followers had just seized control of one of the world's great powers. But Lenin and his successors also devoted the full energy and resources of the Soviet state to promoting and disseminating Marxist doctrine.

They subsidized the translation and publication of Marx's collected works, including the *Marx-Engels-Gesamtausgabe.* They built a personality cult around Marx the man with statues and propaganda posters. They mandated Marxist instruction in schools and universities under their control. They subsidized other Marxist movements around the globe in a militaristic campaign that matched or exceeded any other imperialist regime in history. Even non-Soviet Western Marxists such as the Frankfurt School and its Critical Theory outgrowths, though notoriously schismatic from doctrinaire Marxism, owe their very existence to the aftermath of 1917 on Marx's intellectual reputation.

These findings have attracted some controversy, although mainly for their political implications about Marxism today. Their historical validity is plainly attested in multiple sources, including on the far left. While reviewing printing records of the *Communist Manifesto,* Marxist historian Eric Hobsbawm noticed its spartan circulation in the late nineteenth and early twentieth centuries. Even among the labor-oriented Social Democratic political parties of this era, party-produced print runs amounted to no more than a couple of thousand copies. "This situation changed after the October Revolution," Hobsbawm

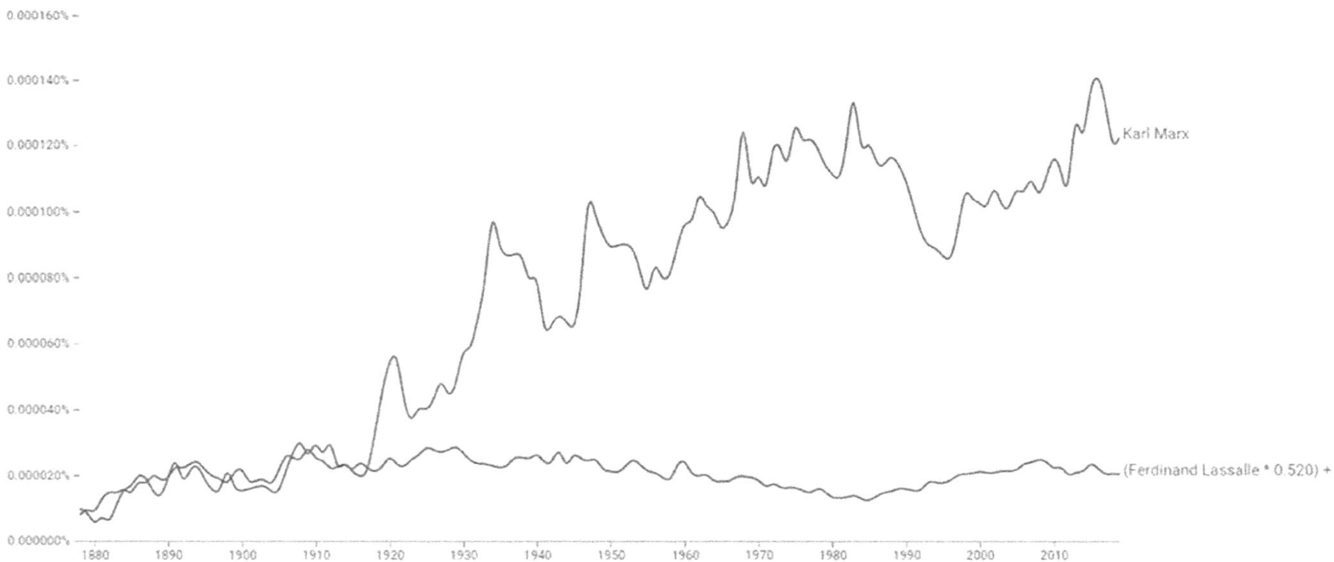


*Note:* Results are tested for statistical significance through 1932. Extrapolation to the present day is included for context, although we acknowledge the role of subsequent treatments in explaining the continued upward trajectory of Marx's citations.
*Source:* Magness and Makovi (2023, Figure 2, p. 1529).

*Figure 2.1* *Karl Marx's Ngram pattern, contrasted with synthetic counterfactual*

continued. "Following Lenin, all leaders were now supposed to be important theorists" and all had to learn Marx. The Soviets embarked on an international publishing spree to spread the word, "all backed by the – for these purposes – unlimited resources of the Soviet Communist Party" (Hobsbawm 1998, pp. 9–10).

Some decades earlier, Ludwig von Mises authored a similar assessment. "The very small groups of zealous Marxians – probably never more than a few hundred persons" in all of Germany before the First World War, "were completely segregated from the rest of the [Social Democratic] party membership." As Mises continued, "The millions voting the Social Democratic ticket paid no attention to these endless theoretical discussions concerning the concentration of capital, the collapse of capitalism, finance capital and imperialism, and the relations between Marxian materialism and Kantian criticism" (Mises 1944, p. 154). Marx's early intellectual champions largely failed at spreading his messages, even in cursory form, beyond their own circles prior to Lenin's intervention in Russia.

Please note that I am not saying that all Marxists today learned from Lenin and Stalin, or that Soviet Marxism is a secret undergirding of every Marxist movement. It is not. But Marx's own reputation itself is inextricably connected to the Bolshevik Revolution, which rescued him from obscurity and put his name at the front of the intellectual map. Marxism today stands on Lenin's shoulders, whether it wishes to admit this reality or not. And Marxist intellectuals remain the secondhand dealers in a theory that is, itself, secondhand dealing of other obscure nineteenth-century socialists.

Hayek's 1949 retrospective took notice of this pattern of dissemination and paired it with another observation about the role of intellectuals in promoting favored ideas. These secondhand dealers, he noted, tend to adopt "views on subjects which have little to do with the merits of the real achievements" of the work they are considering. Intellectual fashionability trumps internal validity – a pattern attested in the readily observed abundance of figures "who have undeservedly achieved a popular reputation as great scientists solely because they hold what the intellectuals regard as 'progressive' political views" (Hayek 1949, p. 419).

Among Marxists, this pattern becomes readily apparent when one recognizes that almost all of Marx's acclaim comes from outside of the economics discipline, despite the fact that Marx addressed his "critique" to economists and considered himself to be a social-scientific contributor to economics. As Hayek notes, "there was probably at no time a majority of economists, who were recognized as such by their peers, favorable to socialism" (1949, p. 419). This remains true three quarters of a century later, with Marxist economists operating on the extreme heterodox periphery of the profession. The decisive defeat of socialism within economics was not sufficient though, as "it is not the predominant views of the experts but the views of a minority, mostly of rather doubtful standing in their profession, which are taken up and spread by the intellectuals" (Hayek 1949, p. 419). Indeed, Marxism likely triumphed in the academy by eschewing specialized expertise. Socialism died in its infancy in economics and then ceded the field, only to take up roost in the English department.

We see this pattern at play in the current homes of academic Marxists, almost all of which sit squarely in the humanities and softer social sciences. As with 1917 before them, this second wave of Marxist theorizing attained its intellectual acclaim through external political events rather than the merit of its ideas. The philosopher Roger Scruton traced these events to the social upheavals of 1968 and its aftermath – a period when far-left activism accelerated on campus, and university administrators responded by opening the doors of the faculty ranks to accommodate radical political causes. Scruton recalled his own experience in struggling to make sense of this sudden surge of acclaim around a system of ideas that had not only lost the battle of ideas in economics, but now had the hindsight of humanitarian disasters over the preceding decades and their revelations about Soviet atrocities. Instead, "the theories of Marx were being recycled as the true account of the sufferings of humanity under 'capitalist' regimes" (Scruton 2019, p. 6). A distinctive feature of this intellectual turn, he continued, was its nearly complete obliviousness to any earlier refutation of the Marxist system. Instead, the intellectual proponents of socialism simply handwaved their opposition away:

> [I]t was rare to find any mention in the left-wing journals of the criticisms that Marx's writings had encountered during the previous century. Marx's theory of history had been put in question by Maitland, Weber and Sombart; his labour theory of value by Böhm-Bawerk, Mises, and many more; his theories of false consciousness, alienation and class struggle by a whole range of thinkers, from Mallock and Sombart to Popper, Hayek and Aron. Not all those critics could be placed on the right of the political spectrum, nor had they all been hostile to the idea of "social justice." Yet none of them, so far as I could discover when I came to write this book, had been answered by the New Left with anything more than a sneer. (Scruton 2016, pp. 6–7)

Scruton was not alone in this observation. Karl Popper, the great philosopher of science, recounted his own rediscovery of the Western Marxist Frankfurt School in the 1960s as an example. Led by Max Horkheimer, Herbert Marcuse, Theodor Adorno, and others, this group of Marxist theoreticians emerged out of the University of Frankfurt in the 1920s. Their founding in 1923 came on the heels of the Soviet Revolution and likely owed itself to this event. Karl Korsch, one of their formative philosophical influences, admitted as much at the group's founding seminar when he credited Lenin with reinvigorating the revolutionary zeal of Marx and rescuing it from Social Democratic electoral politics (Korsch 1970, p. 67). They also provided an early home to a range of Soviet-funded publishing and scholarly projects aiming to disseminate Marx's works before being forced to relocate to Columbia University in the early 1930s to escape Nazi oppression.

The Frankfurt School has since become a storied "non-Soviet" strain of Marxist thought that rejects the revolutionary organizing and political strategies of the Bolsheviks in favor of a philosophical approach, rooted in shifting and upending academic discourse. Their core insight, most closely associated with Horkheimer, divides intellectual life into "traditional" and "critical" theories (Horkheimer 1972). Whereas the former is nominally descriptive and often said to be positivistic, encompassing most conventional academic debate, the Frankfurt theorists interpret it as a mechanism to sustain and reinforce the power structures of capitalism, of bourgeois society, and of "neoliberalism" and a host of other made-up concepts and jargon. Taking inspiration from Marx's dictum "The philosophers have hitherto only interpreted the world in various ways. The point, however, is to change it," these authors placed themselves in a separate classification of Critical Theory. In contrast to Traditional Theory, the expositors of Critical Theory purport to interrogate the world through an "emancipatory" lens, the gist of which conveniently aligns with the uninterrogated political prescriptions of Marxian socialism.

In Popper's telling, "I first heard of the Frankfurt School in the 1930s but decided then, on the basis of some experimental reading, against conscientiously reading its output" (Popper 1994, p. 78). This was a polite way of saying that he saw very little substance to the Critical Theory literature, most of which appeared in Horkheimer's in-house academic journal, *Zeitschrift für Sozialforschung*. Turning again to Ngram, we see that citation patterns for the main Frankfurt School theorists are almost non-existent in this period. Others apparently followed Popper's lead by ignoring this group in its formative years, and for at least a couple of decades afterward.

Critical Theory citations surge suddenly in the late 1960s and have remained fashionable among intellectuals ever since (see Figure 2.2). Popper sat as a witness to these events after being lured into a debate at an academic conference with the comparatively obscure Adorno. As he later recounted, the Critical Theorists used the exercise to incorrectly paint him as a positivist, generally avoiding any substantive engagement with the paper he delivered (Popper 1970). He nonetheless used the occasion to familiarize himself with their works. Much like Scruton, he found only circular reasoning and an a priori assumption of Marxian premises, layered over in dense proprietary jargon. Of Adorno, Popper succinctly concluded that "he has nothing whatever to say; and he says it in Hegelian language" (1994, p. 78). Horkheimer only fared

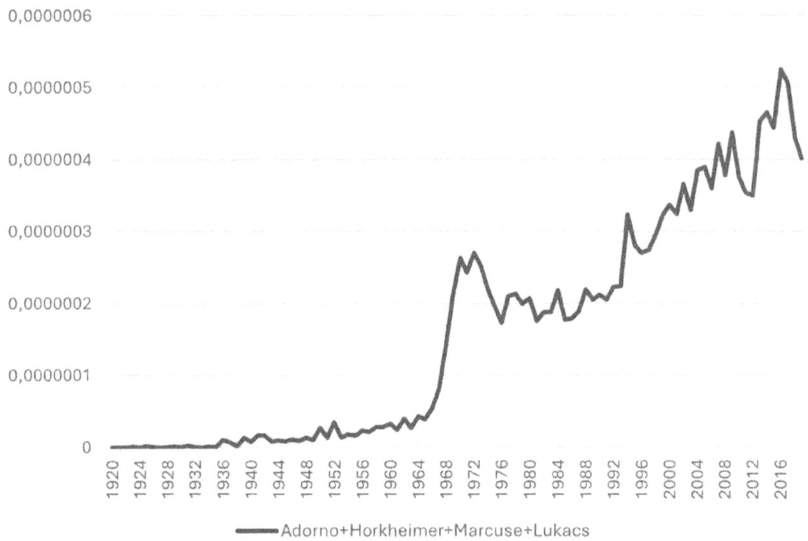


*Source:* Own elaboration.

*Figure 2.2* *Aggregated Frankfurt School Ngram citations*

better by comparison on the basis that his prose was slightly less pretentious than his colleague (Popper 1994, p. 79).

Turning again to citation patterns, we see a remarkable shift in the late 1960s. Whereas the main Frankfurt School theorists had piddled along in relative obscurity for decades, including the prime years of their academic outputs, they suddenly surged after 1968 in conjunction with the campus protest waves. Political fashionability among the secondhand dealers in ideas once again resuscitated Marxist theorizing.

In considering the counterfactuals of history, we might imagine a world in which the Soviets did not succeed or a world in which the campus "New Left" of the 1960s fizzled out of fashion as level-headed voices subjected its underlying literature to rigorous scrutiny and found it wanting. We might also imagine a world in which rigorous expertise and a functional peer review system flushed out obscurantism and penalized philosophical arguments that assumed their own conclusions in their premises.

Marx might still be studied in this world, but as a heterodox figure on the outskirts of intellectual life. There would no doubt be other socialists in the intellectual canon, but a more diverse variety in both emphasis and political methods – perhaps a socialism that followed Lassalle or Rodbertus in seeking a legislative route to its objectives, as opposed to revolutionary violence. Or perhaps we would see socialist schools that followed Proudhon or Bakunin – two contemporary competitors of Marx for leadership of the international socialist movements of his day. Or perhaps political socialism would follow the left-leaning faction of Henry George's movement, which Sun Yat-sen explicitly invoked when proclaiming a non-Marxian socialist Republic of China in 1912. Evincing Balfour's observations from 1885, George's Ngram patterns far outpaced Marx until switching places, shortly after the Russian Revolution.

No thanks to 1917, Marxism emerged as the dominant socialist tradition and effectively sidelined or squeezed out its main socialist competitors during his lifetime and the decades immediately after his death.[7] Successor reinventions of Marx have only served to recycle his theories as axioms, even as they falter under scrutiny.

As we turn our attention to today, we find another unsettling development. Marx has not only attained a hegemonic presence among other socialist theorists – he has also attained a hegemonic presence in intellectual life, placing pressure on all other competitor philosophies and displacing almost all other traditions – liberalism, conservatism, pluralism – as a favored method and approach of the academic elite across fields and disciplines that never even knew or meaningfully considered Marx until some four decades after his lifetime.

Curiously, Marx's track record in practice has done almost nothing to diminish his post-1917 stature. Historical amnesia surrounds the atrocities of his followers, as does an endless stream of dissociation and excuse-making for their failures. The Soviet Union, Maoist China, Kim's North Korea, Pol Pot's Cambodia, Castro's Cuba, Mugabe's Zimbabwe, Chavez and Maduro's Venezuela, and countless other deadly authoritarian regimes – all carried out in Marx's name, and celebrated by Marxists at their inception – are casually dismissed and dissociated from Marx's theories in their destructive aftermaths. They are not "true socialism" or "true Marxism," we are told, and it falls to the next socialist regime to implement Marx "the right way."

A succinct and representative example of this tendency among modern intellectuals may be seen in political theorist Matthew McManus's account of Marx's reputation over time:

> But of course the most substantial objection came from Karl Marx, whose epochal critique of political economy remains in some respects the climax of the modernist project ... Marxism became the chief theoretical outlook for most of the major socialist movements and parties by the end of the 19th century, with many achieving important reforms. But its reputation was seriously tarnished by the totalitarian movements in the Soviet Union, China, Cambodia, and elsewhere, which appealed to Marx's legacy to advance tyranny while taking serious liberties with his thought. With the collapse of the Soviet Empire in 1989, many thought socialisms' days were

> numbered, though it has since enjoyed a resurgence in popularity as the inequalities and vulgarities of neoliberalism became increasingly scrutinized. (McManus 2024, pp. 4–5)

Note that McManus errs in assigning high status to Marx's intellectual following in the late nineteenth century, which, as we have seen, he did not possess at any point in his life or for many decades thereafter. Neither does McManus substantiate his efforts to differentiate the humanitarian abuses of Marx's twentieth-century followers from Marx's own revolutionary theorizing. One is reminded of the quip of French philosopher Michel Foucault, who stated in a rare moment of clarity: "Rather than searching in [Marx's] texts for a condemnation in advance of the Gulag, it is a matter of asking what in those texts could have made the Gulag possible, what might even now continue to justify it, and what makes it intolerable truth still accepted today." "The Gulag question," Foucault continued, "must be posed not in terms of error (reduction of the problem to one of theory) but in terms of reality" (Foucault 1980, p. 135).

The reality of twentieth- and twenty-first-century Marxist governments is an unambiguous track record of tyranny and predation. As the empirical evidence shows, attempts to dissociate Marx from Marxism's track record are not simply a convenient rhetorical ploy – they are historically false and impossible. I cannot claim to know the exact course of the twentieth century in the absence of the Marxist-inspired Bolshevik Revolution, including whether other revolutionary uprisings would have occurred or who they would claim as their intellectual inspirations. But the history is clear that the deadly, illiberal, and tyrannical events of 1917 secured Marx's place in the intellectual canon – a place where he remains today, irrespective of the merits or record of his ideas. When modern Marxist intellectuals attempt to separate themselves from the history of Marxism in practice, they deny a central reason for the continued salience of their ideas: 1917 is the likely progenitor of their own interest in Marx.

Intellectuals – the secondhand dealers – nonetheless remain the primary mechanism for disseminating socialism, and are now reinventing its reputation. A curious feature of this process is the investment that these same disseminators make in maintaining the illusion of merit around their ideas. They proceed as if Marx actually possessed the superior arguments, having tapped the zeitgeist of industrial capitalism and diagnosed both its proximate defects and inevitable collapse in due time. And they proceed as if their prescriptive alternatives of socialism are self-evidently superior approaches to economic organization, glossing over socialism's disastrous performance in the last century or, more often, handwaving those episodes away as irrelevant and "not true socialism."

Alain Badiou, one of the leading figures to emerge from the 1960s New Left in Scruton's diagnostic assessment, offered a surprisingly candid retrospective of this pattern, all while remaining self-assured about the course he desires. After conceding that "around 1850 or 1860, nobody, apart from a tight little circle of activists, had heard of Marx yet," he turns to the role of mythology in sustaining certain intellectual currents. Badiou continues:

> A retrospective Marx was therefore constructed, as though he'd been a great public figure of the nineteenth century. That was not at all the case. He was totally obscure, as, for that matter, was Lenin for a long time ... We need to remember this: the career of revolutionary figures is often subterranean and has already gone through long periods of obscurity in the past. Long periods of obscurity that coincide every time, it must be said, with a boost in capitalism's globalism. (Badiou with Lancelin 2019, p. 60)

The myth, in turn, has become a self-sustaining narrative among the intellectuals who continue to champion socialism.

Note that the validity of Marx and later anti-capitalist causes is seldom questioned in these circles. It is assumed and incorporated into the basis of subsequent revolutionary action. Once again, Hayek's diagnosis seems appropriate:

> It is perhaps the most characteristic feature of the intellectual that he judges new ideas not by their specific merits but by the readiness with which they fit into his general conceptions, into the picture of the world which he regards as modern or advanced. (Hayek 1949, p. 423)

The secondhand dealer is neither a source of new knowledge nor a qualified curator of the same. He is a would-be designer of intellectual currents who picks and chooses his evidence, and even his myths, on the basis of convenience to a prior belief system. Merit has little room in this intellectual world, and neither does factual validity or rigor. For, as in Hayek's time as well as now, the secondhand dealer's "criterion must be consistency with his other views and suitability for combining into a coherent picture of the world" (Hayek 1949, p. 423).

## NOTES

1. Vanguardism traces its origins to Marx and Engels (1970). This text describes the Communists, of which Marx and Engels see themselves as representatives, as "the most advanced and resolute section of the working-class parties of every country, that section which pushes forward all others" (Marx and Engels 1970, p. 81).
2. In their own lifetimes, Rodbertus and Lassalle likely enjoyed greater influence than Marx among fellow socialists. Several late nineteenth-century scholars

of socialism ranked the quality of Rodbertus's theoretical expositions above Marx and assigned the latter to a secondary place in its niche literature. See e.g. Wagner (1878), Osgood (1886), and Andrews (1892). On a similar note, Lassalle was widely renowned for his skills as a political organizer and speaker – characteristics that won him posthumous praise from figures including Otto von Bismarck and Bertrand Russell. Marx, by contrast, eschewed public speaking and had a reputation for being temperamental – even toward his friends and allies.

3. The Scholarometer browser extension is available at https://scholarometer.indiana.edu/#author;4VSRHmIAAAAJ;0.
4. Author's calculations, Open Syllabus Project. http://www.opensyllabus.org.
5. A heterodox school of Marxist economists has existed since the late nineteenth century, albeit without any real influence in the profession. As Stigler (1988, p. 1733) wrote, this tradition comprises "a small minority of modern economists, and (...) their writings have virtually no impact upon the professional work of most economists in major English-language universities."
6. According to the Open Syllabus Project, Freire's *Pedagogy of the Oppressed* (1970) is the fourth most frequently assigned text in university classes on education, being outranked only by commonly used textbooks.
7. For a thoughtful commentary on the implications of this counterfactual scenario, see Rojas (2024).

## REFERENCES

Andrews E. B. (1892). Rodbertus's socialism. *Journal of Political Economy*, 1(1), pp. 50–67.

Badiou A. with Lancelin A. (2019). *In Praise of Politics*. Hoboken, NJ: John Wiley & Sons.

Balfour A. (1885). Land, land reformers, and the nation, in *Industrial Remuneration Conference: The Report of the Papers and Proceedings read in Prince's Hall, Picadilly*. London: Cassell & Company, p. 336–368.

Barker J. (2018). Happy Birthday, Karl Marx. You Were Right! *The New York Times*. https://www.nytimes.com/2018/04/30/opinion/karl-marx-at-200-influence.html [Accessed 21.06.2025].

Böhm-Bawerk E. von (1949). *Karl Marx and the Close of His System*. Edited by P. Sweezy. Translated by A. M. McDonald. New York, NY: Augustus M. Kelley.

Bortkiewicz L. von (1949). On the Correction of Marx's Fundamental Theoretical Construction in the Third Volume of Capital, in Sweezy P. (ed.), *Karl Marx and the Close of His System*. New York, NY: Augustus M. Kelley, pp. 197–221.

Butler C. V. (1907). Capital, by Karl Marx. Vol. II. The process of circulation of capital. Edited by Frederick Engels [review]. *Economic Journal*, 17(68), pp. 558–561.

Carver T. N. (1922). Review of *The Revival of Marxism* by J. Shield Nicholson. *University of Pennsylvania Law Review and American Law Register,* 70(4), pp. 363–365.

Copleston F. (2003). *A History of Philosophy: Volume 7. 18th and 19th century German Philosophy*. London: Continuum.

Coupé T. (2022). Who is the most sought-after economist? Ranking economists using Google Trends. *Southern Economic Journal*, 89(2), pp. 611–642.

Edgeworth F. Y. (1921). Review of *The Revival of Marxism* by J. Shield Nicholson. *Economic Journal*, 31(121), pp. 71–73.

Engels F. (1851). Letter from Engels to Marx 19 May 1851, in *Marx/Engels Collected Works* (MECW), Volume 38. New York, NY: International Publishers, p. 357.

Engels F. (1883). Funeral speech for Karl Marx, March 17, 1883 [Speech transcript], in Foner P. (ed.), *When Karl Marx Died*. New York, NY: International Publishers, pp. 18–19.

Fitzhugh G. (1857). *Cannibals All, or Slaves Without Masters*. Richmond, VA: A. Morris.

Foner P. (1973). *When Karl Marx Died*. New York, NY: International Publishers.

Foucault M. (1980). *Power/Knowledge: Selected Interviews and Other Writings, 1972–1977*. New York, NY: Random House.

Freire P. (1970). *Pedagogy of the Oppressed*. New York, NY: Continuum Books

Green E. (2016). *What are the most-cited publications in the social sciences (according to Google Scholar)?* May 12, 2016, LSE Blog. https://blogs.lse.ac.uk/impactofsocialsciences/2016/05/12/what-are-the-most-cited-publications-in-the-social-sciences-according-to-google-scholar/ [Accessed 21.06.2025].

Gross N., Simmons S. (2007). *The Social and Political Views of American Professors*. Unpublished paper presented at the Symposium on Professors and Their Politics, Harvard University.

Hayek F. von (1949). The intellectuals and socialism. *The University of Chicago Law Review*, 16(3), pp. 417–433.

Hobsbawm E. (1998). Introduction, in Marx K., Engels F. (eds.), *The Communist Manifesto: A Modern Edition*. London and New York: Verso, pp. 9–10.

Horkheimer M. (1972). Traditional and Critical Theory, in *Critical theory: Selected Essays*. Translated by M. O'Connell. New York, NY: Continuum, pp. 188–243.

Hyndman H. (1911). *The Record of an Adventurous Life*. London: Macmillan.

Jevons W. S. (1871). *The Theory of Political Economy*. London: Macmillan.

Keynes J. M. (1931). A short view of Russia, in *Essays in Persuasion*. London: Macmillan, pp. 253–271.

Korsch K. (1970). *Marxism and Philosophy*. Translated by F. Halliday. New York, NY: Monthly Review Press.

Lomasky L. (1989). Socialism as classical political philosophy. *Social Philosophy and Policy*, 6(2), pp. 112–138.

Magness P., Makovi M. (2023). The mainstreaming of Marx: Measuring the effect of the Russian Revolution on Karl Marx's influence. *Journal of Political Economy*, 131(6), pp. 1507–1545.

Magness P., Makovi M. (2024). *Did Karl Marx Party in 1891? The Effect of SPD's Erfurt Program on Karl Marx's Citations*. Working Paper.

Magness P., Waugh D. (2022). The hyperpoliticization of higher ed. *The Independent Review*, 27(3), pp. 359–370.

Marshall A. (1890). *Principles of Economics*. London: Macmillan.

Marx K., Engels F. (1970). *The Communist Manifesto*. New York, NY: Washington Square Press.

McManus M. (2024). *The Political Right and Equality: Turning Back the Tide of Egalitarian Modernity*. Abingdon, UK: Routledge.

Menger C. (2007). *Principles of Economics*. Translated by J. Dingwall, B. Hoselitz. Auburn, AL: Ludwig von Mises Institute.

Mises L. von (1944). *Omnipotent Government: The Rise of the Total State and Total War*. New Haven, CT: Yale University Press.
Mises L. von (1957). *Theory and History*. New Haven, CT: Yale University Press.
Olson M. (1965). *The Logic of Collective Action: Public Goods and the Theory of Groups*. Cambridge, MA: Harvard University Press.
Osgood, H. L. (1886). Scientific socialism. *Political Science Quarterly*, 1(4), pp. 560–594.
Popper K. (1970). Reason or revolution? *European Journal of Sociology*, 11(2), pp. 252–262.
Popper K. (1994). The Frankfurt School, in *The Myth of the Framework: In Defence of Science and Rationality*. London: Routledge, pp. 78–81.
Ramus P., Tcherkesoff W., Labriola E. (1906). *Die Urheberschaft des Kommunistischen Manifests*. Berlin, Germany: Freier Arbeiter-Verlag.
Rodbertus-Jagetzow C. (1850). *Sociale briefe an v. Kirchmann*. Berlin, Germany: F. Gerhard.
Rojas F. (2024). Was Marx a mistake for the Left? *Temple of Sociology*, January 9, 2024. https://templeofsociology.substack.com/p/was-marx-a-mistake-for-the-left [Accessed 23.06.2025].
Samuelson P. (1962). Economists and the history of ideas. *American Economic Review*, 52(1), pp. 1–18.
Scruton R. (2019). *Fools, Frauds, and Firebrands: Thinkers of the New Left*. London: Bloomsbury Continuum.
Stigler G. (1988). Palgrave's Dictionary of Economics. *Journal of Economic Literature*, 26(4), pp. 1729–1736.
Tooze A. (2018). Why Karl Marx is More Relevant than Ever. May 4, 2018. *Financial Times*. https://www.ft.com/content/cf6532dc-4c67-11e8-97e4-13afc22d86d4 [Accessed 21.06.2025].
Wagner A. (1878). *Briefe von Ferdinand Lassalle an Carl Rodbertus-Jagetzow*. Volume 1. Berlin, Germany: Puttkammer & Mühlbrecht.
Waugh D. (2022). The Hyperpoliticization of Higher Ed. *The Independent Review*, 27(3), pp. 359–370.
Wicksteed P. (1885). The Jevonian criticism of Marx. *To-day: Monthly Magazine of Scientific Socialism*, 3(16), pp. 177–179.

# 3. Evolution of institutions and orders of actions in Hayek: two different theories of two distinct spontaneous phenomena

**Stefano Moroni**

## INTRODUCTION

It is common knowledge that "spontaneous order" is one of the pivotal concepts of F.A. Hayek's thought. In this regard, Jason Potts (2013) pointed out that Hayek's work contains two different mechanisms that tend to overlap within this concept of spontaneous order, namely the evolution of rules and network coordination. This chapter[1] intends to delve further into the issue and draw this distinction even more radically. In particular, it will argue that we are not dealing simply with two different mechanisms within a unified theory, but with two distinct *theories* (which may or may not be combined): (i) the theory of the spontaneous evolution of social institutions and (ii) the theory of the spontaneous order of actions.

## TWO THEORIES ABOUT TWO DIFFERENT SPONTANEOUS PHENOMENA

As suggested, it is possible and necessary to establish a clear distinction between two of Hayek's theories on two separate phenomena: first, his theory regarding the spontaneous evolution of social institutions (developed mainly in Hayek, 1982 and 1988); and second, his theory of the spontaneous order of actions (already clear in his early work, e.g. Hayek, 1948). The two theories must be kept distinct because they pivot on: (i) different "unintended (ordered) phenomena" that are "unplanned" in a different sense;[2] (ii) different kinds of "emergence";[3] (iii) different kinds of "knowledge" (available in society); (iv) different kinds of "invisible-hand explanations".[4]

Unfortunately, Hayek's later work tends to blur this distinction, principally because of his rather haphazard and increasingly unfocused use of the term "spontaneous order", a habit followed by many of his disciples. Discussing Hayek's perspective, Kley (1994, p. 26) observes: "While a ubiquitous theme, the idea of a spontaneous order does not receive a sufficiently systematic treatment in his writings. This shows in the secondary literature, where the views about its substance, its scope, and its significance as an analytical concept differ widely." Similarly, Hodgson (1993, p. 177) writes: "A serious shortcoming of Hayek's work [is] a lack of clarity about the crucial concept of spontaneous order".

The confusion has been further exacerbated by Hayek's notorious binary opposition between "constructivism" and "evolutionism". Employed by Hayek to qualify his personal position, the latter term shifts the bulk of the emphasis onto the theory of (spontaneous) evolution, relegating the theory of (spontaneous) order to second place.

For this reason, I shall discuss these two theories separately. For each of them, the following four questions will be considered: (i) What are the basic claims of the theory? (ii) Exactly what unintended ordered phenomenon does it aim to explain? (iii) In what way does it do this (i.e. what kind of invisible-hand explanation does it employ)? (iv) Who were Hayek's precursors and who inspired him to explore this path?

## FIRST THEORY: THE THEORY OF THE SPONTANEOUS EVOLUTION OF SOCIAL INSTITUTIONS

Hayek developed this theory toward the end of his life (although elements of it can be found in earlier works, e.g. Hayek, 1967, it is in Hayek 1982 and, especially, Hayek 1988 that the theory is constructed). As Hodgson (1993, pp. 158–159) notes: "We have to wait until the late 1980s to receive the fullest explicit statement of Hayek's evolutionary conception, in a few pages of *The Fatal Conceit*. Given the significance of an idea of the 'evolution' of social institutions in Hayek's mature work, it is odd that it receives so little elaboration." See also Naomi Beck (2015, p. 85): "Hayek's theory of cultural evolution was slow to mature. Its most detailed account appeared only four years prior to his death, in the incomplete manuscript *The Fatal Conceit* [...]." Compared to the second theory, which is discussed below (the theory of the spontaneous social order of actions), the theory of the spontaneous evolution of social institutions is barely sketched; indeed, Hayek gave it scant treatment. To quote Viktor Vanberg (2001, p. 59): "Hayek's theory of cultural evolution is not a tightly reasoned, well-integrated body of arguments, but, instead, a more loosely connected set of general ideas and conjectures."

## Characteristics

*First question: What are the basic arguments of the theory?* Hayek's theory of the spontaneous evolution of "social institutions" – interpreted as durable and established systems of basic social rules of conduct – puts forward two arguments (Hayek, 1982, 1988). The first argument is that most social institutions are the unintentional outcome of a slow evolution process over a very long time. Evolution, in this case, is a process of trial and error comprised of three steps: (i) the first step is the *generation* of a variety of practices and rules; (ii) the second step is the *competition* among and reduction of the variety of rules via selection; (iii) the third step is the *propagation* and persistence of the solution – that is, the system of rules – selected. The specific mechanism at work here is a form of "group selection": the central idea is that certain rules evolve and spread because members of groups that comply with them enjoy greater success – in particular, in terms of welfare and numerical increase – than do members of groups that do not accept them, or accept different rules.[5] The second argument is that institutions which have evolved over time embody the acquired knowledge/wisdom of several generations: they are a store, a distillate, of successful experimentations; they therefore embody a quantity of knowledge which would be otherwise inaccessible to an individual mind. This accumulated wisdom is therefore of a largely stable and stabilising nature (rather than dynamic and catalysing). As Hayek (1988, p. 75) writes: "Most knowledge [...] is obtained not from immediate experience or observation, but in the continuous process of sifting a learnt tradition, which requires individual recognition and following of [...] traditions." In brief: "Tradition is in some respects superior to, or 'wiser' than, human reason" (Hayek, 1988, p. 75).

*Second question: What type of unintended (emergent) phenomena does the theory aim to explain?* The type of ordered unintended phenomenon covered by the theory is a "system of rules". The spontaneous emergent elements are, in this case, the basic social institutions.

*Third question: What type of reasoning does the theory employ?* The invisible-hand explanation used in this case does not presuppose the existence of given rules, but competitive sets of rules in formation and transformation. This invisible-hand explanation is quite generic: it relies on few conditions from the outset. It employs a form of "conjectural history": that is, a reconstruction of how the systems of rules might have come into being.[6] In other words, conjectural history is a rational reconstruction of a hypothetical kind of social process which may never have been directly observed but which, if it had effectively taken place, would have produced the phenomenon at issue (in our case, the propagation and perpetuation of certain institutions). This is an investigation that tries "to make intelligible why some rules rather than others had prevailed" (Hayek, 1988, p. 69). And it is a kind of *teleological* explanation (even if a very particular one), in that even if it does not imply any design by a voluntary maker, it effectively implies the idea that certain kinds of institutions would not have endured if they had not functioned in a manner likely to produce certain effects (i.e. increasing the number and welfare of the groups adopting them) (Hayek, 1967, pp. 66–81).[7]

*Fourth question: Who were the precursors and inspirers of this aspect of Hayek's work?* Those who preceded and steered Hayek's thought toward this first type of theory include such thinkers as David Hume (2000 [1739]), Adam Ferguson (1995 [1767]), and Edmund Burke (1999 [1790]). Endorsing the assertion that the two theories under discussion – the theory of the spontaneous evolution of institutions, and the theory of the spontaneous order of actions – should be treated as distinct from each other, it may be noted that the three authors just cited furnished considerable inspiration for Hayek's theory of the evolution of institutions, but limited material (and in some cases none) for the theory of the spontaneous order of actions. Ferguson (1995 [1767]), for instance, shows considerable regard and insight on the spontaneous evolution of social institutions, whereas the basic nature and advantages of spontaneous (market) order seem to elude him.[8]

## Clarifications

Evolutionary processes have some similarities in biological and cultural evolution. Three crucial aspects that are particularly important to stress, for both biological and cultural evolution, are the following. First, neither biological evolution nor cultural evolution follows "inevitable laws of historical development"; in other words, they do not conform to predefined specific phases or stages through which evolution must necessarily pass. Evolution is an open-ended process. It is thus not possible to predict future developments in detail. "All evolution [...] is a process of continuous adaptation to unforeseeable events, to contingent circumstances which could not have been forecast. [...] Evolutionary theory can never put us in the position of rationally predicting and controlling future evolution" (Hayek, 1988, p. 25). Second, every evolutionary process is contingent, inasmuch as it could just as easily not have come about – or not happened in the way in which it actually did. Third, every evolutionary process leads to sub-optimal results. An evolutionary process cannot attain optimal results because it acts on certain causal variations and not on all possible variants (Simon, 1983; Elster, 1989; Hodgson, 2004). This notwithstanding, it can achieve crucial results where other mechanisms would have failed.

Two important differences between natural evolution and cultural-institutional evolution are instead the following. First, whilst the contemporary biological evolutionary approach does not rest primarily on the inheritance of acquired characteristics and traits, cultural development rests specifically on such kinds of inheritance: that is, the inheritance of rules of conduct, rules that are not innate but learnt through experience. Each individual then acquires rules of conduct from society at large: cultural evolution comes about through the transmission of information and habits, not solely from the individual's physical parents but also from a large, indefinite number of human ancestors (Hayek, 1988). Second, there is a crucial difference regarding the origin of variations: the raw material upon which natural biological selection acts is supplied by chance genetic mutations; on the contrary, the material on which institutional evolution acts is supplied by human trial and error, by intentional agents trying to deal with life problems.

## SECOND THEORY: THE THEORY OF SPONTANEOUS SOCIAL ORDERS

In contrast with the theory of the spontaneous evolution of social institutions, Hayek began formulating his theory of the spontaneous order of actions early on in his career in the 1930s and, unlike its counterpart, this theory was expanded and developed in great depth throughout his subsequent work.

### Characteristics

*First question: What are the basic arguments of the theory?* The theory of spontaneous social orders pivots largely on two fundamental arguments (Hayek, 1948, 1967, 1982). The first argument posits that complex social orders like the market – that is, orders which entail the spontaneous efficient coordination of innumerable independent individual actions – can come into being if the individuals concerned follow certain abstract rules that allow them to freely pursue their own ends according to their personal abilities and knowledge. In short, the formation of a spontaneous social order is the result of individuals following certain abstract rules in their responses to their immediate environment. "The responses of the individuals to the events in their environment need be similar only in certain abstract aspects to ensure that a determinate overall order will result" (Hayek, 1982, vol. I, p. 44). Consequently, the general spontaneous order that emerges is not part either of the specific ends of the individuals (inasmuch as nobody acts with the aim of establishing an overall order of actions), or of the rules *per se* (inasmuch as no given rule is aimed intentionally at the formation of some overall order of actions). Hence, order itself does not exist *ex ante* – in all its details – in the minds of individuals; rather, it develops *ex post*. In short, the causes behind the emergence of order are endogenous: order is self-organising. Furthermore, this polycentric and non-hierarchic order is flexible and dynamic: it is able to adapt itself to new circumstances. Spontaneous order is therefore a "transcendent" order, a superindividual pattern: that is, an order that may persist even if its various components are different in type or in number. In fact, to ensure that such an order endures over time a certain relational structure must be maintained; its components, that is to say, must remain interrelated in some way. The second argument – to resume the more general discussion – is that complex social orders of this type generate greater knowledge than any other kind, with wide-ranging benefits. Moreover, the kind of knowledge that emerges in this case is – as happens in market systems – dynamic and catalysing (rather than static and stabilising), in the sense that it is continually produced and adjusted by the intrinsic competitive workings of the spontaneous order (Heiner, 1990; Witt, 1997; Chiles et al., 2010).

*Second question: What unintended (emergent) ordered phenomenon does the theory aim to explain?* The type of ordered phenomenon to which the theory refers is an order of actions that depends on certain rules of conduct. The spontaneous aspect is the emergence of a pattern of (unintentional) cooperation. Note that institutions – rules of conduct – ensure a certain kind of correspondence of expectations (a first-level correspondence of expectations), but this does not already constitute the order of society that is crucial for Hayek. The spontaneous order of actions (a second-level correspondence of expectations) is the unplanned result of the fact that individuals follow these rules and freely react to their environmental conditions.

*Third question: What kind of explanation does the theory involve?* The invisible-hand explanation presupposes in this case a certain set of abstract rules, and it takes account of the unintended emergence of a particular form of interrelation between individual actions. This invisible-hand explanation is more specific than the previous one because it can rely upon various preconditions: for example, the existence of certain rules. In the words of Hayek (1967, p. 72), "for the explanation of the functioning of the social order at any one time the rules of individual conduct must be assumed to be given". It is important to stress that the invisible-hand type of explanation applied in this case does not constitute an example of *conjectural history*; in particular, it does not reconstruct any "history". Furthermore, it is not a teleological explanation.

*Fourth question: Who were Hayek's precursors and sources of inspiration on this question?* For this second type of theory, Hayek's sources include Bernard Mandeville (1997 [1714]) and Adam Smith (1993 [1776]). Confirming that the two theories discussed here are distinct, note that while Smith and Mandeville are evident precursors of Hayek's theory on the spontaneous order of actions, their influence is entirely absent from Hayek's theory of the evolution of social institutions. In the early editions of the *Fable of Bees*, Mandeville (1997 [1714]) maintained, in fact, that social institutions and norms of conduct are introduced deliberately: he proposed a "conspiracy theory" on the emergence of social institutions and rules, suggesting that moral conduct is a cunning invention; in other words, Mandeville ruled out the spontaneous emergence of social institutions and norms over time.[9] Smith (1978 [1762]) sketched a generic and tentative stadial theory of development in his *Lectures on Jurisprudence*, but he never constructed an original or significant theory on the evolution of institutions.[10] In short: "A theory of cultural evolution [...] is not present in Smith" (Petsoulas, 2001, p. 147). Here arises a good opportunity to briefly digress also on Darwin. Hayek (1988) maintains that Darwin had derived his ideas for spontaneous evolution from Smith. Darwin had doubtlessly read the work of Smith; but, in light of the above, although he found insights in it on issues concerning social instincts and actions, he would have found nothing to inspire a proper theory of evolution. In short, while it is true that the evolutionary study of society and culture long antedates Darwin (Sahlins and Service, 1960), Smith probably does not figure among the precursors of Darwinian (or some other kind of) evolutionary theory.[11] To conclude: "The search for a sophisticated idea of evolution or anything clearly resembling natural selection in Smith's writings is in vain" (Hodgson, 1993, p. 59).

## Clarifications

Three particular points need stressing: first, we must clarify which rules must be present so that the emergence of a spontaneous order of actions is fostered; second, we must specify the distinction between *systems of rules* and *orders of actions* (a distinction that seems to have eluded many of Hayek's commentators);[12] third, we must bear in mind that the emergence of spontaneous order does not necessarily require rules that are themselves spontaneous in nature (another point that has eluded many of Hayek's commentators and disciples).[13]

Let us start with the issue concerning types of rules. Made orders are regulated by "concrete rules" (i.e. rules of organisation), whereas spontaneous orders are regulated by "abstract rules" (i.e. rules of conduct). Concrete rules are specific, end-state-dependent, short-run oriented and prevalently positive. On the contrary, abstract rules are generic, end-state-independent, long-run oriented, and prevalently negative: that is, they are rules that: (i) refer to general types of situations or actions and apply equally to everyone, or at least to whole classes of individuals (they must be applicable to an unknown and indeterminable number of instances and persons); (ii) are independent of any specific result, outcome or end-state; (iii) must serve in the long run (they must be stable, and adhered to, for long periods); and (iv) merely prohibit individuals from interfering with the protected domain of other individuals rather than imposing some positive duty or action (they merely serve to prevent certain severe conflicts and predefined tangible and direct types of harm).

A second crucial point concerns the necessity to distinguish the spontaneous social order – that is, a situation that entails the unintended reciprocal coordination of actions among individuals – from the system of abstract rules that contribute *indirectly* to its emergence. As noted by Hayek (1967, p. 66) in the introduction to a fundamental chapter in one of his most important books: "The purpose of these notes is to clarify the conceptual tools with which we describe facts [...]. More particularly, their aim is to make clear the important distinction between the systems of rules of conduct which govern the behaviour of the individual members of a group (or of the elements of any order) on the one hand, and, on the other hand, the order or pattern of actions which results from this for the group as a whole." See also Hayek (1967, p. 67): "That the systems of rules of individual conduct and the order of actions which results from the individuals acting in accordance with them are not the same thing should be obvious as soon as it is stated, although the two are in fact frequently confused." This same point is stressed again in Hayek (1982, vol. I, p. 113): "The order of actions is a factual state of affairs distinct from the rules which contribute to its formation." The distinction between the system of rules and the order of actions can be highlighted in a simpler and more immediate way by observing that an order for the whole society does not simply materialise whenever individual behaviours of a certain kind are regular in themselves; it only does so when certain forms of regularity in individual behaviour occur (Hayek, 1982). In any event, in many cases we discover the particular function which certain rules serve only after we have understood the spontaneous order produced by individual actions in accordance with them. As Hayek observes (1982, vol. I, p. 113), regrettably even scholars of law frequently confuse the system of rules of conduct and the order of actions: "Although people are usually well enough aware that in some sense the rules of law are required to preserve 'order', they tend to identify this order with obedience to the rules and will not be aware that the rules serve an order in a different way, namely to effect a certain correspondence between the action of different persons." As already said, the matching of certain expectations granted by the existence of certain abstract rules does not already represent order in society; compliance with such abstract rules is actually a simple precondition for order – an order of actions that effectively depends upon both general rule-following *and* individual adjustment. To conclude: observe how, whilst in the case of a "spontaneous order" (e.g. the market) the system of rules and the order of actions do not coincide, in the case of a "made order" (e.g. an organisation) the system of rules and the order of actions tend to coincide.

A third important issue concerns the not necessarily spontaneous nature of the rules in question. The spontaneous and unintended nature attributed to the complex orders of actions discussed above does not necessarily clash with the deliberate introduction of rules and regulatory systems, at least those of a certain kind. In other words, spontaneous orders of actions do not perforce or exclusively require spontaneous rules. As Hayek (1978, p. 74) writes: "A spontaneous order may rest in part on regularities which are not spontaneous but imposed." See also Hayek (1982, vol. I, p. 45):

> The spontaneous character of the resulting order must [...] be distinguished from the spontaneous origin of the rules on which it rests, and it is possible that an order which would still have to be described as spontaneous rests on rules which are entirely the result of deliberate design [...]. That even an order which rests on made rules may be spontaneous in character is shown by the fact that its particular manifestation will always depend on many circumstances which the designer of these rules did not and could not know.

## THE MARKET AS A SPONTANEOUS INSTITUTION, THE MARKET AS A SPONTANEOUS ORDER

In this section, the distinction between the theory of spontaneous evolution of social institutions and the theory of spontaneous social order is used to draw a clear demarcation line – contrary to some current trends – between the market as a spontaneous *institution* and the market as a spontaneous *order*. This demarcation does not imply a simple distinction between long-term and short-term (market) dynamics, but a more fundamental distinction between different types of emergent phenomena and social dynamics. Drawing a distinction between the market as a spontaneous institution and as a spontaneous order within Hayek's perspective seems feasible both *historically* (in his early studies Hayek neatly explained the functioning of a spontaneous market order without referring to the idea of the spontaneous evolution of institutions, a concept he introduced later), and *theoretically* (the Hayekian explanation of the market's functioning – and of the formation of an order of actions within it – is possible and interesting whether we suppose either that the underlying rules of conduct evolved spontaneously or that they were deliberately introduced).

### The Market as a Spontaneous Institution

If we embrace Hayek's theory of the spontaneous evolution of social institutions, we can argue that the market system – as a specific form of institution – is "spontaneous" because nobody deliberately invented or set it up at any particular time in history. Instead, it emerged spontaneously and unintentionally over a long period of time. (By the same logic, language itself is a "spontaneous" phenomenon.) Hayek speaks of a process of trial and error which overall lasted hundreds of thousands of years before producing the distinctive set of abstract rules that characterise current market systems. The theory of the spontaneous evolution of social institutions therefore explains how and why certain types of institutions (i.e. a market structure) superseded other types of institutions (i.e. non-market structures).

It is the idea of the market as a social institution that Hayek (1978, p. 11) had in mind when he observed that the market system could not have been invented deliberately: "This follows from the fact that the result could not have been foreseen. None of our ancestors could have known that the protection of property and contracts would lead to an extensive division of labour, specialisation and the establishment of markets." He reiterated this point frequently in his work: "We have never designed our economic system. We were not intelligent enough for that" (Hayek, 1982, vol. III, p. 164).

Similarly, the market as a spontaneous institution was what Herbert Simon (1981, p. 47) had in mind when he wrote (in a text in which he acknowledged the important contribution of Hayek's theoretical works): "No one supposes that a modern organisation-&-market economy is the product of deliberate design. Surely it evolved from earlier subsistence economies (...) over thousands of years".

## The Market as Spontaneous Order

If we embrace Hayek's theory of spontaneous order, we can argue that the market is "spontaneous" because the rules of conduct typically associated with it do not contain instructions directly aimed at constructing the order of actions that emerges. The mutual matching of individual expectations that emerge within a market system – thanks also to the mechanism of pricing that works like a telecommunication system – is therefore, in that sense, utterly unplanned.

It is the idea of the market as a social order of actions that Hayek had in mind when he noted how the market is a self-organising mechanism that enables the individuals taking part in exchanges to have greater opportunities than are offered by any other known economic system. This idea of the market was what James Buchanan (1977, pp. 25–39) also had in mind when he wrote – in a chapter in which he discussed Hayek's contribution – that the crucial principle to be highlighted in economics is the principle of the spontaneous order of the market: Buchanan was thinking of the principle whereby – in a market system that has no top-down planning – supermarket shelves supply such desired goods as tomato sauce.

Note that the coordination of independent actions, the efficient use of dispersed know-how, and the creation of widespread prosperity are possible in a market system thanks to the *combined* functioning of a framework of rules and the price system. Certainly, in his early work Hayek placed the main emphasis on the role of prices, whereas in later works he laid greater stress on the abstract rules. The point is not that in later Hayek the abstract rules tend to supersede the price system in fostering the coordination and employment of dispersed knowledge (Fleetwood, 1997); rather, more simply, it is that those abstract rules are combined with the price system in carrying out this role (Runde, 1997). Notably, in their reflections on how to reduce the uncertainties of the social world through forms of coordination, many sociologists have tended to foreground only the former aspect – the importance of social rules and institutions – while many economists have stressed the latter – the importance of orders of actions. The originality of Hayek's thought is that it considers both these aspects jointly.

As stated above, the theory of spontaneous order only explains the *role* – the function, the importance – of certain rules; it does not explain their *genesis* (which is the province of the theory of the spontaneous evolution of institutions discussed earlier).

It should also be noted that, by interpreting the market as principally a spontaneous *institution* rather than a spontaneous *order*, we cannot deploy Hayek's well-known "epistemic" critique of centralised planning.[14] In contrast, note that it was only by considering the market principally as a spontaneous *order* and not so much as a spontaneous *institution* that Hayek was able to conduct his renowned epistemic critique of centralised planning. As is well known, this critique holds that it is not possible to introduce a form of intentional organisation and coordination of the various actions and activities that can guarantee the activation and efficient use of dispersed knowledge in the same way as it is possible to obtain it via a spontaneous type of order (i.e. the market). More precisely, it is impossible intentionally to concentrate the dispersed knowledge that enables complex economic systems to function because this knowledge is: (i) *situated* (i.e. it is know-how – and not know-that – specific in space and time); (ii) *tacit* (i.e. it is know-how acquired through a process of "learning by doing", and therefore one that is internalised in the minds of individuals, who make use of it without deliberate, explicit reflection); and (iii) *dynamic* (i.e. it changes over time, sometimes rapidly). It is therefore intrinsically impossible intentionally to make dispersed knowledge "public". An attempt to do so – that is, intentionally to centralise knowledge and guide the economy – would result in a drop in productivity and efficiency due to the fact that we would be forcing the system to use less than the knowledge actually available in society, and thereby reducing the opportunities for experimentation.

It is important to note that the market does not merely "gather" dispersed knowledge; rather, it incentivises individuals to "generate" it (Butos and McQuade, 2002). Even Hayek himself, who placed little emphasis on this aspect in his early writings, later wrote that to define the problem of economic competition solely "as one of utilising knowledge dispersed among hundreds of thousands of individuals still over-simplifies its character"; indeed: "it is not merely a task of utilising information about particular concrete facts which the individuals already possess, but one of using their abilities of discovering such facts as will be relevant [...] in the particular situation" (Hayek, 1982, vol. III, p. 190).

## REFLECTIONS ON THE "DEGREE OF RELATION" BETWEEN THE THEORY OF SPONTANEOUS EVOLUTION AND THE THEORY OF SPONTANEOUS ORDER

So far I have argued that the theory of the evolution of social institutions and the theory of spontaneous social order are two distinct theories. That said, while they are distinct, can we say that they are in some way "relatives"? In certain passages it would appear that Hayek himself (1967, p. 77; 1978, p. 250; 1982, vol. III, p. 158, and 1988, p. 146) considered the two ideas of the evolution of institutions and of spontaneous order to be "twins", but unfortunately his statements to this effect were very ambiguous, and he did nothing to spell out exactly what he meant. As Petsoulas (2001, p. 16) writes: "This is one of the most puzzling statements in his social theory, for it is never systematically explored". See also Schmidtchen (2000, p. 32): "Hayek never delivered a formal model of the 'twin ideas' hypothesis". And Kley (1994, p. 39): "He never explains satisfactorily what renders the idea of a spontaneous order and the theory of cultural evolution 'twin conceptions'."

If we hypothesise that somehow the two theories could be "twins", there are five possible ways in which this could happen (and Hayek seems to oscillate among them); they concern: (i) commonality; (ii) compatibility; (iii) inseparability; (iv) interchangeability; and (v) genesis.

The first possible reason for their being twin theories is that they have several significant characteristics in common – they might be said to be recognisable among many other theories because of certain "family traits", as it were: for instance, they both give precedence to unintended (ordered and emergent) phenomena; they give preference to invisible-hand explanations; and they acknowledge a central role of the institutions. To my mind, this first interpretation is highly plausible.

The second possible reason for their being considered twin theories is that they are "compatible"; in other words, they are not incompatible and can "operate in parallel". This too seems reasonably plausible. (To say that the two theories are compatible does not necessarily mean that they are also interdependent – which effectively they are not.[15])

A third possible reason is that the two theories are inseparable: that is, they always operate in tandem. This seems only partly plausible. Although the two theories may go hand in hand (as stated above, they are in fact compatible), they can also come about separately. Hayek himself often points out that a spontaneous order of actions can come about even if the abstract rules that fostered its emergence were introduced deliberately.

A fourth possible reason for their being twins is that the former is the "clone" of the latter; that is to say, the theory of the spontaneous evolution of institutions is by and large a re-proposal of the original theory of spontaneous order, set in another ambit.[16] This explanation seems unconvincing, given that Hayek's theory of the spontaneous evolution of social institutions is not merely a "projection" of his theory of spontaneous order onto another reality, but in many respects an entirely new theory in its own right.

A fifth possible reason for their being twin theories is that they are the offspring of the same "mother theory", namely a unified theory of unintended ordered phenomena. There can be no doubt that from the outset Hayek (1952) had a general theory of this type in mind, but he did not develop it; nor, to my knowledge, have others done so.[17]

To conclude, the theory of spontaneous social order and the theory of the spontaneous evolution of social institutions share certain similarities in how they are formulated; they often operate in tandem (though not necessarily always); and they can also be complementary – but this in no way entails that the two are indistinguishable from each other. The degree of relation between the two theories is therefore not as close as might appear at first sight; let us therefore say that they are more "cousins" than "twins" in their kinship.

## TWO EXPLANATORY THEORIES

There is one last vital point that should be clarified before concluding. At every stage of my argument for drawing a distinction between the theory of the spontaneous evolution of social institutions and that of spontaneous social order, and for treating the two as separate but compatible, I have assumed that both of them are theories of a descriptive-explanatory nature, and not axiological-normative. While this assumption is quite plausible for the latter of the two theories, it is admittedly problematic as regards the former.

Some critics in fact argue that Hayek implied that the theory of the spontaneous evolution of social institutions also (some say mainly) had a *normative* element, and hence that it would deem evolutive outcomes as positive in themselves. In other words, they charge Hayek with subscribing to a form of "evolutionary ethics" (Walker, 1986, pp. 53–54; Kley, 1994, pp. 137–138). I think such claims are inaccurate, while acknowledging that a more systematic inquiry by Hayek himself would have been useful.

Hayek did not claim that the outcomes of the spontaneous evolution of social institutions are above criticism, but rather that such criticism should be partial and gradual. As Hayek (1988, p. 27) himself notes: "I do not claim that the results of group selection of traditions are necessarily 'good' – any more than I claim that other things that have long survived in the course of evolution, such as cockroaches, have moral value." Therefore: "Recognising that rules generally tend to be selected, via competition, on the basis of their human survival-value certainly does not protect those rules from critical scrutiny" (Hayek, 1988, p. 20). See also Hayek (1960, p. 36): "It is, of course, a mistake to believe that we can draw conclusions about what our values ought to be simply because we realise that they are a product of evolution." The kind of scrutiny applicable to systems of rules that have percolated down through time should be a type of "immanent criticism"; one that focuses on discrete issues, one at a time, proceeding gradually (Hayek, 1978, pp. 18–22; 1982, vol. I, pp. 118–122 and vol II, pp. 24–27). In short: while certain institutions and traditions cannot be justified and "demonstrated" in the way that scientistic rationalism demanded, their long processes of formation and development can be reconstructed thanks to an evolutionary view. In doing so we can to some degree understand how they work, and to the extent that we succeed in this endeavour, we can revise and improve our institutions by remedying recognisable defects through gradual improvement (Hayek, 1988).

In conclusion, to claim that the acceptance of an evolutionary theory of social institutions entails the absolute impossibility of reforming those institutions would have quite simply been an error of logic (Goodin, 1996, pp. 27–30; Ruttan, 2003, pp. 4–8, 271–272; Alexander, 2011). On the contrary: "reform of the basic rules of the game in a democratic society is fully compatible with an evolutionary view of social change" (Vaughn, 1994, p. 229).[18] The crucial point is simply that accepting an evolutionary theory of social institutions (i.e. an empirical theory of the emergence of institutions – albeit empirical in a special sense) implies that only certain specific types of deliberate institutional reform are possible, and not others (Moroni, 2010 and 2011). In particular, it is better to use a dynamic, strictly "non-engineerist" approach that: (i) acknowledges the distinctive nature of social institutions (in particular, their difference from organisations); (ii) recognises the non-tabula-rasa scenario in which the problem of reforming them normally arises (reformed institutions are always successor institutions); (iii) encourages humility (very often the point is not to "invent" institutions, but to be able to recognise and implement those institutions that have evolved over time and have proved to foster beneficial forms of cooperation) and gradualism (i.e. incremental improvement) (Moroni, 2021). The issue is not simply one of being conservative or not, of recognising or not the possibility of transcending our "institutional embeddedness" (in both cases, the answer lies somewhere in between). It is to recognise that institutions are entirely different from the other elements that we usually manage. Consequently, we must adopt a wholly different approach if we want to comprehend them and, especially, if we intend to deal with them properly.

## CONCLUSION

In conclusion, the importance of considering the theory of spontaneous order of actions and the theory of spontaneous evolution of institutions as separate theories should be reiterated. Many commentators and followers of Hayek still fail to appreciate this important distinction,[19] a failure which can generate some undesirable overlaps among explanatory levels and concepts. It is an interesting challenge to assess whether and how it is possible to devise a more general theory of spontaneous phenomena that covers a variety of different types of unintended patterns (diZerega, 2013). To my mind, this challenge is still ongoing, and I hope that the discussion of Hayek's work conducted in this chapter will shed some light on the intricacies, opportunities, and difficulties of this enterprise.

## NOTES

1. This chapter is a substantially revised version of Moroni (2014).
2. Unintentional consequences of human actions (i.e. consequences that diverge from the individuals' intentions) make it impossible to reduce social theory to mere questions of psychology (Hayek, 1952; Popper, 1945; Watkins, 1968). The central questions which the social sciences address arise precisely because the intentional activities of individuals generate forms of regularity that are not foreseen, nor intended by any of them (Moroni, 2012).
3. "Emergent properties" stand in contrast to "aggregate properties": emergent phenomena depend on their constituent parts but are *irreducible* to them (Polanyi, 1958; Popper, 1972). The idea of emergence suggests that reality is stratified (Lewis, 2011, 2012); it entails genuine novelty (Foster and Metcalfe, 2012). Of particular relevance to the following discussion is Martin and Sunley's (2012) study on different *levels* of emergence in the social sphere.
4. "Invisible-hand explanations" take account of the formation of an "ordered" phenomenon without presupposing the presence of an "ordinator". Invisible-hand explanations therefore often supplant visible-hand (e.g. conspiratorial) ones, positing *complex* and *indirect* cause-and-effect relations in place of more *simple* and *direct* ones (Nozick, 1974, pp. 18–22, 1997, pp. 191–197). Therefore, invisible-hand explanations often contain an element of "surprise" (Ullmann-Margalit, 1978).
5. As many have pointed out, there are doubts as to whether Hayek's idea of group selection is actually compatible with the methodological individualism that he initially professed; interesting as this point is, I shall not deal with it here (on this, see Moroni, 2005, pp. 87–113).
6. The notion of *conjectural history* was first introduced by Dougald Stewart (1829 [1793], p. 31): "In examining the history of mankind [...] when we cannot trace the process by which an event *has been* produced, it is often of importance to be able to show how it *may have been produced*." "To this

species of philosophical investigation [...] I shall take the liberty of giving the title of *Theoretical* or *Conjectural History*" (Stewart, 1829 [1793], p. 31).

7. On the idea that this is still an invisible-hand explanation, even if it is one of a very particular (functional-evolutionary) kind, see in particular Ullmann-Margalit (1978). See also Heath (1992).
8. Here are three verdicts by Ferguson on commercial societies (characterised by the division of labour) that take a position opposite to that of the Hayekian theory of spontaneous market order. "In every commercial state, notwithstanding any pretension to equal rights, the exaltation of a few must depress the many" (Ferguson, 1995 [1767], p. 177). "The desire of profit stifles the love of perfection. Interest cools the imagination, and hardens the heart" (Ferguson, 1995 [1767], p. 206). "The separation of profession, while it seems to promise improvement of skills, [...] serves, in some measure, to break the bonds of society" (Ferguson, 1995 [1767], p. 207).
9. "It is evident that the first rudiments of morality, broached by skilful politicians, to render men useful to each other as well as tractable, were chiefly contrived that the ambitious might reap the more benefit from, and govern vast numbers of them" (Mandeville, 1997 [1714], p. 39). "By society I understand a body politic, in which man, either subdued by superior force or by persuasion drawn from his savage state, has become a disciplined creature that can find his own ends in labouring for others, and where under one head or other forms of government each member is rendered subservient to the whole, and all of them by cunning management are made to act as one" (Mandeville, 1997 [1714], p. 137). I think (see also Petsoulas, 2001, pp. 78–106) it is difficult to maintain that in his *Dialogues Between Horatio and Cleomenes,* Mandeville (1997 [1729]) later developed an authentic evolutionary theory of social institutions, as claimed by Goldsmith (1985).
10. This point was made clear by Menger (1985 [1883], p. 172):

    > What Adam Smith and even those of his followers who have most successfully developed political economy can actually be charged with is not the failure to recognise the obvious significance of the study of history for the politician. Nor is it a failure to recognise the just as obvious principle that various economic institutions [...] correspond to various temporal and spatial conditions of economy. It is their defective understanding of the unintentionally created social institutions and their significance for economy. It is the opinion appearing chiefly in their writings that the institutions of economy are always the intended product of the common will of society as such, results of expressed agreement of members of society or of positive legislation. [...] The result is that the broad realm of unintentionally created social structures remains closed to their theoretical comprehension.

    (Notably, this passage from Menger – which many considered incomprehensible or erroneous – acquires significance as soon as we draw a distinction between the theory of the spontaneous evolution of institutions and the theory of the spontaneous order of actions.) In short: the originality that some (e.g.

Meek, 1971) have attributed to the "stadial theory" sketched out in Smith's *Lectures on Jurisprudence* is hard to detect at all (Pesciarelli, 1986).

11. As Beck (2016, p. 50) writes: "There is no direct evidence [...] that Smith's principle of a self-regulating market influenced Darwin's reflections on natural selection". In light of our reasoning, it is so because the principle of "self-regulating market" and "natural selection" concern two different questions. Beck herself recognises that Hayek created a certain confusion in this regard. As she stresses: "The spontaneous order, as understood by Hayek, and evolution constitute [...] two disparate concepts. And Hayek's attempt to collapse one into the other [...] remains unconvincing" (Beck, 2016, p. 55).
12. Among the few who have clearly recognised this distinction are Galeotti (1991, pp. 288, 292), Streit (1997, pp. 39–42), Kasper and Streit (1998, pp. 147–152), Van den Hauwe (1998), Gloria-Palermo (1999, p. 33), Gaus (2006), Whitman (2009), Postema (2011), Lewis (2016), Rizzo (2021), and Festré (2019).
13. Among those who have clearly recognised this aspect, see Ottonelli (1995, p. 32), Vanberg (2001, p. 69), and Ioannides (2003).
14. At most (by taking the market to be a spontaneous institution), we can say that any deliberate intervention aimed at radically modifying certain social institutions would risk jeopardising the inherent capacity to stabilise and orientate that they have acquired over time (Leoni, 1961). On this, see the discussion by Vanberg (2001, pp. 78–80) about "constructivistic rationalism I" (the view contested by the Hayekian critique of the central planning of economic activities) and "constructivistic rationalism II" (the view contested by the Hayekian critique of totally top-down institutional design).
15. To say (as Hayek does) that certain rules are selected because they contribute to the formation of beneficial spontaneous social orders does not reduce the *difference* between the two theories: it simply elaborates *one of them*, namely the theory of the spontaneous evolution of institutions.
16. See for instance Gedeon (2015, p. 6): "Since Hayek's theory of socio-cultural evolution is the generalisation of the theory of spontaneous market order, understanding the former presumes the knowledge of the latter."
17. This is a significant point and worth elaborating further. In this, as in any other case, it is clearly always possible to construct a more general "mother" theory that comprises others as simple specifications. We must ask ourselves if the price to pay is too steep. In Hayek's case, my belief is that the price is exceedingly high. As matters now stand, it would be a case of a very generic theory that limited itself to affirming that it is possible for disparate elements to combine unintentionally in an ordered structure, without, however, affirming anything of relevance about the conditions and ways in which this has happened.
18. See also Prychitko (1994), Vanberg (2001, pp. 78–80, 2006), and Buchanan (2005, p. 31).
19. Even those commentators who appreciate the distinction between the two theories (such as Barry, 1982, Galeotti, 1991) do not seem to have grasped how

important it is. Alternatively, as happens in Kirzner (1992, pp. 163–179), they arrive at the distinction via tortuous paths (after erroneously assuming that the two theories describe an identical mechanism). Those who, to my mind, clearly grasp the issue at hand include Klein (1997), Schmidtchen (2000), Petsoulas (2001, pp. 12–52), Gaus (2006), and Postema (2011). Another author who recognises the distinction between the two theories with sufficient clarity is Kley (1994, p. 21). The differences between Kley's approach and my own are the following: first, Kley severs the two theories from each other in order to facilitate his critique (driven by a questionable hypercritical standpoint that, to my mind, is partially preconceived) of each one separately; whereas I divide them for the purpose of highlighting the importance and originality of both. Furthermore, Kley (1994, p. 158) maintains that the two theories actually collide; whereas I believe that they are perfectly compatible.

## REFERENCES

Alexander E. (2011). An Evolutionary Theory of Institutions. Prescriptive Implications. *Planning Theory*, 10(2), pp. 187–189.

Barry N. (1982). The Tradition of Spontaneous Order. *Literature of Liberty*, 5(2), pp. 7–58.

Beck N. (2015). The Garden of Orderly Polity: F. A. Hayek and T. H. Huxley's Views on Social Evolution. *Journal of Bioeconomics*, 17, pp. 83–96.

Beck N. (2016). The Spontaneous Market Order and Evolution. *Studies in History and Philosophy of Science Part C: Studies in History and Philosophy of Biological and Biomedical Sciences*, 58, pp. 49–55.

Buchanan J. (1977). *Freedom in Constitutional Contract*. College Station. TX: Texas A&M University Press.

Buchanan J. (2005). *Why, I, Too, Am Not a Conservative*. Cheltenham, UK: Edward Elgar Publishing.

Burke E. (1999 [1790]). *Reflections on the Revolution in France*. Oxford, UK: Oxford University Press.

Butos W., McQuade T. (2002). Mind, market and institutions. The knowledge problem in Hayek's thought, in Birner J., Garrouste P., Aimar T. (eds.), *F. von Hayek as a Political Economist*. London: Routledge, pp. 113–133.

Chiles T. Tuggle C., McMullen J., Bierman L., Greening D. (2010). Dynamic Creation: Extending the Radical Austrian Approach to Entrepreneurship. *Organization Studies*, 31, pp. 7–46.

diZerega G. (2013). Outlining a New Paradigm. *Cosmos & Taxis*, 1(1), pp. 3–20.

Elster J. (1989). *Nuts and Bolts for the Social Sciences*. Cambridge, UK: Cambridge University Press.

Ferguson A. (1995 [1767]). *An Essay on the History of Civil Society*. Cambridge, UK: Cambridge University Press.

Festré A. (2019). Hayek on Expectations: The Interplay between Two Complex Systems. *The European Journal of the History of Economic Thought*, 26(5), pp. 911–941.

Fleetwood S. (1997). Hayek III: The necessity of social rules of conduct, in Frowen S. (ed.), *Hayek: Economist and Social Philosopher*. London: Macmillan, pp. 155–178.

Foster J., Metcalfe J.S. (2012). Economic Emergence: An Evolutionary Economic Perspective. *Journal of Economic Behavior & Organization*, 82, pp. 420–432.

Galeotti A.E. (1991). Individualism, social rules, tradition: The case of Friedrich A. Hayek, in Wood J.C., Woods R. (eds.), *Friedrich A. Hayek. Critical Assessment*, volume IV. London: Routledge, pp. 281–296.

Gaus G. (2006). Hayek on the evolution of society and mind, in Feser E. (ed.), *The Cambridge Companion to Hayek*. Cambridge, UK: Cambridge University Press, pp. 232–258.

Gedeon P. (2015). Spontaneous Order and Social Norms. Hayek's Theory of Socio-cultural Evolution. *Society and Economy*, 37(1), pp. 1–29.

Gloria-Palermo S. (1999). An Austrian Dilemma: Necessity and Impossibly of a Theory of Institutions. *Review of Austrian Economics*, 11, pp. 31–45.

Goldsmith M.M. (1985). *Private Vices, Public Benefits. Bernard Mandeville's Social and Political Thought*. Cambridge, UK: Cambridge University Press.

Goodin R. (1996). Institutions and their design, in Goodin R. (ed.), *The Theory of Institutional Design*. Cambridge, UK: Cambridge University Press, pp. 1–53.

Hayek F. von (1948). *Individualism and Economic Order*. Chicago, IL: University of Chicago Press.

Hayek F. von (1952). *The Counter-Revolution of Science*. Glencoe, CA: The Free Press.

Hayek F. von (1960). *The Constitution of Liberty*. Chicago, IL: University of Chicago Press.

Hayek F. von (1967). *Studies in Philosophy, Politics and Economics*. London: Routledge.

Hayek F. von (1978). *New Studies in Philosophy, Politics, Economics and the History of Ideas*. London: Routledge.

Hayek F. von (1982). *Law, Legislation and Liberty*. London: Routledge.

Hayek F. von (1988). *The Fatal Conceit*. London: Routledge.

Heath E. (1992). Rules, Function, and Invisible Hand. *Philosophy of the Social Sciences*, 22(1), pp. 28–45.

Heiner R. (1990). Hayek Competition: From Coordination to Creation. *Cultural Dynamics*, 3, pp. 49–60.

Hodgson G. (1993). *Economics and Evolution*. Ann Arbor, MI: University of Michigan Press.

Hodgson G. (2004). *The Evolution of Institutional Economics*. London: Routledge.

Hume D. (2000 [1739]). *A Treatise of Human Nature*. Oxford, UK: Oxford University Press.

Ioannides S. (2003). Orders and Organizations. *American Journal of Economics and Sociology*, 62(3), pp. 533–566.

Kasper W., Streit M.E. (1998). *Institutional Economics*. Cheltenham, UK: Edward Elgar Publishing.

Kirzner I. (1992). *The Meaning of Market Process*. London: Routledge.

Klein D. (1997). Convention, Social Order, and the Two Coordinations. *Constitutional Political Economy*, 8(4), pp. 319–335.

Kley R. (1994). *Hayek's Social and Political Thought*. Oxford, UK: Clarendon Press.

Leoni B. (1961). *Freedom and the Law*. Princeton, NJ: Van Nostrand.

Lewis P. (2011). Varieties of Emergence: Minds, Markets and Novelty. *Studies in Emergent Order*, 4, pp. 170–192.

Lewis P. (2012). Emergent Properties in the Work of Friedrich Hayek. *Journal of Economic Behavior & Organization*, 82, pp. 368–378.

Lewis P. (2016). Systems, structural properties and levels of organisation: The influence of Ludwig Von Bertalanffy on the work of F.A. Hayek, in Fiorito L.,

Scheall S., Suprinyak C.E. (eds.), *Research in the History of Economic Thought and Methodology,* volume 34A. Leeds, UK: Emerald Group Publishing, pp. 125–159.
Mandeville B. (1997 [1714]). *The Fable of the Bees.* Indianapolis, IN: Hackett Publishing.
Mandeville B. (1997 [1729]). *The Fable of the Bees. Part II: Dialogues Between Horatio and Cleomenes.* Indianapolis, IN: Hackett Publishing.
Martin R., Sunley P. (2012). Forms of Emergence and the Evolution of Economic Landscapes. *Journal of Economic Behavior & Organization*, 82, pp. 338–351.
Meek R.L. (1971). Smith, Turgot, and the Four Stages Theory. *History of Political Economy*, 3(1), pp. 9–27.
Menger C. (1985 [1883]). *Investigations into the Method of Social Sciences with Special Reference to Economics.* Translated by F.J. Nock. New York and London: New York University Press.
Moroni S. (2005). *L'ordine sociale spontaneo.* Torino: Utet.
Moroni S. (2010). An Evolutionary Theory of Institutions and a Dynamic Approach to Reform. *Planning Theory*, 9(4), pp. 275–297.
Moroni S. (2011). The Role of Deliberate Intervention on Organizations and Institutions. *Planning Theory*, 10(2), pp. 190–197.
Moroni S. (2012). Land-use planning and the question of unintended consequences, in Andersson, D. (ed.), *The Spatial Market Process.* Bingley: Emerald Group Publishing, pp. 265–288.
Moroni S. (2014). Two Different Theories of Two Distinct Spontaneous Phenomena: Orders of Actions and Evolution of Institutions in Hayek. *Cosmos & Taxis. Studies in Emergent Order and Organization*, 1/2, pp. 9–23.
Moroni S. (2021). Evolutionary Approaches and Planning: Dynamics of Activities and Dynamics of Institutions. *Scienze Regionali*, 20(2), pp. 267–288.
Nozick R. (1974). *Anarchy, State and Utopia.* New York, NY: Basic Books.
Nozick R. (1997). *Socratic Puzzles.* Cambridge, MA: Harvard University Press.
Ottonelli V. (1995). *L'ordine senza volontà. Il liberalismo di Hayek.* Torino: Giappichelli.
Pesciarelli E. (1986), On Adam Smith's Lectures on Jurisprudence. *Scottish Journal of Political Economy*, 33(1), pp. 74–85.
Petsoulas C. (2001). *Hayek's Liberalism and Its Origins.* London: Routledge.
Polanyi M. (1958). *Personal Knowledge.* London: Routledge.
Popper K. (1945). *The Open Society and its Enemies.* London: Routledge.
Popper K. (1972). *Objective Knowledge.* Oxford: Clarendon Press.
Postema G. (2011). Nature as first custom: Hayek on the evolution of social rules, in Boettke P., Zywicki T. (eds.), *Research Handbook on Austrian Law and Economics.* Cheltenham, UK: Edward Elgar Publishing, pp. 65–91.
Potts J. (2013). Rules of Spontaneous Order. *Cosmos and Taxis*, 1(1), pp. 30–41.
Prychitko D. (1994). Socialism as Cartesian legacy, in Boettke P., Prychitko D. (eds.), *The Market Process.* Aldershot, UK: Edward Elgar Publishing, pp. 261–73.
Rizzo M. (2021). Abstract rules for complex systems. *European Journal of Law and Economics*, 52(2), pp. 209–227.
Runde J. (1997). Comment: Rules for prices? in Frowen S. (ed.), *Hayek: Economist and Social Philosopher.* London: Macmillan, pp. 179–183.
Ruttan V.W. (2003). *Social Science Knowledge and Economic Development.* Ann Arbor, MI: University of Michigan Press.
Sahlins M.D., Service E.R. (1960). *Evolution and Culture.* Ann Arbor, MI: University of Michigan Press.

Schmidtchen D. (2000). Rules and order, in Bouckaert B., Godart-van der Kroon A. (eds.), *Hayek Revisited*. Cheltenham: Edward Elgar Publishing, pp. 32–45.
Simon H. (1981). *The Sciences of the Artificial*. Cambridge, MA: The MIT Press.
Simon H. (1983). *Reason in Human Affairs*. Redwood City, CA: Stanford University Press.
Smith A. (1978 [1762]). *Lectures on Jurisprudence*. Oxford: Clarendon Press.
Smith A. (1993 [1776]). *An Enquiry into the Nature and Causes of the Wealth of Nations*. Indianapolis, IN: Hackett Publishing.
Stewart D. (1829 [1793]). Account of the life and writings of Adam Smith, in *The Works of Dugald Stewart*. Cambridge, UK: Hilliard and Brown, pp. 3–75.
Streit M. (1997). Constitutional ignorance, spontaneous order and rule orientation: Hayekian paradigms from a policy perspective, in Frowen S. (ed.), *Hayek: Economist and Social Philosopher*. London: Macmillan, pp. 37–58.
Ullmann-Margalit E. (1978). Invisible-hand Explanations. *Synthese*, 39, pp. 263–291.
Vanberg V. (2001). *The Constitution of Markets*. London: Routledge.
Vanberg V. (2006). Human Intentionality and design in cultural evolution, in Schubert C., Wangenheim G. von (eds.), *Evolution and Design of Institutions*. London: Routledge, pp. 197–212.
Van den Hauwe L. (1998). Evolution and the Production of Rules. *European Journal of Law and Economics*, 5(1), pp. 81–117.
Vaughn K. (1994). Can democratic society reform itself? The limits of constructive change, in Boettke P., Prychitko D. (eds.), *The Market Process*. Aldershot, UK: Edward Elgar Publishing, pp. 229–243.
Walker G. (1986). *The Ethics of F.A. Hayek*. Lanham, MD: University Press of America.
Watkins J.W.N. (1968). Methodological individualism and social tendencies, in Brodbeck M. (ed.), *Readings in the Philosophy of the Social Sciences*. New York, NY: Macmillan, pp. 269–280.
Whitman D. (2009). The rules of abstraction. *The Review of Austrian Economics* 22, pp. 21–41.
Witt U. (1997). Self-Organization and Economics – What is New? *Structural Change and Economic Dynamics* 8, pp. 489–507.

# 4. Hayek on welfare state

**Mihaela Ifrim**

At first glance, the welfare state issue seems to be limited to the need to increase the role of governments, in particular by correcting the main claimed shortcoming of the market economy, income inequality. A favorite theme of socialists when criticizing capitalism, the fight against inequality and poverty is proving to be a crucial ingredient in political discourses and in the actions of various organizations that are promising a better world. Although it is recognized for its superior efficiency in terms of production, capitalism, or the social order of the market economy, loses the sympathy of those who do not recognize its humanity, equity, or fairness in terms of redistribution. The unmitigated failure of socialism, experienced despite the theoretical demonstration of its impossibility, has not put an end to the mirage of egalitarianism and communitarian nostalgia. But, if common ownership of the means of production has already proved its inefficiency, individual freedom and the right of private property are now increasingly threatened by the expansion of government regulations and by more and more interventions in the name of the so-called 'social justice.' And who could be against such actions that promise social justice and extended benefits 'from the cradle to the grave?'

Understanding the implications of the welfare state goes beyond a simple economic analysis in terms of costs–benefits and implies questioning the very principle of liberty. In addition, an important role is played by the unintended consequences of government intervention, but also by understanding the errors that fuel the welfarist claims. The Hayekian position towards the welfare state, which this chapter aims to systematize, will appear as a puzzle made up of elements that seem disparate, but which have been identified as possible pieces after reading some of the chapters directly or indirectly dedicated to the subject in his *The Constitution of Liberty*, *Law, Legislation and Liberty*, *The Atavism of Social Justice*, and *The Fatal Conceit.* I have chosen to reproduce in extenso most of the quotes to avoid truncating or taking Hayek's standpoint out of context.

## THE SOCIALISM IS DEAD, LONG LIVE THE WELFARE STATE!?

When socialism failed in its promise of providing social justice, while capitalism retained its supremacy in the efficient provision of goods and services, the trade-off in the Western world involved combining the production of the market economy with the redistribution of incomes through government action. The state has ceased to be reduced to the minimal functions outlined by the classical economists, and its supply of goods and services and its areas of intervention have expanded significantly. A representative figure of the defenders of liberty and a tireless critic of socialism, Friedrich von Hayek didn't share libertarian enthusiasm, rationalism, or constructivism. Going through that beautiful chapter 'Freedom, Reason, and Tradition' in *The Constitution of Liberty*, it is easy to identify the tradition of liberty with which Hayek associates himself. It is the British, evolutionist tradition, which identifies the social order in the process of selecting those customs and institutions that have proved most effective for the welfare of individuals. This is opposed to the French approach to liberty, essentially a rationalist one, which, centered around the concept of laissez faire, has proven to be more anarchist. This distinction between the two types of freedom is important in order to understand that Hayek was not against any action taken by the state, but he was against the coercion that the state can use:

> Freedom of economic activity had meant freedom under the law, not the absence of all government action. (Hayek 1960, p. 220)

> A functioning market economy presupposes certain activities on the part of the state; there are some other such activities by which its functioning will be assisted; and it can tolerate many more, provided that they are of the kind which are compatible with a functioning market. (Hayek 1960, p. 222)

> Though government must not use its power of coercion to reserve for itself activities which have nothing to do with the enforcement of the general rules of law, there is no violation of principle in its engaging in all sorts of activities on the same terms as the citizens. (Hayek 1960, p. 223)

These concessions made to governmental actions were, of course, a source of complaints among the libertarian wing of the Austrian school of economics. In introducing the welfare state concept in the chapter dealing with this subject in *The Constitution of Liberty*, Hayek argued that:

> limiting the role of the state to the defense of law and order cannot be justified by the principle of liberty. Only the coercive measures of government need be strictly limited. We have already seen … that there is undeniably a wide field for

> non-coercive activities of government and that there is a clear need for financing them by taxation. (Hayek 1960, p. 257)

This statement, anyway, is far from being a proof in placing Hayek among those who favor welfarist actions. It is vital to look at the whole, not just at some fragments that may prove to be misleading. Actually, Hayek referred to this term cautiously. "Unlike socialism, the conception of the welfare state has no precise meaning" (Hayek 1960, p. 257). This fact makes the dangers that it implies for a free society not very easy to identify, at first sight:

> So long as the danger came from socialism of the frankly collectivist kind, it was possible to argue that the tenets of the socialists were simply false: that socialism would not achieve what the socialists wanted and that it would produce other consequences which they would not like. We cannot argue similarly against the welfare state, for this term does not designate a definite system. What goes under that name is a conglomerate of so many diverse and even contradictory elements that, while some of them may make a free society more attractive, others are incompatible with it or may at least constitute potential threats to its existence. (Hayek 1960, pp. 258–259)

The threats to the existence of a free society derive from the exploitation of certain human instincts and the proliferation of some terms that evoke strong individual feelings and which, transformed from good intentions into state action lines, eventually legitimize the coercive power of the state.

## EVOLUTION, ORDER, AND AN ATAVISM

The emergence of open societies and the evolution of civilization are due to the replacement of the specific objectives of small communities with abstract rules, which have been subject to a long process of selection, in which human reason has played virtually no role (Hayek 1978; Hayek 1979). This perspective on the evolution of society, the emergence of spontaneous order, and the inevitable conflict between some innate values and the rules of conduct that have not been deliberately imposed is a defining element of Friedrich Hayek's position in the never-ending dispute between those who defend the free, competitive market and those who advocate the planning of human interactions. The free market, seen as a game of catallaxy (Hayek 1978), where price signals guide supply and demand, has enabled a significant improvement in individuals' living conditions, although this doesn't mean the equalization of incomes, the rewarding of merits, or the recognition of needs. The problem comes when the rules learned in order to benefit from the fruits of the civilized world clash with the primitive instincts specific to living in small communities, the inherited heritage of tribal life. "Mankind achieved civilization by developing and learning to follow rules … that often forbade him to do what his instincts demanded and no longer depended on a common perception of events" (Hayek 1988, p. 12):

> Part of our present difficulty is that we must constantly adjust our lives, our thoughts and our emotions, in order to live simultaneously within different kinds of orders according to different rules. If we were to apply the unmodified, uncurbed, rules of the micro-cosmos (i.e., of the small band or troop, or of, say, our families) to the macro-cosmos (our wider civilisation), as our instincts and sentimental yearnings often make us wish to do, *we would destroy it.* Yet if we were always to apply the rules of the extended order to our more intimate groupings, *we would crush them.* So, we must learn to live in two sorts of world at once. (Hayek 1988, p. 18, emphases in original)

Still, on the same page, he repeats the warning that "our instincts often threaten to topple the whole edifice." According to Hayek, when individuals fail to separate the two types of order, when they do not understand the logic of the market economy, they fall into the trap of the promises of a rationally designed social order:

> Their demand for a just distribution in which organized power is to be used to allocate to each what he deserves is thus strictly an *atavism*, based on primordial emotions. And it is these widely prevalent feelings to which prophets, moral philosophers, and constructivists appeal by their plans for the deliberate creation of a new type of society. (Hayek 1979, p. 176, emphasis in original)

Somehow, there occurs a dissonance between accepting the game of catallaxy, which has proven to provide the most efficient allocation of resources, and advocating the action of the state in distributing the outcomes. Although Hayek did not exclude the provision of a minimum income for those who cannot obtain it by participating in the market game, he made it clear that these actions should be undertaken outside the market mechanism:

> If they accept their winnings from the game, it is cheating for individuals or groups to invoke the powers of government to divert the flow of good things in their favour – whatever we may do outside this game of the market to provide a decent minimum for those for whom the game did not supply it. (Hayek 1978, p. 64)

The claim for a fair distribution through the actions of the state is the result of a collectivist, atavistic mentality, which is not compatible with the rules of the civilized world, where the remunerations determined by means of market prices are the only ones that can be fair (Hayek 1978, p. 64). But the welfare state has a strong incentive to perpetuate this mentality.

## WELFARE STATE AND SOCIAL JUSTICE

The philosophical foundation of a welfare state is the concept of social justice (Caldwell 2004), highly criticized by Hayek in a period of great effervescence of governmental actions in Western societies. If the term welfare state is a vague one, that of social justice is an "empty formula, conventionally used to assert that a particular claim is justified without giving any reason" (Hayek 1978, p. 60), and, at the same time, is both "misleading and meaningless" (Butler 2012, p. 83). Only human actions can be just or unjust, despite the frequent tendency to extend justice to a state of affairs. The social order of the free market implies justice in the way competition takes place between market agents, and not in terms of its results. It is enough to lack fraud, violence, and monopoly to be able to talk about just prices, the only ones that can indicate the relationship between demand and supply:

> Justice has meaning only as a rule of human conduct, and no conceivable rules for the conduct of individuals supplying each other with goods and services in a market economy would produce a distribution which could be meaningfully described as just or unjust. Individuals might conduct themselves as justly as possible, but as the results for separate individuals would be neither intended nor foreseeable by others, the resulting state of affairs could neither be called just nor unjust. (Hayek 1978, p. 61)

The mechanism of allocating resources in the market order does not need corrections justified by a supposed social justice. This is nothing, in fact, but another name for the distribution of incomes between individuals, and distribution can have nothing in common with the market. Also, in the name of the same redistribution, another fictional term is often used – 'value to society.' The incomes obtained by individuals on the market are only related to "what these services are worth to those who receive them" (Hayek 1976, p. 76). Thus:

> Services can have value only to particular people (or an organization), and any particular service will have very different values for different members of the same society. To regard them differently is to treat society not as a spontaneous order of free men but as an organization whose members are all made to serve a single hierarchy of ends. This would necessarily be a totalitarian system in which personal freedom would be absent. (Hayek 1976, pp. 75–76)

Pretending the existence of a value for society demonstrates, in fact, the misunderstanding of the subjective theory of value and the use of a variety of terms that resort to collective feelings, without having any consistency and coherence:

> Although it is tempting to speak of a "value to society" instead of a man's value to his fellows, it is in fact highly misleading if we say, e.g., that a man who supplies matches to millions and thereby earns $200,000 a year is worth more "to society" than a man who supplies great wisdom or exquisite pleasure to a few thousand and thereby earns $20,000 a year. Even the performance of a Beethoven sonata, a painting by Leonardo or a play by Shakespeare have no "value to society" but a value only to those who know and appreciate them. … The point is not that the true values are different, but that the values attached to the different services by different groups of people are incommensurable. (Hayek 1976, p. 76)

All these attempts to justify governmental intervention in the name of so-called 'social justice' are in fact without foundation. However, they are part of the effervescence that comes with all things connected to social. It is useful here to revisit *The Fatal Conceit*, where Hayek described 'social' as being a weasel word, depriving of content any term to which it is prefixed, while seemingly leaving it untouched. 'Social,' which has probably become "the most confusing expression in our entire moral and political vocabulary" (Hayek 1988, p. 114) is found by him in more than 160 words.

Therefore, 'social justice' is, in fact, a term that gains support by appealing to public sensitivities when, in fact, it means nothing more than the redistribution of income through government action:

> Though a redistribution of incomes was never the avowed initial purpose of the apparatus of social security, it has now become the actual and admitted aim everywhere. No system of monopolistic compulsory insurance has resisted this transformation into something quite different, an instrument for the compulsory redistribution of income. (…) At the moment we are concerned only with the process by which an apparatus originally meant to relieve poverty is generally being turned into a tool of egalitarian redistribution. It is as a means of socializing income, of creating a sort of household, state which allocates benefits in money or in kind to those who are thought to be most deserving, that the welfare state has for many become the substitute for old-fashioned socialism. (Hayek 1960, p. 289)

## WELFARE STATE AND THE PROBLEM OF KNOWLEDGE

Even if we refer only to the good intentions of governments, we cannot omit the existence of the problem of knowledge. "Knowledge exists only as the knowledge of individuals" (Hayek 1960, p. 24). But it remains an open question to what extent governments are able not only to provide the goods and services desired by individuals, but also to identify the minimum necessary income or to draw the line between the arbitrary and the moderation in its distributive actions. "Such an order involving an adjustment to circumstances, knowledge of which is dispersed among a great many people, cannot be established by central direction" (Hayek 1960, p. 160). Lacking the individually dispersed knowledge, governments should be primarily concerned with providing the conditions that allow these individuals to satisfy their own needs:

> Even in the modern welfare societies the great majority and the most important of the daily needs of the great masses are met as a result of processes whose particulars government does not and cannot know. The most important of the public goods for which government is required is thus not the direct satisfaction of any particular needs, but the securing of conditions in which the individuals and smaller groups will have favourable opportunities of mutually providing for their respective needs. ... The prime public concern must be directed not towards particular known needs but towards the conditions for the preservation of a spontaneous order which enables the individuals to provide for their needs in manners not known to authority... (Hayek 1976, p. 2)

Individuals can direct their efforts toward satisfying their own needs as long as they can have freedom of choice within a coherent institutional framework, where the rules of the game are clear and respected. Creating this framework is the most important public good, Hayek said.

## WELFARE STATE AND FREEDOM

Although Hayek is denounced by some libertarian authors as making important concessions to state intervention through his position regarding the activities that government could undertake in society, his permanent concern to preserve and defend individual freedom is beyond any doubt. Hans-Hermann Hoppe called him a moderate social democrat because:

> according to Hayek, government is "necessary" to fulfill the following tasks: not merely for "law enforcement" and "defense against external enemies" but "in an advanced society government ought to use its power of raising funds by taxation to provide a number of services which for various reasons cannot be provided, or cannot be provided adequately, by the market". (Hoppe 2011)

Always existing an infinite number of goods and services that the market does not provide, Hayek gave government a blank check, Hoppe believes. Indeed, we can find in *The Constitution of Liberty* a generous list of activities that can be provided by the state (the provision of a reliable and efficient monetary system, the setting of standards of weights and measures; the providing of information gathered from surveying, land registration, statistics, etc.; and the support, if not also the organization, of some kind of education) (Hayek 1960, p. 223). All these activities of government are part of its effort to provide a favorable framework for individual decisions, added Hayek. In addition, there is a series of public goods whose offering through collective effort is in favor of all members of society – parks, museums, sports facilities. But Hayek made an important clarification, which Hoppe omitted – the state does not violate any principle regarding freedom by engaging in different activities, as long as it does so from the same positions as the individuals (Hayek 1960, p. 223). But, when the state uses its coercive powers and claims to have exclusive rights in some areas, freedom is threatened.

In addition to public goods, provided through common efforts, there may be common risks that can be reduced through government intervention. But Hayek emphasized the difference between limited security, by ensuring a minimum of subsistence for all citizens, without any kind of privileges, and absolute security, which involves ensuring a certain standard of living, based on some comparisons, to some people who are supposed to deserve this income and do not obtain it on the free market (Hayek 1960, p. 259). Such discriminatory treatment, Hayek said, is nothing but a form of income redistribution, which has nothing in common with a free society, but leads to socialism:

> Insofar as this means that the coercive powers of government are to be used to insure that particular people get particular things, it requires a kind of discrimination between, and an unequal treatment of different people which is irreconcilable with a free society. This is the kind of welfare state that aims at "social justice" and becomes "primarily a redistributor of income." It is bound to lead back to socialism and its coercive and essentially arbitrary methods. (Hayek 1960, pp. 259–260)

## WELFARE STATE AND THE ROAD TO SOCIALISM

Although socialism no longer represented, in the years in which *The Constitution of Liberty* was written, the main threat to Western society, Hayek drew attention to the fact that good intentions behind the actions of political reformers will directly lead to more and more planning and control. Somehow, socialism no longer needs to eliminate private property to achieve its goal. The regulation and taxation of revenues generated by the use of private property will generate the redistribution of revenues. Russian-type socialism was replaced by social democratic socialism, to use the taxonomy proposed by Hoppe in his *Theory of Socialism and Capitalism* (1989). And Hayek cannot be suspected of having favored this latest version, as he was accused by Hoppe, as can be easily observed in the following paragraph:

> Though socialism has been generally abandoned as a goal to be deliberately striven for, it is by no means certain that we shall not still establish it, albeit unintentionally. The reformers who confine themselves to whatever methods appear to be the most effective for their particular purposes and pay no attention to what is necessary to preserve an effective market mechanism are likely to be led to impose more and more central control over economic decisions (though private property may be preserved in name) until we get that very system of central planning which few

> now consciously wish to see established. Furthermore, many of the old socialists have discovered that we have already drifted so far in the direction of a redistributive state that it now appears much easier to push further in that direction than to press for the somewhat discredited socialization of the means of production. They seem to have recognized that by increasing governmental control of what nominally remains private industry, they can more easily achieve that redistribution of incomes that had been the real aim of the more spectacular policy of expropriation. (Hayek 1960, pp. 256–257)

The same idea can be found a few pages further:

> Seen as an alternative to the now discredited method of directly steering production, the technique of the welfare state, which attempts to bring about a "just distribution" by handing out income in such proportions and forms as it sees fit, is indeed merely a new method of pursuing the old aims of socialism. (Hayek 1960, p. 289)

There is no doubt, from these paragraphs, that Hayek was not only far from sympathizing with this metamorphosis of the state into a social bulwark, but he clearly understood the resurgent dangers of old socialism and the renewed threats to the free world. The Beveridgean catchphrase 'from the cradle to the grave' seems to have been conceived for our times. Just as Hayek also seems to have written for our times. His objections and doubts about the welfare state are even more relevant today, since it is much more inflated than in the years when Hayek wrote about it. Every expansion of its role, every new and promising 'social' measure means increased government spending, with significant fiscal and monetary implications. The game of the market is constantly threatened by the distortion of price signals, with important consequences for individual incentives and actions. The mirage of intervention in the name of 'social' ideals is highly disruptive to the proper application of the rules of catallaxy. The welfare state, with all its good intentions, remains a sum of governmental actions that can pave the road to serfdom, and Hayek's work remains proof of his deep commitment to the defense of individual freedom.

## REFERENCES

Butler E. (2012). *Friedrich Hayek: The Ideas and Influence of the Libertarian Economist*. Petersfield, Hampshire, UK: Harriman House.

Caldwell B. (2004). *Hayek's Challenge. An Intellectual Biography of F. A. Hayek*. Chicago, IL: The University of Chicago Press.

Hayek F. von (1960). *The Constitution of Liberty*. Chicago, IL: University of Chicago Press.

Hayek F. von (1976). *Law, Legislation and Liberty, Volume 2: The Mirage of Social Justice*. Chicago, IL: University of Chicago Press.

Hayek F. von (1978). The atavism of social justice, in Hayek F. von (ed.), *New Studies in Philosophy, Politics, Economics and the History of Ideas.* Chicago, IL: University of Chicago Press, pp. 57–68.

Hayek F. von (1979). The three sources of human values, in Hayek F. von (ed.), *Law, Legislation and Liberty*, vol. 3. Chicago, IL: University of Chicago Press, pp. 153–176.

Hayek F. von (1988). *The Fatal Conceit. The Errors of Socialism.* London and New York: Routledge.

Hoppe H.-H. (1989). *A Theory of Socialism and Capitalism.* Auburn, AL: Ludwig von Mises Institute.

Hoppe H.-H. (2011). *Why Mises (and not Hayek)?* https://mises.org/mises-daily/why-mises-and-not-hayek [Accessed: 21.06.2025].

# 5. Hayek on religion and social evolution

**Tomáš Krištofóry and Josef Šíma**

## INTRODUCTION

Hayek was a humble student of spontaneous orders: "he began with the market order, then became aware of the existence of orders in many other areas" (Caldwell 2014, p. 35). Leading Hayek scholars lately identified orders in many areas of Hayek's ever-broadening body of thought (Horwitz 2008; Lewis 2015; Lewis 2016a; Lewis 2016b; Oliva 2016; Vanberg 2017). These researchers follow Hayek's thought from the 1920s up to his book *Law, Legislation, and Liberty* (1982). But Hayek lived until 1992 and published *The Fatal Conceit* in 1988. Did Hayek add any new type of order in the 1980s? We maintain that religion and social morals is roughly a 1970s and especially 1980s addition to his body of thought and as such should be a matter of interest in the literature examining Hayek's science of complex orders. Scholars, however, typically don't understand that this was the case. This oversight forms the gap this chapter aims to address.[1]

In studying this, we don't need to rely on *The Fatal Conceit*, which is problematic in some respects. Already in the 1978 autobiographical interviews, Hayek emphasized that the moral order of our civilization is in fact a result of religion which itself is an order:

> Yes, I think it goes to the question which people try to answer by religion: that there are in the surrounding world a great many orderly phenomena which we cannot understand and which we have to accept. In a way, I've recently discovered that the polytheistic religions of Buddhism appeal rather more to me than the monotheistic religions of the West. If they confine themselves, as some Buddhists do, to a profound respect for the existence of other orderly structures in the world, which they admit they cannot fully understand and interpret, I think it's an admirable position. (Hayek 1983b, p. 489)[2]

Here, Hayek does not advocate for any specific religion; rather, he underscores the essential linkage between religious and other societal orders. This chapter explores this linkage, investigating Hayek's integration of religion into his broader theoretical framework on the evolution of orders. We offer a synoptic view of the various aspects of Hayek's theory of social evolution in relation to religion. We do not investigate in depth these individual aspects.

The objectives of our research are to:

(1) Discuss the use of Hayek's papers from the time span 1978 to 1985, which was his last active period in life, for reconstruction of his theory of moral order vis-à-vis *The Fatal Conceit*. While the downside of the former ones is that these materials are not systematic, their upside is that this is Hayek, using his parlance, connects this new theory to his previous ones. There is no concern whether Hayek wrote these papers because Bartley was not yet involved. We primarily use his writings up to 1985 in this chapter.

(2) Examine Hayek as a value-free scientist of morals and demonstrate that, at least in his writings up to 1985, Hayek considered both economics and religion crucial to understanding the main topic of *The Fatal Conceit*, that is, explain and uphold some systems of morals, those that are better adapted to catallaxy;

(2.1) explain in which direction Hayek further developed his idea of immanent criticism which he previously used in the second volume of *Law, Legislation and Liberty*. Now, Hayek offers immanent criticism as a tool to religious leaders to better adapt their morals to catallaxy. We provide Hayek's examples of immanent criticism;

(2.2) offer a bit of Hayek's conjectural history of the emergence of commercial morals, something he alluded to in the Epilogue to *Law, Legislation and Liberty* (Caldwell 2004, p. 319) in relation to religion. Hayek doesn't justify any particular religion. Rather, he identifies criteria for the group selection of a religion to the status of World religions in the very long run. No religion supports morals that are fully adapted; all of them would better use immanent criticism continuously to better adapt;[3]

(2.3) describe religion as Hayek's next chapter in the debate on economic calculation. Morals are evolutionary, not revolutionary as socialists thought them to be. Socialist morals are maladapted; in the very long run, they will be ruled out in the cultural evolution. Like they were in 1989;

(2.4) highlight the role of religious freedom. Although cultural evolution also operates under oppressive totalitarian regimes, thriving religious competition serves as a discovery procedure in morals.

(3) Explain why religious support for the institutions of family and several property is the criterion of the group selection of religions.

(4) Explain why Hayek refuted (in connection to religion) the utilitarianism of rules and any kind of moral utilitarianism. Moral utilitarians—including Hayek's master Ludwig von Mises, and Hayek's earlier views—admit

that we, the people, have a choice between commercial morals and non-commercial morals. Hayek emphasizes we don't have this freedom of choice. Hence, socialism is impossible.

(5) Extend Hayek's analysis to explain recent religious developments and outline Hayekian pattern prediction of variant future developments.

## CONTEXT OF THE HAYEKIAN THEORY OF RELIGIOUS EVOLUTION

Our approach to reconstructing Hayek's views on religion and social evolution in the 1980s is based on his writings and interviews from the 1980s. Between 1978 and 1985, Hayek developed his theory in a scattered form that can only be reconstructed retrospectively. Why these dates? Late in 1978, Hayek finished writing *Law, Legislation and Liberty*. In its Epilogue (Hayek 1982, vol. III, p. 176), he indicated that he was willing to write another book. He thus launched *The Fatal Conceit* book project. It is an established fact that Hayek fell ill in summer 1985 and never truly recovered (Hennecke 2000, p. 367; Ebenstein 2003, pp. 230–235; Caldwell 2004, p. 362; Cubitt 2006, p. 167). This is why he needed W. W. Bartley to finish *The Fatal Conceit*. Many judgments were uttered about that book and about Bartley's participation. Instead of entering this minefield, we rely on material that is safely Hayek's. That is, up to the summer of 1985.[4]

How much did Hayek write in that period? Scholars may still consider Gray (1982; 1998) as the main source for Hayek's bibliography, especially when Gray gets a reference from one of Hayek's biographers (Ebenstein 2001, p. 334). Scholars should be aware that Gray wrote his bibliography in 1982 while Hayek was still figuring out how social evolution was functioning and was actually only to write key papers on the topic of religious evolution. In fact, Gray admitted as much in 1984: "In the fundamental case of the competition of religions—which Hayek has addressed profoundly *in his as yet unpublished writings*—there seems no necessary clash, then, between the economic approach and the Hayekian rule-following conception" (Gray 1998, p. 46). To get a better idea of how much Hayek was writing in the 1980s, we must turn to Hans Jörg Hennecke.

In his intellectual biography of Hayek, Hennecke quoted almost a hundred of Hayek's texts in the period 1978 to 1985 (Hennecke 2000, pp. 404–408). Hennecke didn't write this to assemble Hayek's complete bibliography. Nevertheless, the German Hayek Society proudly presents Hennecke's list of Hayek's references as the Hayek bibliography.[5] Hennecke's bibliography is an appropriate starting point for scholars willing to focus on Hayek's 1980s.

Hayek's papers are highly repetitive, an observation which won't surprise anybody knowledgeable about Hayek's 1980s and his *The Fatal Conceit*.[6] But is this a problem rather than an opportunity? We opt for the latter. To answer, we must remember Hayek's way of thinking. Hayek was putting together pieces of the puzzle, trying to find words for the abstract structures he felt or saw in front of him. In his *Two Types of Mind*, Hayek describes his way of thinking as the mind of a puzzler (Hayek 1978). Repetitiveness might be a part of the puzzler's life. To describe how the pieces fit, he would have to explore, describing each piece's relations to other ones at a time. At the beginning, he perhaps didn't yet know how pieces fit together and hence repetitiveness. We admit that perhaps Hayek grew more repetitive in the 1980s, which may have been caused by his old age or by his interest in a new field, morals.[7] A new field would require more rethinking from a puzzler. In our approach, we maintain that his way of thinking is an opportunity rather than a problem. We only need to follow his way of thinking. We observe that in various of his articles, the core of the cultural evolution argument was the same and thus repetitive, but usually a new aspect of the problem was introduced. Just as we would have expected from a puzzler. Our experience is that one only begins to realize this if he or she reads at least a dozen of these articles in quick succession, perhaps concentrating on one particular Hayekian theory.

So where do we have Hayek's papers collected to read them? The quick but imprecise answer in this digital age is the internet. After his Nobel Prize in 1974, his articles were published by institutes and regional newspapers around the world because Hayek traveled a lot to lecture (Caldwell 2016). While some of these institutes and journals no longer exist, surviving institutes and journals dug out some of these articles and videos from their archives and made them available online, which helped us greatly. If one prefers printed resources, the most that we have together in print is a 1983 volume assembled by the Adam Smith Institute, which contains four of Hayek's papers (Hayek 1983a). This is not too much, but this book may serve as a good beginning. Apart from this one, the best advice we have is to start with Hennecke's bibliography and search items of interest on the internet or in your library. Serious scholars, however, will study them in the archives.[8]

We then have plenty of resources. But aren't they contaminated by the problems connected to oral history? A considerable part of the 1980s papers was intended to be the autobiographical material (Hayek 1983b; Hayek 1994). This material is tricky (Caldwell 2007). The criticism was based on the fact that (1) Hayek's memory often failed him in dating his past theoretical advances, (2) even if he wanted to remember correctly, "in autobiographical accounts, whatever gets selected is then integrated into a larger narrative—we construct stories about our lives" and that ultimately we are persuaded that the story is true, and (3) that we all want to look good (Caldwell 2007, p. 345). Two further reasons could be added: (4) Hayek wanted his stories to be funny: "He very often related his own misadventures, which were not necessarily as funny as he thought them to be" (Cubitt 2006, p. 5), and (5) Hayek reinterpreted his earlier achievements in the light of his present concern. We admit that Caldwell's criticism is true in general. Hayek continued to have a problem with memory in the 1980s. Nevertheless, this criticism applies much more to the case when Hayek spoke about his earlier periods in life than when he spoke about something he was doing right at that time or was about to write. Actually, reasons two and five assure us in using Hayek's 1980s materials to our benefit. There might be problems with details but we do not consider Caldwell's criticism of Hayek's 1980s materials devastating vis-à-vis our approach as a whole. With all these potential problems in mind, we turn next to a stepwise reconstruction of Hayek's theory of religious evolution.

## RECONSTRUCTION OF THE HAYEKIAN THEORY OF RELIGIOUS EVOLUTION

If an economist is to say anything about morality, he or she should be aware of the presupposition of value freedom, which is usually interpreted as a prerequisite of positive science. Hayek, influenced in this respect by David Hume and Max Weber, was fully aware of this problem. In 1978, Hayek wanted to support Mises' criticism of socialism and its morality. By then he had learned that a scientific defense of capitalist morality would have to be free of value judgments. At the same time, he felt the urgent need to develop a scientific theory of morality:

> It is indeed necessary in this connection to be very careful, and even pedantic, with regard to the expressions one chooses, because there exists a real danger of inadvertently slipping value judgments on an illegitimate manner into a scientific discussion, and also because those defending their socialist ideals are now mostly trained to use "freedom from value judgments" as a sort of paradoxical defense mechanism for their creed, and are constantly on the look-out to catch their critics out in some incautious formulations. (Hayek 1978, p. 297)

Striving for a scientific theory of morals actually became his main concern. He didn't fail this principle when working on *The Fatal Conceit*:

> I have chosen the clumsy title under which this lecture was announced ('The Origins and Effects of Our Morals: A Problem for Science') in order to make it clear from the outset that in discussing morals I shall not transgress the sound principle that science cannot produce value judgments. David Hume established this truth two centuries before Max Weber and it would have been much better if I had chosen Hume's brief statement of this truth as the title of my lecture. It is that "The rules of morality are not the conclusions of our reason." (Hayek 1984c, p. 35)[9]

Hayek derived an important scientific question from Hume's is-ought problem and Max Weber's rejection of value judgments in science:[10] If it is true, as Hume claimed, that the rules of morality are not the conclusions of human reason, then where do they come from? In 1983 and 1984, Hayek worked particularly hard on this problem. In a flurry of articles, some of which we have already quoted, he made it clear that Hume didn't give an answer to his own question and that he identified Adam Smith as the one who did. Hayek identifies Smith's answer as the "selective evolution" of religions that sanction market morality better than competing religions (Hayek 1983c, p. 24; Hayek 1983d; Hayek 1984b, p. 322; Hayek 1984c, p. 39; Hayek 1984d, pp. 2, 4). Here we come to our subject. The evolution of morality is a scientific problem that avoids the trap of value judgments in scholarly reasoning. At the same time, in upholding certain systems of morality, we need to rely on an active role of religions rather than commit a naturalistic fallacy.

For Hayek, the spontaneous evolution of morals is a result of both economics and religion: "Our morals, like many other aspects of our culture, developed concurrently with our reason, not as its product. *To understand this, both economics and religion come into play*; the first helping to explain how moral orders evolve and how they can assist us where reason falters; the second, as an aid in upholding some systems of morality against the premature assaults of reason" (Hayek 1986b).[11]

How may an individual religion advance the evolutionary status of its morals? In connection to this, Jeremy Shearmur had the following problem with religious evolution in Hayek's thought: "It is not clear how the conservative citizen is to choose what it is that he should accept, and what he should be critical of" (Shearmur 1996, p. 84).[12] If Hayek's argument isn't to collapse to evolutionary fatalism, and if religion plays an active role in maintaining adapted morality, then there must be some mechanism by which religion can improve the evolutionary status of its morality.

## IMMANENT CRITICISM OF TRADITIONS

Hayek dealt with the concept of immanent criticism of our traditions before *The Fatal Conceit*. He developed it in *Law, Legislation and Liberty* and reconstructed that the forefathers of this method were David Hume and Immanuel Kant. Immanent criticism, according to Hayek, was a method by which the judge arrived at the new precedent (Hayek 1982, vol. I, p. 118; Hayek 1982, vol. II, pp. 24, 26). In the 1980s, he developed these ideas further (Hayek 1984b; Hayek 1984c). He applied them not only to the problem of the evolution of the value of several properties (Kreuzer, Hayek, Dahrendorf 1983, p. 38) which is reproduced in *The Fatal Conceit* (Hayek 1988, p. 69), but also to some of our religious traditions:

> The moral tradition remains a treasure which reason cannot replace, but can only endeavour to improve by immanent criticism, that is, by endeavouring to make a system which we cannot create as a whole, serve more consistently the same set of effects. (Hayek 1984b, p. 329)[13]

With the help of his immanent criticism concept, Hayek criticized the theology of liberation, a distinctly Marxist doctrine within Catholic theology, first in private, later in public. He criticized it at the meeting with Pope John Paul II in 1980 as a warning against the destruction of values by scientific error,[14] he criticized it in the correspondence with Cardinal König prior to the conference on cultural evolution (Hoover Institution Archives, Hayek's files, box 31, folder 21) and he later wrote an evolutionary critique of liberation theology in 1985 (Hayek 1985b, pp. 52–53; Hayek 1986a, p. 20; Hayek 1986b). This critique is reproduced in some form in *The Fatal Conceit* (Hayek 1988, p. 51). If immanent criticism led to the conclusion that there's nothing to adapt, because the whole is maladapted, then Hayek's setup ruled out such morals. Hayek's immanent criticism led to the conclusion that liberation theology is maladapted and if Catholicism wishes to improve its adaptation to catallaxy, it would better get rid of it as a whole.

More tellingly, he used immanent criticism to suggest the future development of Weberian Protestant ethics.

A reader might ask: is the Protestant Ethics Thesis (Weber 2002) behind Hayek's argument? As an agnostic, Hayek denied this, just as he denied believing in other religions. Still, we have his answer. In an interview with John O'Sullivan in 1985,[15] Hayek answered, giving an example of immanent criticism:

> ...even that puritan ethics has element in it, which is not quite compatible. It assumes, that hard work must bring its proper reward and I think we have to reconcile our facts that even hard work is not a guaranty, so the success must be up to a point a matter of accident (Hayek 1985c).

Even the Protestant doctrine had a maladaptive aspect: the doctrine forming an expectation that if you work hard, you will be rewarded on this earth. As an immanent criticism, Hayek suggests that Protestant theologians find ways to inhibit the self-destructive potential of this part of the doctrine. According to Hayek, material success on this earth is also a matter of luck. If Protestants expect they will be rewarded for their earthly efforts, it may to some degree promote other types of morality than market morality.

Moreover, the differentiation of Protestant religions in the Reformation allowed the evolutionary selection of religions to operate once again:

> The much-discussed problem of Max Weber about why were the Protestants economically more successful than the Catholics seems precisely to be based on this fact [religious evolution]. At least some Protestant sects apparently put greater weight on this part of religious morality, which allowed them to operate the extended order, as I call it, on a larger scale. (Hayek 1985a, p. 11)[16]

It is also earlier on, in the third volume of the *Law, Legislation and Liberty,* that Hayek challenged Max Weber:

> Long before Calvin the Italian and Dutch commercial towns had practiced and later the Spanish schoolmen codified the rules which made the modern market economy possible. See in this connection particularly H. M. Robertson, *Aspects of the Rise of Economic Individualism*, a book which, if it had not appeared at a time when it practically remained unknown in Germany, should have disposed once and for all of the Weberian myth of the Protestant source of capitalist ethics. He shows that if any religious influences were at work, it was much more the Jesuits than the Calvinists who assisted the rise of the "capitalist spirit". (Hayek 1982, vol. III, p. 203)

Hayek's argument is not a defense of any particular religion, but rather a theory of religious evolution that provides religious thought with the arguments and tools to enhance its long-term survival while helping to sustain the economic order that transcends the capacities of human reason.

## INSTITUTIONS AND "COMMERCIAL" MORALS

By his conjectural history of morals, Hayek had in mind a story of the rise and fall of civilizations as based on the interplay of morals and institutions: "I sometimes wonder whether this interaction, in which moral beliefs create institutions which, in turn, produce moral conceptions very different from those that gave rise to the institutions, is not the true story of the rise and fall of civilizations" (Hayek 1980, pp. 46–47).[17]

Contrary to conservative interpretations, Hayek maintained that the moral teachings of Judaism and Christianity are of older origin than conservatives would like to hear:

> When I pass from the morals of the hunting band in which man spent most of his history, to the morals which made possible the market order of the open society, *I am jumping over a long intermediate stage*, much shorter than man's life in the small band, but still of much greater length than the urban and commercial society has enjoyed yet, and important because *from it date those codifications of ethics which became embodied in the teaching of the monotheistic religions*. It is the period of man's life in tribal society. (Hayek 1978, p. 61)

Hayek suggested that Judaism and Christianity were established in the only part of the world where the institution of private property was sanctioned more than 2000 years ago, that is, in Greece: "I may also add that the European civilization could develop in the *only* area world in which the institution of private property was fully developed over two thousand years ago" (Hayek 1983c, p. 26). This implies that in other parts of the world maladapted religions prevailed that prevented a rise of catallactic civilization.

Hayek believed that if other than adapted morals came upon a civilization and it didn't adapt, the civilization then fell. He thought that Gibbon was partly right that ancient Rome fell due to adopting the Christian morals, which were incapable of maintaining the Roman civilization. Christianity built another one:

> This commercial spirit was temporarily—I'm afraid I agree here, to some extent, with Gibbon—destroyed under the influence of Christianity and again revived in modern times. By the eighteenth or early nineteenth centuries, these new morals, which I will call the "commercial" morals, had, in the Western industrial world, spread almost universally. (Hayek 1983a, p. 33)

From some other of Hayek's articles it follows that the civil code of Justinian from the sixth century established the foundations of the rule of law, which developed very slowly but steadily until the end of the Middle Ages (Hayek 1978, p. 123). During the Reformation, those Protestant religions that sanctioned the values of the family and multiple property prevailed like we have already seen (Hayek 1985a). Many heretical religions appeared, Manicheans, Bogomils, etc., that disapproved of family and several property, but overall they didn't last in the long run: "If you look at the great heretical movements of the last 2000 years, whether they are the Gnostics, the Manichaeans, the Bogomils, the Cathars, the Socialists or whatever you like, the two things in the Western traditions that they all fought against are private property and the family" (Hayek 1985b, pp. 49–50).[18] He characterized this long run as about 100 years. This is the time frame in which group selection operates due to the resulting differences in economic productivity.

## RELIGIOUS EVOLUTION AS A NEXT CHAPTER IN THE CALCULATION DEBATE

Hayek believed that among the contemporary religions and quasi-religions, only communism opposes family and private property. Therefore, the pattern prediction follows that communism as a quasi-religion will be excluded in the future religious evolution:

> The only religions that have survived are those which support property and the family. If you look at the present world, you will find that, with the exception of communism, all the world-wide religions (whether the monotheistic creeds of the West, or the exotic religions of the East)[19] support the two principles of private property and the family. Even though thousands of religious founders have reacted against this and have advocated religious beliefs opposed to these two institutions, their religions have not lasted very long. "Not very long", in this sense, means not more than roughly a hundred years. I think that we are presently watching one such experiment already in the state of decline before its hundred years are over. Communism, is, of course, one of these religions which are anti-property, and anti-religion, which had its time, and which is now declining rapidly. We are watching one instance where the process of the natural selection of religious beliefs disposes of yet another mistaken one, and restores the basic beliefs in property and the family. (Hayek 1983a, p. 48)

Hayek related his new research program to an updated view of the calculation debate. In February 1979, when he had already been writing *The Fatal Conceit* for several months, he reflected on why the Paris Challenge failed.[20] Apart from practical reasons, some of the socialists he was contemplating inviting withdrew their socialist opinions. They had been persuaded without a discussion. Hayek reflected that the reason for their conversion was really conversion, even in religious terms. Hayek would reflect deeply. Now, Hayek needed to rethink the calculation debate. Previously, he had not been quite right about it. He reflected on previous events:

> Now, sitting down and writing this out, I found that merely explaining, as I had done as basis for a debate in somewhat theoretical terms, *the reasons why I believed that socialism could not possibly work* and that the whole scheme was a mistake, *would not be adequate*. (Hayek 1983a, p. 28)

Thus, the argument of religious evolution basically becomes an argument against the rationality of socialism; it is a continuation and extension of the socialist calculation debate with a different analytical tool. Quasi-religions of socialism or social justice are the last of the false religions, which are unlikely to survive their hundredth year—the pattern prediction that proved true for socialism in 1989.[21]

## COMPETITION OF RELIGIONS AS A DISCOVERY PROCEDURE

We have just seen that "symbolically true" religions (Hayek 2013b, p. 254) got rid of the social evolution of the communist heresy. However, for Hayek, a thriving moral evolution presupposed more than the unnoticed growth of secret, underground churches which unexpectedly turned into victory in 1989.

We can see in the example of Solzhenitsyn that the defeat of the socialist heresy is not an occasion for "symbolically true" religions in Eastern Europe to run their post-historic victory laps. They are never "above" or "after" social evolution, but they continue to develop. Or they may decide not to develop any further. To continue developing in an adaptive way, a thriving religious competition is necessary. In 1985, John O'Sullivan asked Hayek for his opinion on Solzhenitsyn, which may serve us as a proxy for Eastern European morals. Hayek said that Solzhenitsyn was a religious person and was unhappy in the West because he considered it "such an irreligious society" (Hayek 1985c). Solzhenitsyn was capable of tearing down the mask of the maladapted socialism, but didn't see a way to the catallaxy. Notice a flagrant difference from the Far Eastern religions, respecting *other* orderly phenomena in the world, which Hayek admired in 1978.

In this regard, we may formulate something as Hayek's conception of competition of religions as a discovery procedure. He developed it mainly in the interview with John O'Sullivan in 1985, which was one of his last interviews. Hayek probably didn't have enough time to work these aspects into a coherent text of his. But we may incorporate these pieces of the puzzle.

For future religious evolution, Hayek outlined two possible courses of evolution: if constructivist rationalism with its constructivist morals succeeds in substantially reducing the level and diversity of religious beliefs, there is a danger of the fall of our civilization (Hayek 1985c). The second, more optimistic possibility is that the future religious evolution of our civilization will be driven mainly by the new religious ideas flowing out of the USA in the next 100 or 200 years:

> Americans were evidently very flexible in their moral approaches ... The moral views of the next 100 or 200 years are going to be determined by the United States more than any country... Our instincts will have to learn, we shall perhaps for generations still be fighting the problem and fluctuate from the one partition to another. (Hayek 1985c)[22]

But Hayek isn't a fatalist in his quest to rejuvenate Western civilization. Even if the first, gloomy option, namely a decline of the West—which Hayek certainly didn't want—turned out to be correct, some civilization would eventually grow on its ashes. Hayek was drawn to Chinese history, which is precisely the case for many centuries. In the same interview with John O'Sullivan, Hayek tells the story of cultural development in China:

> *O'Sullivan:* Could I raise just very elementary objection to your argument. And that is cultural evolution seems to me to come up against a one basic point, namely that a primitive, but a militarily effective society might

very well overwhelm one which is by most standards superior but which nonetheless is some sense decadent?

*Hayek:* Yes, it might happen. But in fact history shows that very largely what was temporarily overwhelmed—the basic local tradition survived and reemerged.

*O'Sullivan:* I have in mind obviously the Soviet domination of Eastern Europe.

*Hayek:* Yes, well, so how that will end. My most interesting example is that we have the longest history the case of China where it seems that temporarily strong government stopped further cultural evolution with a temporary decline and only when government become weak again, cultural evolution resumed. And that there remainders of the old tradition remained in existence for a long period to reemerge at a later stage. Although the very efficient strong government caused long periods of stagnation. (Hayek 1985c)

Miss Cubitt also reports that in 1984 a Chinese scholar invited Hayek to visit China, but this never happened, in part because of Hayek's illness. The Chinese scholar "reminded Hayek of his letter and his wish to study China's 'interrupted history'" (Cubitt 2006, p. 114).

All of the above specifications—if included in Hayek's *The Fatal Conceit*, which they were not—could have prevented accusations of Hayek being Panglossian, committing the naturalistic fallacy, and similar criticisms (Whitman 1998; Denis 2002; Angner 2004).

Hayek argued that we need new religious ideas of good and bad. In defending Mandeville, Hayek argued that we will have to learn that good and bad are something else in raw bands and in commercial society (Kreuzer, Hayek, Dahrendorf 1983, pp. 31–33). Hayek may even have hoped to remedy some of the drawbacks of current religions, namely their anthropomorphism (Hayek 2013b, p. 250; Hayek 1988, pp. 56–57). If this is true, it would help religions to come closer to an understanding of transcendence far beyond our imagination than anthropomorphic ones. This would perhaps help to better ground the market order, which is "literally transcendent" to our cognitive capacities (Hayek 1984a, p. 8; Hayek 1988, p. 72).

It is noteworthy that Hayek encouraged the development of a religion called the Unification Church, a small church that organized conferences on religion and science and was opposed to socialism and which is sometimes considered controversial.[23] Hayek prepared two keynote lectures for them, of which the latter should have been *The Presumption of Reason*. Instead, Bartley presented it in Hayek's name.[24] Finding a replacement was unfortunate both for Hayek and for ICUS, though declining the lecture altogether would have been still worse. It was unfortunate for the conference organizers because they were planning to give Hayek their award or "the Moonie award" (Cubitt 2006, pp.

206–207).[25] They organized a substitute award celebration which happened in April 1986 in Freiburg where Hayek was living, now destined by his illness to stay there until his death. On that occasion, Hayek delivered a short acceptance speech. In it, he described that initially he was somewhat unsure that the interaction with ICUS was a good idea but then recollected that he previously spoke to Pope John Paul II and participated in the scholarly conference organized by Cardinal König. He provided this as a reason why he would eventually participate in their activities, demonstrating his religious tolerance (Hoover Institution Archives, Hayek's files, box 111, folder 13).

Even if we don't mean to judge *The Fatal Conceit*, of the above-mentioned aspects of the theory of religious evolution, only a few are mentioned in *The Fatal Conceit*: heretics, the quasi-religion of socialism, and the possible collapse of our civilization if most people cease to believe in supernatural beliefs, a note, which is, nevertheless, Jeffrey Friedman's.[26]

## FAMILY AS A MEANS OF PASSING ON MORALS

Hayek's argument is that the religions that survive in the long run are those that support the institutions of the family and private or several property. Why these institutions? Hayek, the economist, was aware of the urgency of the problem:

> I must still explain why I believe that the belief in the institution of private property—or, as I prefer to call it, several property, because it is not necessarily the property of individuals but the properties of any group—is an essential condition of the development of the extended order of human co-operation. (Hayek 1983a, p. 49)

The reason for several properties is that it enables and deepens the division of labor:

> Private property, of course, was never "invented" in the sense that people foresaw what its benefits would be. Its main benefit turned out to be the division of labour which it brought about. That in turn increased the possibility of maintaining a larger number of people because it generated an increase in productivity by enabling us to utilize a much greater variety of information than could ever be possessed by any single agent. (Hayek 1983a, p. 49)

The family has been selected because it best preserves its several properties while teaching children the morals that will enable them to become members of the extended economic order of capitalism. Regarding the family, there is an interesting note in connection with demography, especially in developing countries. If they want to become "full members" of Western civilization, they will have to change their family morals and adjust their planning of the number of children accordingly:

> we are living in period of the most rapid multiplication of mankind, observing the traditional rules which were selected because they were most beneficial to the multiplication of mankind, does not lead to an indefinite multiplication. It is a process, which is self-regulating. As the advance order of society expands the part of the world where people have learned to control their numbers, the periphery of people who profit from it and are thus enabled still to satisfy their primitive instinct of providing many children, will become smaller. (Hayek 1983a, pp. 51–52)

Their original traditional morals of having as many children as possible were adapted to a time when a third of children died shortly after birth and only about half of children could be expected to live to adulthood. Under conditions of increased wealth, improved health care, nutrition, and other services, virtually no children die, so there is a good hope that one can have only two children and they will live long into adulthood. Moreover, in our civilization, the division of labor has led to the invention of machines, and the labor force needs a certain amount of education to participate in the division of labor and the creation of wealth. The "quality" and quantity of children seem to be substitutes under these conditions. Therefore, the shrinking of the nuclear family is the adaptive behavior of contemporary families. Thus, Hayek's theory is not a Panglossian demographic theory, as identified by Naomi Beck, who bases her criticism on *The Fatal Conceit*, which is retrograde in this respect (Beck 2011). It can easily be described by Hayek's theory of cultural evolution and was used as a tool for family policy analysis (Horwitz 2015).

## MISESIAN LEGACY AND THE DENIAL OF THE RULE UTILITARIANISM IN THE EMERGENCE OF MORALS

Hayek himself said in retrospect that he started from the position of utilitarianism (Hayek 1987, p. 39), which can be documented by *The Constitution of Liberty*, his 1960 book (Hayek 2013a). By the 1980s he had freed himself from these notions to such an extent that both in the 1980s articles and in *The Fatal Conceit* he denied the possibility of explaining and improving our morals with the help of utilitarianism. In 1978, Hayek identified the problem with utilitarianism in the legacy of Ludwig von Mises, his great teacher and mentor.[27]

Hayek maintained this in a foreword to the 1981 edition of Mises' book *Socialism*. Hayek wrote his Foreword earlier on, already in August 1978 (Hayek 1992, pp. 136–143) which is the time when Hayek started *The Fatal Conceit* project. In his Foreword, Hayek arrives at a striking criticism of Mises' moral utilitarianism. Hayek informs that he would no longer share it. For Mises, liberalism "regards all social cooperation as an emanation of rationally recognized utility" (Hayek 1992, p. 142), a position Hayek criticized for its "extreme rationalism." Hayek is not a thorough critic of his mentor and friend. To the contrary, he credits Mises for helping us understand the spontaneous order that nobody has designed: "It is greatly to Mises' credit that he largely emancipated himself from that rationalist-constructivist starting point, but that task is still to be completed" (Hayek 1992, p. 142). Hayek would adopt the research program stimulated by Mises. At the same time, Hayek would work on getting rid of the constructivist rationalism and utilitarianism in morals. One of Hayek's tasks while working on *The Fatal Conceit* was to battle moral utilitarianism. He wanted to provide a scholarly demonstration that we are not free to choose the alternative, that is, socialist morals. That is also a devastating argument of the last, moral stronghold of socialism, and is thus also Hayek's last substantial argument in the economic calculation debate. It is therefore paradoxical that he is still considered a moral utilitarian (Yeager 1985; Yeager 1989). In the 1980s, scholars were apparently missing an idea of where Hayek's research was heading.

The problem with utilitarianism in morals can be illustrated by an example from Neolithic religion. Shamans didn't choose to deny some people access to "sacred" bulls *in order to establish institutions* of agricultural civilization that could feed more people in a more humane way (Lewis-Williams, Pearce 2005). The shamans did this for religious reasons—and perhaps for their own satisfaction, but certainly not for rule-utilitarian reasons. Hayek himself used another example, that of Protestant religions. Did Calvin invent a religion to create a morality that would ultimately allow for a more advanced economic order? Albert O. Hirschman denied the possibility of such far-reaching providence on the part of those acting during the Reformation. Hayek used the quotation from Hirschman's 1981 edition (Hirschman 1997; Hayek 2013b, p. 242). If we follow the rules of spontaneous order, we're creating an "unknown civilization" to which Hayek dedicated his *Constitution of Liberty* (Hayek 2013a; Hayek 1985c).

The danger of the utilitarian understanding of the emergence of morals can be seen in the softest form of utilitarianism, the so-called "rule-utilitarianism ex post."[28] It's the position that only after cultural evolution is complete can we look back and see what rules have survived, and then say that it will be rational to follow those rules in the future. Hayek's late writings deny this stance. When can we say that we are on top of cultural evolution? If someone says that we are "after cultural evolution," then which religion best supports the ideal morals achieved?[29] Such thoughts could lead out of the realm of science and certainly out of Hayek's theory. It would be reminiscent of Hayek's idea of synoptic delusion, according to which the human mind, in a miraculous moment, out of the blue, recognizes all the dispersed facts of time and space, including itself, to which facts we have to adapt (Hayek 1974). Hayek was of the opinion that even institutions of several property and family will need more adaptations to the ever-expanding order, so that the present form cannot be conserved and maintained to be rational or definite. What reason can accomplish is the immanent criticism that can help religious leaders to better adapt our institutions to the unknown facts of our environment. Hayek spoke to religious leaders in this manner. If a theory of the spontaneous evolution of morals is to be more fully developed, both in its economic part and in its religious part, the error of rule-utilitarianism must be combated.

## CONCLUSION

Hayek's theory of the evolution of morals and religions provides a more solid foundation for our understanding of social evolution than is usually acknowledged. To do so, we reconstructed his contributions. Our chapter provides a historical reconstruction of his theory from the materials of the 1980s. Starting in 1978, Hayek wrote another hundred articles. We rely on them rather than on *The Fatal Conceit.*

The first is the methodological presupposition of value neutrality in an economist's study of morals. Hayek used Hume's version of the is-ought distinction, that one can never derive morals from reason. For Hayek, a research question followed from Hume's stance: if not from reason, then where do moral rules come from? In Hayek's view, Adam Smith gave the correct answer to Hume's research question, namely that religions sanctioned moral rules before reason. Hayek sees here a foreshadowing of his own argument of cultural evolution based on the principle of group selection.

Religion played an immensely important role in this for Hayek. In fact, *economics and religion* are the two intended tools that help Hayek achieve his goal which he had by 1985 with his project on *The Fatal Conceit*, which is the evolutionary theory of morals. Even if the chapter about religion was not in the original plan of *The Fatal Conceit* (Ebenstein 2003, pp. 218–219, 224), its inclusion is in line with his research interests in the 1980s. It is unclear, however, from *The Fatal Conceit* whether and how the concept of immanent criticism applies to religion. An active rather than passive role of religion is needed to make adjustments for the future adaptation of morals to the economic order. We offer Hayek's examples of such immanent criticism. That would have solved the problem of Hayek's methodological individualism versus his group selection, which scholars overemphasize.

Moreover, the historical course of the evolution of religions was omitted from *The Fatal Conceit.* We have provided some evidence of this evolution, such as the religious reasons for the rise and fall of ancient Greece and Rome, and then the rise of European civilization in the Middle Ages and later in the Reformation. Most interesting in this history, however, are the patterns that predict future religious evolution. One of them is that (1) either the constructivist rationalist religious or socialist sects will deprive believers of their faith and our civilization and its market order will crumble or (2) a new religious energy will spring from the process of discovering morals (namely, religious freedom in the USA). Hayek believed that since the number of new religious ideas is the highest in the USA, they will provide our civilization with the adaptations of our moral order to the facts, which nobody can know in its entirety.

We acknowledge that Hayek's theory was far from complete at the time of its fullest development and that it needs to be supplemented to become a convincing theory of the "rise and fall of civilizations" and their economic orders. However, Hayek's explanation of the role of religions in social evolution, as we find it in his 1980s papers, is more convincing than is usually understood. Hayek nested his 1980s ideas on religion and social evolution neatly so that they are consistent with his previous ideas.

## NOTES

1. We thank the participants of the Wirth Institute conference about Hayek that took place in June 2024 in Kraków for their remarks. Alberto Mingardi, Mark Pennington, and Eamonn Butler were particularly helpful. All of the remaining errors are ours, however. We should also note that all translations are ours. All *italics* in quoted passages are ours. All footnotes within the quoted passages are also ours.
2. Prior to these talks, Hayek went to Japan where he was exploring Far Eastern religions, see Yoshino (2017). We thank Eamonn Butler for directing our attention to the Far East. Hayek explored religion as a complex order in his 1982 lecture *The Overrated Reason* (Hayek 2013b, pp. 247–252). We do not follow his discussion here. We, however, note that the venue where Hayek delivered this lecture demonstrates his heightened interest in religion. He offered that speech at the conference commemorating Charles Darwin's centenary at the session on cultural evolution. The conference was organized by the Catholic prelate, Franz Cardinal König (Hoover Institution Archives, Hayek's files, box 31, folder 21).
3. Erwin Dekker suggested to us that we're actually explaining the tension between Hayek the methodological individualist and Hayek the group selectionist that scholars think is a big problem of Hayek in the 1980s (Vanberg 1985; Buchanan 1988–1989). Up until 1985, Hayek conceived of *The Fatal Conceit* book project neither as a book on constitutional development nor a book on economics, but as a book on morals.
4. We thank Alberto Mingardi, who suggested at the June 2024 conference in Kraków that we didn't need to utter derogatory comments about *The Fatal Conceit*, which is, after all, a good book. We previously launched unnecessary attacks at *The Fatal Conceit* that led us astray. Mingardi's advice helped us focus better.

5. See https://hayek.de/bibliographie/.
6. Charlotte Cubitt, Hayek's secretary in the 1980s, mentioned the word "repetitive" or "repetitions" in connection to Hayek's writing no less than 27 times (Cubitt 2006). The lead author of this chapter once asked Bruce Caldwell to send some of Hayek's articles from the 1980s. Caldwell was very kind and sent the papers. At the same time, he warned that they are very repetitive and they might therefore contain only very little value added.
7. Hayek was open with his audience about his writing issues in the 1980s. He would tell his audiences during this period that he was "making an experiment on them," "trying out some new ideas" with them (Hayek 1983d). In saying this, he was honest. To grasp the bigger idea he was after, we need to read them all.
8. We proceeded with our research in the order just described. We recommend to the reader a study guide to Hayek's papers at the Hoover Institution Archives: https://oac.cdlib.org/findaid/ark:/13030/kt3v19n8zw/entire_text/. To help the reader spare some of our toil, we provide links to some of the materials we found on the internet in our list of references. As far as we know, the most complete internet guide to Hayek's materials is this one: https://contemporarythinkers.org/friedrich-hayek/
9. Here we see Hayek's repetitive but explorative work in action. He delivered this lecture under the title *The Rules of Morality are not the Conclusions of our Reason* for the Unification Church conference called the International Conference on the Unity of Sciences (ICUS) on November 25, 1983. He is mentioning another title under which the lecture was previously advertised. He delivered a lecture with that title, *The Origins and Effects of Our Morals: A Problem for Science* several weeks before at the Hoover Institution on November 1, 1983 (Hayek 1984b, p. 318). He apparently was not comfortable with the latter title, changing it before the ICUS conference in Chicago. Hayek also held a lecture named *The Rules of Morality are not the Conclusions of our Reason* at George Mason University (Hayek 1983d). Although we don't know the date of the George Mason lecture, it falls to this period. Apart from the changing titles of his lectures, the important part for us here is his task of formulating a value-free theory of morals and its emergence which he elaborated from several angles in these articles.
10. Though Hayek wanted to be a positive scientist, he was no positivist. A positive science of morals would not commit value judgments but would explain the emergence of morals. We thank Erwin Dekker for this insight.
11. The quoted resource is the first translation by Bartley of Hayek's German article that was named *Die Überheblichkeit der Vernunft*, of which two original German versions appear; the version Bartley apparently used for translation does not contain the passage we quote. For a somewhat similar passage in that original, see Hayek (1986a, p. 10). To help remedy a possible problem of Bartley's involvement, let us also quote from the earlier one of these two German originals, in support of our argument that we need both economics

*and* religion to understand the theme of *The Fatal Conceit*, at least according to Hayek in 1985:

> Finally, it is the by-product of the *study of economics* that we are compelled to recognize that, in addition to the explanatory reason of the individual, we owe our civilization to an independent moral tradition, not created by reason, which scientists have often rejected because it is the result of superstition or the result of a theistic religion. *We must recognize* that the order in which we live today is not our creation of an impersonal process of evolution which has left us, in addition to reason, an endowment consisting of *a moral conviction* which includes all sorts of things, but certainly two: the recognition of the institution of private property and the recognition of the institution of the family. (Hayek 1985b, p. 55)

In addition to value-free economics or catallaxy, we must recognize a moral conviction of religions.

12. The concept of immanent criticism, Hayek's tool to achieve this goal, is introduced in *The Fatal Conceit* and illustrated in the economics of property rights, but no one knows from *The Fatal Conceit* whether and how to use immanent criticism in religion.
13. In the realm of morals, Erwin Dekker suggested to us that Hayek's immanent criticism as a tool for religious leaders mimics the method of development of the dogmas of the Catholic Church in ecumenical councils throughout two millennia, and was a part of the cultural milieu of Hayek's Vienna. Also see Dekker's work (Dekker 2016).
14. See Ebenstein (2001, pp. 301–302) with quotes from Hayek's address.
15. The interview was supposed to be about Hayek's life and works, but at times it turned out to be a schooling in Hayek's most novel aspects of the theory of the evolution of religions.
16. According to Scott Yenor, in the early modern period, the progress toward capitalism was achieved only after a great religious revolution rather than its evolution. Yenor argued that the British crown intervened in the Roman Church, thus implying the Church was a retrograde institution, impossible of further evolution. Yenor contrasts this with Hayek (Yenor 2007, p. 114), but it doesn't contradict Hayek's 1980s materials.
17. In a 1977 interview, Hayek used similar expressions: "So we have this strange interaction between morality – institution – and morality. I suspect more and more that the rise and fall of cultures can be explained to a large extent by this interaction" (Hayek 1977). In *The Fatal Conceit* "the undoubted historical connection between religion and the values that have shaped and furthered our civilisation" (Hayek 1988, p. 137), this connection was only postulated. Religion is missing in the first couple of chapters of *The Fatal Conceit*, where Hayek provides a piece of conjectural history of how our moral traditions developed. We remedy that in our account which follows Hayek's depiction of the evolution of civilization in connection to religion.

18. Also see Hayek's other draft of *Die Überheblichkeit der Vernunft* (Hayek 1986a, p. 12) and its translation that Bartley prepared (Hayek 1986b). Bartley's translation reproduces this argument.
19. Notice that in the autobiographical interviews in 1978 Hayek felt more attracted to tolerant polytheist Far East religions that respected other complex orders in the world, referring to Japan. Prior to these discussions, Hayek visited Japan (Cubitt 2006, p. 27).
20. Hayek wanted to organize a grand debate of twelve defenders of capitalism and twelve of their socialist counterparts. He was imagining that the discussion would happen in Paris. He contemplated organizing the Paris Challenge for the greater part of the year 1978 (Cubitt 2006, pp. 23–26).
21. We should also read some demographic examinations of Hayek's thesis in this light. Michael Blume examines whether Amish fertility confirms Hayek's theory (Blume 2010). Hayek wasn't interested in religion demography per se where Amish fertility has been a striking phenomenon. Instead, he was interested in the emergence of world morals, catallactic morals that are upheld primarily by world religions in which then, Hayek was interested primarily.
22. Notice that Hayek's judgment about America as a religious country is contrasted by Solzhenitsyn's view.
23. Bartley and Radnitzky were inviting Hayek to those conferences continuously (Cubitt 2006, p. 40, pp. 106–107) for some years before Hayek delivered his plenary lecture *The Rules of Morality are not the Conclusions of Our Reason* at their yearly conference in November 1983 (Hayek 1984c). Hayek's secretary would refer to them as "the Moonies, or ICUS, as Hayek preferred to call them in public" (Cubitt 2006, p. 40). Hayek was also to give the keynote at the November 1985 ICUS conference. It is for this conference that Bartley translated Hayek's *Die Überheblichkeit der Vernunft* into *The Presumption of Reason* and presented it instead of Hayek. Bartley translated it for Hayek who became almost mortally ill in late summer 1985. When learning the news about how the conference went on, Hayek, already ill, had one of his better days. He labeled Bartley's lecture a "bastard lecture" but was still in an unusually good mood that his health status normally allowed: "He then talked about the Moonie presentation, during which he said that Bartley's 'bastard lecture' had caused much interest and a lively debate" (Cubitt 2006, p. 183). This was Bartley's first service directly involving Hayek's texts. We already noticed that Bartley didn't translate it one to one but at present we don't know whether Hayek was involved in these alterations. For the time being, we refrain from judging Bartley.
24. In the German original, *Die Überheblichkeit der Vernunft*, Hayek mentioned his encounter with Franz Cardinal König and the story of how he came up with the expression "symbolic truth" of religion at the conference organized by Cardinal König in 1982 (Hennecke 2000, p. 376). This passage is not included in Bartley's translation for the Unification Church conference, *The Presumption of Reason*.

25. For Hayek, if for no other reason, it was unfortunate that he hadn't secured the monetary reward for the prize.
26. The last two sentences of *The Fatal Conceit* are written by a red pen on the margins of the draft labeled, by the same red pen, "Jeff's copy" (Hoover Institution archives, Hayek's files, box 111, folder 20 and folder 21). In 2017, the lead coauthor of this chapter presented that material at the Summer Seminar in the History of Economics, claiming that the red pen was Hayek's. Bruce Caldwell was in the audience. He asked who Jeff was. Caldwell suggested Jeffrey Friedman was the one. That is a convincing explanation. We thank Bruce Caldwell for this note. Jeffrey Friedman served as Bartley's research assistant (Caldwell 2004, p. 317). We don't aim to assess religion in *The Fatal Conceit*. We merely quote *The Fatal Conceit* to alert the reader to the value of the 1980s papers.
27. We elaborate on Hayek's Misesian legacy in studying spontaneous order in morals in a separate paper that is going to be published as a chapter in the book on Hayek under the auspices of the Adam Smith Institute, London (Krištofóry, Šíma 2025). The present chapter offers our synoptic view of Hayek's theory of social evolution in the context of religion. We are persuaded that more papers can be written on tiny aspects of Hayek's theory like we are doing in our other paper.
28. We like the expression of rule utilitarianism *ex post* as differentiated from rule utilitarianism *ex ante*. Ján Pavlík, a former teacher of the lead coauthor and a former colleague of the second coauthor, liked these expressions in the context of Hayek (Pavlík 1999). Pavlík also realized that Hayek mimicked Kant in limiting reason to give space to religion (Pavlík 2004, pp. 536–564). Pavlík taught us a lot about Hayek and spontaneous orders. Even if we highly value what he's done for us intellectually, we must distance ourselves from his deeds as one of the representatives of the Faculty of Economics at the University of Economics in Prague. His deeds contributed to the decline of the faculty so that scholars like Peter Boettke, Dan B. Klein, or Deirdre McCloskey, who previously cherished their stays at "our" institution, will never come again. Pavlík's deeds also contributed to the fact that although present work is to a great degree his grandchild, none of the two coauthors of this chapter now work at the Faculty of Economics at UEP, the institution with which we had been associating our careers and career prospects.
29. Hayek's value-free approach would forbid a scholarly answer. He would have said, "well, you have a number of religious or agnostic approaches toward social morals. Choose your own, but it will be your personal decision, not a scientific conclusion."

## REFERENCES

Angner E. (2004). Did Hayek Commit the Naturalistic Fallacy? *Journal of the History of Economic Thought*, 26(3), pp. 349–361.

Beck N. (2011). Be Fruitful and Multiply: Growth, Reason, and Cultural Group Selection in Hayek and Darwin. *Biological Theory,* 6(4), pp. 413–423.

Blume M. (2010). Von Hayek and the Amish fertility how religious communities manage to be fruitful and multiply–a case study, in Frey U. (ed.), *The Nature of God – Evolution and Religion*. Baden-Baden: Tectum, pp. 159–175.
Buchanan J. (1988–1989). Hayek and the Forces of History. *Humane Studies Review*, 6, pp. 3–4.
Caldwell B. (2004). *Hayek's Challenge: an Intellectual Biography of F. A. Hayek*. Chicago, IL: University of Chicago Press.
Caldwell B. (2007). Life Writings: On-the-Job Training with F. A. Hayek. *History of Political Economy*, 39 (annual supplement), pp. 342–354.
Caldwell B. (2014). Introduction, in Hayek, F. von (ed.), *The Market and Other Orders. The Collected Works of F. A. Hayek, vol. XV.* Chicago, IL: University of Chicago Press, pp. 1–35.
Caldwell B. (2016). Hayek's Nobel, in Boettke P., Storr V. H. (eds.), *Revisiting Hayek's Political Economy*, Advances in Austrian Economics volume 21. Bingley, UK: Emerald Group Publishing, pp. 1–19.
Cubitt C. (2006). *A Life of Friedrich August von Hayek*. London: Authors OnLine.
Dekker E. (2016). *The Viennese Students of Civilization*. Cambridge, UK: Cambridge University Press.
Denis A. (2002). Was Hayek a panglossian evolutionary theorist? A reply to Whitman. *Constitutional Political Economy*, 13(3), pp. 275–285.
Ebenstein A. (2001). *Hayek: A Biography*. London: Palgrave Macmillan.
Ebenstein A. (2003). *Hayek's Journey: The Mind of Friedrich Hayek*. Berlin, Heidelberg, Dordrecht, New York: Springer.
Gray J. (1982). Hayek and classical liberalism: A bibliographical essay. *Literature of Liberty*, 5(4), pp. 19–101.
Gray J. (1998). *Hayek on Liberty*. London: Routledge.
Hayek F. von (1974). *Law, Legislation and Liberty. Volume 1: Rules and Order.* London: Routledge.
Hayek F. von (1977). Den Markt besser begreifen, *Wirtschaftswoche*, 11.2.1977. https://www.wiwo.de/politik/deutschland/nachdruck-aus-heft-8-1977-den-markt-besser-begreifen/5678832.html [Accessed 21.06.2025].
Hayek F. von (1978). *New Studies in Philosophy, Politics, Economics, and the History of Ideas*. Chicago, IL: University of Chicago Press.
Hayek F. von (1980). *1980s Unemployment and the Unions*. Hobart paper 87. London: Institute of Economic Affairs.
Hayek F. von (1982). *Law, Legislation and Liberty. Volumes 1–3*. London: Routledge & Kegan Paul.
Hayek F. von (1983a). *Knowledge, Evolution and Society*. London: Adam Smith Institute.
Hayek F. von (1983b). *Nobel Prize-winning Economist F. A. Hayek*. Oral history program, University of California, Los Angeles.
Hayek F. von (1983c). Sitte, Ordnung und Nahrung. Über die Ethik des Eigentums und die Entwicklung der Kulturen. *Gießener Universitätsblätter*, 1, pp. 23–30.
Hayek F. von (1983d). The rules of morality are not the conclusions of our reason. A video recording of a 1983 lecture at George Mason University with a Q & A session. https://www.youtube.com/watch?v=uv2aMKr7kTc [Accessed 21.06.2025].
Hayek F. von (1984a). Die ausgedehnte Ordnung menschlicher Zusammenarbeit. *Bayerischer Monatsspiegel*, 20(6), pp. 8–12.

Hayek F. von (1984b). The origins and effects of our morals: a problem for science, in Leube K., Nishyiama Ch. (eds.), *The Essence of Hayek.* Stanford, CA: Hoover Institution Press, pp. 318–330.

Hayek F. von (1984c). The rules of morality are not the conclusions of our reason, in *Commemorative Volume of the Twelfth International Conference on the Unity of the Sciences* (delivered in Chicago in November 1983), New York, pp. 35–42.

Hayek F. von (1984d). Über die Grenzen der individuellen Vernunft und die Macht und die Labilität der Moral. *Orientierungen (Ludwig-Erhard-Stiftung)*, 20(2), pp. 2–6.

Hayek F. von (1985a). *Die Freie Marktwirtschaft und ihre Moralische Grundlagen.* Lecture delivered in Vienna. https://web.archive.org/web/20160305084445/http://www.europainstitut.at/upload/publikationen/publikation_23.pdf [Accessed 23.06.2025].

Hayek F. von (1985b). Die Überheblichkeit der Vernunft. *Veröffentlichungen der Hanns-Martin-Schleyer-Stiftung, Band*, 19, pp. 47–55.

Hayek F. von (1985c). *Friedrich von Hayek: His Life and Thought. Hayek interviewed by John O'Sullivan.* https://www.youtube.com/watch?v=LtCvJeRK3lE [Accessed 23.06.2025].

Hayek F. von (1986a). Die Überheblichkeit der Vernunft: Inaugural address to the Alpbach Forum 1985, in Molden O. (ed.), *Evolution und die Zukunft der Menschheit: Europäisches Forum Alpbach 1985.* Vienna: Österreichisches College, pp. 7–20.

Hayek F. von (1986b). The presumption of reason, in Bartley W. W., III (ed.), *Fourteenth International Conference on the Unity of Sciences: Absolute Values and the New Cultural Revolution*, New York: I.C.U.S. Books. http://blog.ganderson.us/2011/12/the-presumption-of-reason/ [Accessed 23.06.2025].

Hayek F. von (1987). Individual and collective aims, in Mendus S., Edwards D. (eds.), *On Toleration.* Oxford, UK: Oxford University Press, pp. 35–48.

Hayek F. von (1988). *The Fatal Conceit.* Edited by W. W. Bartley III. London: Routledge.

Hayek F. von (1992). *The Fortunes of Liberalism: Essays on Austrian Economics and the Ideal of Freedom.* Chicago IL, University of Chicago Press.

Hayek F. von (1994). *Hayek on Hayek.* Edited by L. Wenar, S. Kresge. Chicago, IL: University of Chicago Press.

Hayek F. von (2013a). *The Constitution of Liberty: the Definitive Edition. Collected Works of F. A. Hayek, Volume 17.* Chicago, IL: University of Chicago Press.

Hayek F. von (2013b). The overrated reason. *Journal of the History of Economic Thought,* 35(2), pp. 239–256.

Hennecke H. (2000). *Friedrich August von Hayek: Die Tradition Der Freiheit.* Düsseldorf: Verlag Wirtschaft und Finanzen.

Hirschman A. (1997). *The Passions and the Interests: Political Arguments for Capitalism Before its Triumph.* Princeton, NJ: Princeton University Press.

Horwitz S. (2008). Analogous models of complexity: The Austrian theory of capital and Hayek's theory of cognition as adaptive classifying systems, in Koppl R. (ed.), *Explorations in Austrian Economics,* Advances in Austrian Economics, Volume 11. Leeds, UK: Emerald Group Publishing, pp. 143–166.

Horwitz S. (2015). *Hayek's Modern Family: Classical Liberalism and the Evolution of Social Institutions.* London: Palgrave Macmillan.

Kreuzer F., Hayek F. von, Dahrendorf R. (1983). *Markt, Plan, Freiheit: Franz Kreuzer im Gespräch mit Friedrich von Hayek und Ralf Dahrendorf.* Leipzig: Deuticke.

Krištofóry T., Šíma J. (2025). *Hayek on Religion and Social Evolution in the 1980s – Mises-related Insights.* London: Adam Smith Institute.

Lewis P. (2015). Orders, orders, everywhere... on Hayek's *The Market and Other Orders. Cosmos+Taxis,* 2(2), pp. 1–17.
Lewis P. (2016a). The emergence of "emergence" in the work of F. A. Hayek: A historical analysis. *History of Political Economy,* 48(1), pp. 111–150.
Lewis P. (2016b). Systems, Structural Properties and Levels of Organisation: The Influence of Ludwig Von Bertalanffy on the Work of F. A. Hayek, in Fiorito L., Scheall S., Suprinyak C. E. (eds.), *Research in the History of Economic Thought and Methodology,* volume 34A. Leeds, UK: Emerald Group Publishing, pp. 125–159.
Lewis-Williams D., Pearce D. (2005). *Inside the Neolithic Mind: Consciousness, Cosmos, and the Realm of the Gods.* London: Thames & Hudson.
Oliva G. 2016. The Road to Servomechanisms: the Influence of Cybernetics on Hayek from The Sensory Order to the Social Order, in Fiorito L., Scheall S., Suprinyak C. E. (eds.), *Research in the History of Economic Thought and Methodology,* volume 34A. Leeds, UK: Emerald Group Publishing, pp. 161–198.
Pavlík J. (1999). About the role of morality and religion in the market system. *E-Logos. Electronic Journal for Philosophy,* 6(1). https://elogos.vse.cz/pdfs/elg/1999/01/22.pdf [Accessed 21.06.2025].
Pavlík J. (2004). *F. A. Hayek a teorie spontánního řádu.* Praha: Professional Publishing.
Shearmur J. (1996). *Hayek and After: Hayekian Liberalism as a Research Programme.* London: Routledge.
Vanberg V. (1985). Cultural evolution vs. rationalism in Hayek's thought. *Cato Policy Report,* 7(1), pp. 3–5.
Vanberg V. (2017). The "Knowledge Problem" as the Integrating Theme of F. A. Hayek's Oeuvre: An Introduction to The Sensory Order, in Vanberg V. (ed.), *The Sensory Order and Other Writings on the Foundations of Theoretical Psychology.* Chicago, IL: University of Chicago Press, pp. 1–111.
Weber M. (2002). *The Protestant Ethic and the Spirit of Capitalism, and Other Writings.* London: Penguin.
Whitman D. (1998). Hayek contra Pangloss on evolutionary systems. *Constitutional Political Economy,* 9(1), pp. 45–66.
Yeager L. (1985). Rights, contract, and utility in policy espousal. *Cato Journal* 5(1), pp. 259–294.
Yeager L. (1989). Reason and cultural evolution. *Critical Review* 3(2), pp. 324–335.
Yenor S. (2007). Spontaneous order and the problem of religious revolution, in Hunt L., McNamara P., (eds.), *Liberalism, Conservatism, and Hayek's Idea of Spontaneous Order.* New York, NY: Palgrave Macmillan, pp. 107–126.
Yoshino Y. (2017). Beyond Darwinism: Examining the Hayek-Imanishi dialogues, in Leeson, R. (ed.), *Hayek: A Collaborative Biography: Part X: Eugenics, Cultural Evolution, and The Fatal Conceit.* Cham: Springer International Publishing, pp. 419–433.

# 6. F.A. Hayek, reader of Hume's *Treatise*

**Emilio Mazza and Alberto Mingardi**

## "MY GREAT IDOL DAVID HUME"

According to F.A. Hayek, David Hume was not only "the greatest legal philosopher whom England has produced before Bentham", he was also the "outstanding philosopher of liberal political and legal theory" (Hayek 1991, p. 105).[1] As Hayek puts it in 1982, he was "my great idol David Hume" (Hayek 2001, p. 35). Hayek saw his own liberalism as in continuity with Hume's: Hume, he thought, "gives us probably the only comprehensive statement of the legal and political philosophy which later became known as liberalism" (Hayek 1991, p. 105). Hayek's own effort as a political theorist, in works such as *The Constitution of Liberty* and *Law, Legislation and Liberty*, can perhaps be seen in the same way.

If we consider the *corpus* of Hayekian writings, we can say that, as Hayek develops his social theory, Hume's influence is growing in importance. *The Road to Serfdom* opens with two epigraphs, one from Hume and the other from Tocqueville; but whereas Tocqueville is mentioned in salient passages of the book, there is only one reference to Hume in a list of classical liberal thinkers. In *The Counter-revolution of Science* Hume is mentioned 9 times and Adam Smith 20. In *The Constitution of Liberty*, Hume is mentioned 10 times, Tocqueville and Smith only 7. In *Law, Legislation and Liberty* Hume's name occurs 52 times, Smith 22 and Tocqueville 4 times.

When illustrating his view of spontaneous order, Hayek often referred to Adam Ferguson's *Essay*: "[social institutions] are indeed the result of human action, but not the execution of any human design" (e.g. Hayek 1988, p. 20; 2011, p. 112; see also Ferguson 1767, p. 187); yet, to explain the same concept, he later often resorted to Hume's *Treatise*: "the rules of morality are not conclusions of our reason" (e.g. Hayek 1988, pp. 8, 66, 69; 1991, p. 107; 2011, p. 124; see also Hume 1890, vol. 2, p. 235).

The point we want to make is that Hayek not only *used* Hume instrumentally to argue for his own ideas. He *studied* Hume and, in 1963, he published one major scholarly article on him. Still, the scholarly interest in Hayek and

Hume is limited. This can be partly explained by the fact that Hayek is usually considered an economist; but it partly reveals a substantial lack of interest in *Hayek as Humean* (so Donald Livingston titled a review of Chandra Kukathas' *Hayek and Modern Liberalism*) from both Hayek's and Hume's scholars. This, in spite of many being aware, as John Gray was, of Hayek's "debts to David Hume, whose influence upon Hayek's moral and political philosophy is ubiquitous and profound" (Gray 1998, p. 56). Shirley Letwin (1976, p. 153), a remarkable scholar of both, observed that "Hayek rightly felt a special affinity" for Hume. Hayek's political theory has been described as "a deontic moral system for the free society" (Radnitzky 1994, p. 82). It could be a good description of the political theory expressed in Hume's *Treatise*.

On this occasion, we will present some evidence of Hayek's careful study of Hume, taking advantage of the available literature and of our own (attempts at) reading of Hayek's *marginalia* to Hume's *Treatise*. We shall also formulate some hypotheses about the time, place and manner in which such "special affinity" began.

## THE MAKING OF A TRADITION

Did Hayek *need* Hume? Hayek devoted substantial efforts to establishing his own readings of the classical liberal tradition in which he placed himself.

In "Individualism: True and False" (1948), he sketched a general scheme in the history of thought: modern Europe has been shaped by a conflict between a tradition of "true" and one of "false" individualism. The former "accounts for most of the order which we find in human affairs as the unforeseen result of individual actions", the latter maintains "that everything which man achieves is the direct result of, and therefore subject to, the control of individual reason" (Hayek 1948, p. 8). This tension is a recurring theme for Hayek. In his Nobel Lecture, he explains that the social reformer or true individualist should not be a "craftsman" who shapes the social order; like a "gardener", he "cultivate[s] a growth by providing the appropriate environment" (Hayek 1989, p. 7).

Under the label of "true individualism", Hayek connects the Austrian school of economics and, in particular, the work of Carl Menger, both as an economist (Menger 2007) and as a social theorist (Menger 1985), with some alleged forerunners: Mandeville, Hume and Smith.[2] Hayek deemed nineteenth-century British liberalism to have drifted towards Thomas Green's "new liberalism" and hence it was safer to search for older roots. Ironically, Hume may have been Green's "great idol" too, as Green himself was the editor of Hume's philosophical works and the author of a 300-page Introduction to Hume's *Treatise*, which Hayek did not underline or annotate.

To Hayek, liberalism is a set of ideas shaped by institutions that have evolved over time, rather than a doctrine that designs and moulds those institutions from the outset. Thinkers register and interpret existing social realities, rather than reality conforming to their theoretical blueprints, and in this story Hume plays a central role in the development of liberalism so understood.

In the 1940s Hayek engaged in an "Abuse of Reason project", as Bruce Caldwell (2004, pp. 232–260) noted, which was a reaction to the British intelligentsia's drift towards planning. If Hayek arrived in England in the early 1930s assuming he was landing in a country where the classical liberal legacy was still strong, he was soon disillusioned. The predominance of "new liberals" certainly prompted a response, but equally important, in his "rediscovering" of a tradition of "true" individualism, was the fact that many a brilliant mind thought that socialism and science went hand-in-hand. One of Hayek's lifelong attempts is the clarification of the nature of knowledge (and, hence, its dispersion rather than concentration in society). To explore the intellectual mistakes in the opposing beliefs, Hayek "envisioned a study with four parts": (1) an overview of "the individualistic theories of the eighteenth century"; (2) an examination of "the intellectual sources of hostility towards those theories"; (3) a historical account of "the spread of the anti-individualist ideas from their origins in France to Germany, England and the United States"; and finally, (4) an examination of "the decay of reason in the twentieth century under fascism and communism" (Caldwell 2004, pp. 240–241).

"Individualism: True and False" reads like a smart summary of the first part; part 3, the historical account of anti-individualism, limited to France, became *The Counter-Revolution of Society* (*Studies on the Abuse of Reason*) and a version of part 4 became *The Road to Serfdom*. "Intellectual history" was indeed "always an important component of Hayek's work" (Caldwell 2014, p. 26). In the genealogy of the tradition of which Hayek presents himself as the heir, Hume occupies the position of one of the founders.

## HOW DID HAYEK MEET HUME?

### What We Know

Part of Hayek's books are now in the Law Department Library at the University of Salzburg, where Hayek lived between 1969 and 1977.[3] The collection includes a few of Hume's works: *Treatise of Human Nature* (Hume 1890),[4] the *Abstract* of the *Treatise* (Hume 1938), the *Essays* (Hume 1875),[5] the *Enquiries* (Hume 1875a), the *Natural History of Religion* (Hume 1875a; 1956), the *Dialogues Concerning Natural Religion* (Hume 1874a), the *Letters* (Hume 1932; 1954).

It is unclear to us *when* exactly Hayek started to be interested in Hume (we would welcome hints and suggestions), and if he was first interested in Hume as "one of the founders of economic theory" or as "the founder of the modern theory of knowledge" or as "the greatest legal philosopher". We do not know *which* Hume Hayek approached first.

In *The Constitution of Liberty*, after quoting the *Treatise* on "The origin of justice and property", and the moral *Enquiry* on "Some Farther Considerations with Regard to Justice", Hayek credits Plant for having alerted him to the importance "of Hume's discussions of such issues": it was "Sir Arnold Plant, who many years ago first drew my attention to the importance of Hume's discussions of these issues" (Hayek 2011, p. 227 n. 19). Plant confirmed Hayek's version but seemed to confine his recommendation to Hume's moral *Enquiry*: "I recall his excitement when I called his attention to the profound discussion of these matters in David Hume's *Inquiry concerning the Principles of Morals*: section III, 'Of Justice'" (Plant 1970, p. 5; cf. Gray 1998, p. 168 n. 3; Ebenstein 2003, p. 65; see n. 26 of this chapter).

In "The legal and political philosophy of David Hume", a 1963 lecture, Hayek again mentions Plant as having drawn his attention to "this respect" of Hume's thought:

> My own attention was first drawn to Hume in this respect [i.e. philosophy of law or legal philosophy] many years ago [the early 1930s] by Professor Sir Arnold Plant, whose development of the Humean theory of property we are still eagerly awaiting. (Hayek 1963, p. 693 n. 3a)[6]

Is he referring to Hume *exclusively* as a "legal philosopher"? (Hayek 1991, p. 104) Is he referring to Hume's *Treatise*, moral *Enquiry* or *Essays*?

In his autobiographical recollections, Hayek remembers that "by the end of the 20s" he was acquainted with the English monetary theory, hence with Hume's essays on debt and money, included in the *Political Discourses*. He indeed quotes the *Political Discourse* in *Prices and Production*. At the end of the 20s (possibly in 1929), Hayek had finished writing the chapter "Genesis of the Gold Standard in Response to English Coinage Policy in the 17th and 18th Centuries".[7] Here he devotes two paragraphs to Hume: his doctrines "undoubtedly constitute a first pinnacle in the development of monetary theory" (Hayek 1991, p. 150).[8]

Though he maintains that "[Hayek's] attraction to Hume, whom he quoted more than anyone else in his major works, stemmed from several sources", Alan Ebenstein seems convinced that the first exposition to "a thinker who would later become more important to him generally in societal thought" (Ebenstein 2003, p. 100) came likely through these monetary studies.

Fast forward to 1938: Hayek published a short notice of the *Abstract* of the *Treatise of Human Nature* edited by John Maynard Keynes and Piero Sraffa (Hayek 1938), in *Economica*, then edited by Lionel Robbins. Robbins obviously thought that his friend was qualified to comment on a matter of Humean philology.

Thus, we can say that by the early 1930s Hayek was acquainted with some of Hume's writings, as he moved to London and worked on his 1930s economic papers.

Concerning Hume's place in the "abuse of reason" project: we know that in August 1939 Hayek announced his plan for a study on "the abuse of reason" in a letter to Fritz Machlup (Caldwell 2010, p. 1). In the second volume of Hayek's copy of *The Letters of David Hume*, we found a blank piece of paper, with the letterhead of the LSE wartime address in Cambridge; a *hint*, if not *evidence*, that during the war years Hayek may have dug seriously into Hume's work.

## Some Hypotheses

Hayek's relation with philosophy is complicated and almost intermittent. During the *Gymnasium,* he felt a first inclination towards it. When he declared "he intended to study 'ethics'", his father presented him with four works of Ludwig Feuerbach. He "found this particular philosopher merely a bore and only much later gained access to serious philosophy" (Hayek 1994, p. 47).

When Hayek says that he "only much later gained access to serious philosophy", it is unclear when his *personal* interest in philosophy developed—perhaps in 1919–1920, when he encountered Ernst Mach's works.[9] Hayek's *professional* interest in philosophy deepened in the 1940s, when he increasingly moved from economics to political theory and history of ideas and when he was struggling with the "Abuse of Reason" project.

Hayek's interest in Hume may have been stimulated by Ludwig von Mises, who played a crucial role in his life as a mentor.[10] In his 1927 *Liberalism*, Mises puts Hume's *Essays Moral, Political, and Literary* as the first text (followed by Smith's *Wealth of Nations* and Bentham's *Defense of Usury*) among the suggested readings "on the literature of liberalism". If "liberal ideas are already to be found in the works of many of the earlier writers", Mises comments, "the great English and Scotch thinkers of the eighteenth and the beginning of the nineteenth century were the first to formulate these ideas into a system" (Mises 2005, p. 153).

Mises certainly had a strong appreciation for Hume. In his 1949 *opus magnum*, *Human Action*, he writes:

> The historical role of the theory of the division of labor as elaborated by British political economy from Hume to Ricardo consisted in the complete demolition of all metaphysical doctrines concerning the origin and the operation of social cooperation. (Mises 2007, p. 147)

Besides quoting him on monetary economics, Mises appeals to Hume to rebuke Voltaire for having believed in the fallacy that "a country cannot profit but at the expense of another". If Voltaire read Hume's essays, "he would have learned how false it is to identify war and foreign trade" (Mises 2007, p. 666).

Thus, Mises could have easily recommended young Hayek to get his hands on Hume's books.

Of course, if Hayek ever considered a philosopher an intellectual comrade, that philosopher was Karl Popper, whom Hayek helped substantially in getting out of New Zealand and in publishing *The Open Society and Its Enemies.*[11] Again, in *The Logic of Scientfic Discovery* (first published in 1935), Popper discusses Hume's problem, or "the problem of induction", and quotes the *Enquiry Concerning Human Understanding*(Popper 1935, pp. 3, 7–8, 14, 225 n. 2). Hence, it is plausible that Hayek's reading of Popper prompeted him to turn to the *Treatise*.

Did Hayek first read the *Political Discourses*, following Menger or Mises (the latter made him "familiar with utilitarianism"):[12] or did he first read the *Treatise*, following Schlick and Popper, and distancing himself from Mises' rationalism?[13] If, as Andrew Gamble remarks, "in his epistemology Hayek's general drift throughout his career is towards Popper and Hume, and away from Mises and Kant" (Gamble 2006, p. 118), then the relevant question is not *when* Hayek read Hume, but *which* work he read first.

By browsing what remains of his library in Salzburg, we can say that Hayek was acquainted with a small part of Hume's literature. For example, he had Eugene Rotwein's long and important Introduction to Hume's economical writings (Rotwein 1955, pp. ix-cxi).[14] In Hayek's library, there is a copy of John Laird's 1932 *Hume's Philosophy of Human Nature* (Laird 1932).[15] There are not many notes in Hayek's copy of Laird's book (and most of them are related to Mandeville and Cicero).

Yet in Hayek's manufacturing of a tradition which ultimately bridged eighteenth-century Scotland and nineteenth-century Austria, one of the most important elements is his view of Hume as being in continuity with Bernard de Mandeville, who "made Hume possible" (Hayek 1991, p. 95). Was Laird's work a source for Hayek or did it just corroborate such an intuition?

## HAYEK AND THE HUMEANS

Hayek published his 1963 essay on Hume in Bruno Leoni's journal *Il politico* and, three years afterwards, he republished it in Vere Chappell's collection on *Hume*. The collection contained the essays of important philosophers and (Humean) scholars: Mossner, Jessop, Popkin, Penelhum, MacIntyre, Flew, Noxon, Stove and others.

An interesting connection is that with Louis Schneider, professor of sociology at Purdue.

In 1967 Schneider edited *The Scottish Moralists on Human Nature and Society*, where he declares: "I am much indebted to Friedrich A. Hayek, who directed my particular attention to the Scottish moralists" (Schneider 1967, acknowledgments). In 1963 Schneider edited the English translation of Menger's *Investigations Into the Method of the Social Sciences*, which Hayek would consider the most significant "Austrian translation" of Mandeville's and Hume's understanding of unintended consequences.[16] According to Schneider, Hayek "has, without any doubt, been directly influenced by the Scottish moralists and by Mandeville" (Schneider 1967, p. xlvi); and "important in the background of Hayek's thought on these lines ['not-of-human-design' perspective], also, is Carl Menger" (Schneider 1967, p. xlvi n. 78; cf. Menger 1985).[17]

When Hayek published the "Legal and Political Philosophy", he was not an unknown post-doc. He had already published the *Constitution of Liberty* and the *Sensory Order*, the "Use of Knowledge in Society", and *The Road to Serfdom*. He was not a *dilettante* in the field of the history of ideas, as he had already published *The Counter-Revolution of Science*—a work in the history of political thought that few could accuse of lacking in depth and originality—as well as his edition of the correspondence of John Stuart Mill and Harriet Taylor (Hayek 1951). In 1948 he published *Individualism and Economic Order*, and in 1974 he was to share the Nobel Memorial Prize in Economic Sciences with Gunnar Myrdal for his work on money.

Why is such a celebrated author so neglected by the Humeans as a serious Hume scholar?

Perhaps Hayek knew the literature on Hume from the early 1930s to the early 1980s (Basson, Broad, Flew, Gaskin, Haakonssen, Laird, Mossner, Penelhum, Rotwein and Strawson) better than Hume scholars knew Hayek. Major Hume scholars who commented on Hayek include Flew, Livingston and Berry—but these are mostly occasional comments, though Flew and Livingston certainly had a genuine appreciation of Hayek's work.

In 2013 Angela Coventry and Alexander Sager programmatically suggested that "contemporary political philosophy would benefit from a more explicit examination of its Humean influence", and gave "special attention to John Rawls and Friedrich Hayek, both of whom read Hume widely and carefully throughout their careers, and to evolutionary approaches to social cooperation pioneered by Hume" (Coventry, Sager 2013, pp. 588, 589). But when in 2019 they edited a beautiful collection of essays on Hume, *The Humean Mind*, with a section on "Twentieth-twenty-first century", the discussion of Hayek's views is confined to a few pages by Eléonore Le Jallé on justice, conventions, property and social order.

We could make a short list of those Hume scholars who briefly discuss Hayek's reading. Yet, as we say in Italian, one swallow does not make a summer. There is no essay on "Hayek and Hume", and almost no traces of Hayek in the Oxford and Cambridge *Companions* to Hume, in the Oxford Handbook, or in Hume's *Intellectual Biography.*

## HAYEK AND HUME ON THE LAW

It is hardly surprising that Hayek insists on Hume as a "legal and political philosopher".

Hayek's views on the law evolve from *The Constitution of Liberty* (2011), originally published in 1960, to *Law, Legislation and Liberty* (1982), originally published in 1973–1979, and end up in a more consistent symmetry between his overall thinking and his legal thinking.

As virtually all post-Second World War classical liberals (think of Ordoliberalism or constitutional political economy), Hayek sees a law-based order as the only chance to restore some liberal elements to contemporary society. At first, he classifies the issue as one of securing legal certainty, as established on a constitutional order. Such order he identifies with the Rechtsstaat: a system of general rules, uniformly applicable, but *legislated* by a lawmaking assembly. While Hayek always had an antipathy for the elbow room inherent in the managing of an administrative state, he first saw the Rechtsstaat as a continental "translation" of the English "rule of law", based on a common law system. But later his views changed.

In this process, a significant part is played by his encounter with Bruno Leoni, who criticizes Hayek's understanding of the Rechtstaat as analogous to the English "rule of law" in his *Freedom and the Law* and suggests a parallel between legislation and top-down economic planning on the one hand, and the common law (or, more broadly speaking, custom, judge-discovered law) and the market process on the other (Leoni 1961).[18] Leoni's contribution is explicitly founded on an understanding of the law as a "spontaneous order".

After his encounter with Leoni—and after his article on Hume—Hayek shifted "toward a new understanding of law itself and the ideal of law". As aptly summarized by Stringham and Zywicki:

> Hayek came to believe that the bottom-up lawmaking process of the common law was more conducive to liberty, coordination of individual expectations, and efficient use of dispersed knowledge than the top-down legislature-focused approach of those earlier works. In large part this preference arose from Hayek's understanding of the common law as being analogous to a market process. (Stringham, Zywicki 2011, pp. 298–299)

But if Leoni alerts Hayek to an issue well within the scope of his own thinking, Zywicki and Stringham point out that it is his acquaintance with Hume that makes Hayek see a way forward in terms of superior consistency. It is through Humean lenses that Hayek understands that "the essence of law is not created by the state, but rather preexists in the conventions and understandings of the individuals that compose a given community" (Stringham, Zywicki 2011, p. 293).

Hence, Hayek came to reject "a conception of law as being simply the command of the sovereign, as has been championed by legal positivists since Hobbes", arguing that it may "undermine the legal order of a free society" (Shearmur 2011, p. xxi). Hayek's criticism of legal positivism is not embedded in a natural law/natural rights account. Instead it builds on "a view of law as a form of spontaneous order, developing from shared customs, but gradually being refined and developed by judges". Indeed, "there are parallels between Hayek's views here and those of common law theorists such as Sir Edward Coke [Hayek made a connexion between Coke and Hume], and also of the Scottish philosopher David Hume" (Shearmur 2011, p. xxii). As Hume "remains faithful to the basic ideas he develops in the *Treatise*" in his essays and his *History of England*, where "he offers a different sort of analysis—one that draws on concrete examples and cases" (McArthur 2018, p. 353), he could provide an approach that bridged a theory which envisions order as an externality and a history that provided examples of such a phenomenon. Indeed, Hayek himself saw Hume's *History* as a continuation of his philosophical work and the book which contributed the most to spread "Whig liberalism" throughout Europe in the eighteenth century (Hayek 1991, p. 106).

For Hayek, Hume's legal theory built on "his anti-rationalist theory of morals which shows that, so far as the creation of moral rules is concerned, 'reason of itself is utterly impotent' and that 'the rules of morality are not conclusions of our reason'" (Hayek 1991, p. 107). This brings Hume to see moral beliefs, and hence rules of conduct and jurisprudential norms, as "artifacts" but unintended ones: offspring of cultural evolution rather than conscious creations of the lawmaker's mind. Quoting Christian Bay on Hume as a "precursor of Darwin in the field of ethics" (Hayek will often refer to Hume, Smith and Ferguson as "Darwinians before Darwin"), Hayek endorses a doctrine of "the survival of the fittest among human conventions—fittest not in terms of good teeth but in terms of maximum social utility" (Hayek 1991, p. 107).

As he deals with Hume, Hayek emphasizes how the Scottish philosopher came to an evolutionary theory of social institutions; how he stresses the difference between "the general and abstract rules of justice and the particular and concrete aims of individual and public action" (Hayek 1991, p. 112) (an argument dear to Hayek, who will reject "social justice" on its very basis); how there is a parallel between Hume's understanding of cultural evolution and organic evolution (again, a theme dear to Hayek). If "The legal and political philosophy of David Hume" paper does not directly address the issue of common law versus statutes, it sets the stage for Hayek's transition towards a wider appreciation of the common law (evolved law) which does not disavow his stress over general rules uniformly applicable as the essence of a liberal order.

Such a Hayekian emphasis on Hume as a legal philosopher may be puzzling, since, according to Neil McArthur, in "rare cases" Hume's work has been considered in relation to the common law (McArthur 2005). Hayek agreed, as he attempted to counter "the common misunderstanding and neglect" of Hume as a liberal political and legal philosopher (Hayek 1991, p. 105). Hayek does not display the careful and discriminating reading of Hume on the common law that McArthur recommends, but has at least two common traits with Hume. On the one hand, he prizes stability and evolution through time. On the other hand, he opposes discretion and supports general law.

All of the above creates some expectations concerning Hayek's reading of the *Treatise.*

## THE FRESH AND REASONED "TREATISE"

The *Treatise*, Hayek writes in 1963, "is today universally acknowledged as [Hume's] greatest achievement" (Hayek 1991, p. 103), following Green who called it "intrinsically the best representation of his philosophy" (Green, Grose 1874, p. v). The *Essays*, the moral *Enquiry* and the *History*, Hayek goes on, "added little that is new to the first statement", even though they contain "sometimes improved formulations" and are "much more effective in spreading his ideas" (Hayek 1991, p. 103). Hume develops his legal and political ideas in his "philosophical" rather than in his historical works. If we want an "explicit and reasoned" statement of the ideal of Whig liberalism (we won't comment on how Hayek uses the word "Whig", out of charity for the audience), "we must turn to his philosophical works" (Hayek 1991, p. 106).

"Almost all" Hume's important and anti-rationalist ideas can be found in the third book of the *Treatise*, Hayek maintains in 1963.[19] According to him, the section "Of the Origin of Justice and Property" is his "most significant contribution" in legal and political theory (Hayek 1991, p. 108). The legal ideas were "first developed" in the *Treatise*, where their "fuller statements" can be found, and "the individual statements often have greater freshness" ("even though the exposition as a whole is sometimes rather prolix") (Hayek 1991, p. 111). Hayek declares that he will quote "mainly", if not "exclusively", from it (Hayek 1991, p. 110).[20] Given Hayek's interest in Hume as a legal philosopher, the reader would naturally expect that the book *Of Morals*, where his anti-rationalist ideas can be found, will be for Hayek the most important. But this is only partly true, at least according to Hayek's copy of the *Treatise*, that is, by the way, the Green and Grose 1890 edition in two volumes.[21]

Hayek's annotations are of several kinds: marginal remarks, underlinings, marginal vertical lines, question marks, small crosses or exes and internal references. The marginal remarks are short summaries, questions and critical observations. The question marks denounce obscurities and (alleged) contradictions, or express perplexities and signal searches for definitions.[22] The underlinings place the emphasis on single words or propositions; the marginal vertical lines (sometimes double) put the emphasis on one or more lines of the text. The small crosses seem to us to add some emphasis. In one circumstance, Hayek also draws a diagram on a loose sheet of paper: a square.

Hayek questions Hume's text,[23] asks for a clarification of the terms,[24] makes some ironic remarks[25] and often advances his own objections to Hume's observations by several but-propositions.[26] It is that kind of "constant carping criticism" which, so Hayek claims in his *Autobiographical Dialogue*, made Othmar Spann throw him out of his seminar because he "confused the younger members" (Hayek 1994, p. 54). In general, Hayek highlights Humean topics and views, for example, the force of sentiment and its relation with reason, and translates Hume's arguments in his own language. It is a careful study of the *Treatise* and a close confrontation with it as a contemporary book.

Should we judge Hayek's interest by the number of annotations and signs, our expectations of him getting a grip on Hume's legal philosophy by reading the *Treatise* would quickly fade away. He seems to read the *Treatise* also thinking of his other interests: first and foremost, the theory of the human mind. Hayek is most captivated by Book I *Of the Understanding* (145 marked passages), then by Book II *Of the Passions* (91 passages). Book III *Of Morals* scored third, with 53 passages. The longest marginal notes are to the Book *Of the Passions* (there are none in *Of Morals*), and its first part "Of Pride and Humility".

While he is studying the *Treatise*, and scribbling his *marginalia*, Hayek's attention is more attracted by associationism than by moral philosophy, by the reflection on the weakness of our faculties, and the limits of our knowledge, than by the account of passions and morals, the influencing motives of the will, and the origin of justice and property. In the *Sensory Order*, he acknowledges "the connection between [his] theory and a familiar older view [...] the obvious relations [...] between it and the basic ideas of the old association psychology" (Hayek 2017, p. 267). Several marginal notes and vertical lines are related to association, and Hayek highlights Hume's remark that "Nothing is more apt to make us mistake one idea for another, than any relation betwixt them, which associates them together in the imagination, and makes it pass with facility from one to the other" (Hume 2007, vol. I, p. 135; SBN 203).

The lower number of *marginalia* doesn't mean Hayek is not interested in the third book *Of Morals*. His interest does go beyond the third section "Of Justice" of the moral *Enquiry*, to which Plant "called his attention", as we saw, at the beginning of the 1930s[27] (Hayek underlines the section and also the third Appendix "Some farther Considerations with regard to Justice") (Hume 2010, pp. 97–101; SBN 303–311).

With regard to the *Treatise*, after underlining some passages of the first section on "Moral distinctions not derived on reason", he concentrates on part II *Of justice and injustice*, especially the section "Of the origin of justice and property". He highlights the role of the rules, by underlining Hume's assertion that, having once "experienc'd the impossibility of preserving any order in society, while every one is his own master", men "naturally run into the invention of government, and put it out of their own power, as far as possible, to transgress the rules of justice" (Hume 2007, vol. I, pp. 354–355; SBN 554). Speculative reasonings, he says underlining Hume's text, "which cost so much pains to philosophers, are often form'd by the world naturally, and without reflection" (Hume 2007, p. 365; SBN 572).

## THE SQUARE

In the book on the passions, where he discusses the proper object of love and hate, and pride and humility, Hume considers their situation "with respect to each other":

> Here – he writes – are four affections, plac'd, as it were, in a square or regular connexion with, and distance from each other. The[y] […] are connected together by the identity of their object, which to the first set of passions is self, to the second some other person. These two lines of communication or connexion form two opposite sides of the square. Again, pride and love are agreeable passions; hatred and humility uneasy. This similitude of sensation betwixt pride and love, and that betwixt humility and hatred form a new connexion, and may be consider'd as the other two sides of the square. (Hume 2007, p. 216; SBN 333)

Hume sums up: "pride is connected with humility, love with hatred, by their objects or ideas: Pride with love, humility with hatred, by their sensations or impressions" (Hume 2007, p. 216; SBN 333). It is the Humean simplified version (no diagonal lines) of the traditional Aristotelian square diagram. Hayek underlines Hume's *resumé* by a marginal line and draws a diagram on a loose piece of paper (see Figure 6.1).

In drawing this diagram, Hayek is in good company among philosophers and Hume scholars. In 1946, Quine gives a lecture on Hume's philosophy (Quine 2003, p. 241; 2008 p. 122) and makes his own scheme; in 1966, Árdal, the author of *Passion and Value in Hume's Treatise*, declares: "it may be

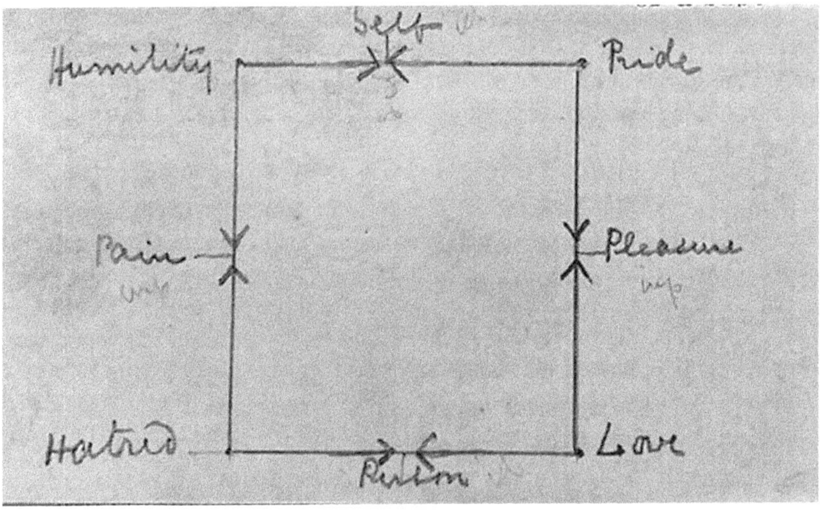


*Source:* Hayek handwritten notes to Hume's *Treatise*, Law Department Library, University of Salzburg.

*Figure 6.1* *Drawing of Hume's square diagram*

helpful to represent some of the relations between the basic indirect passions by drawing up a square according to Hume's description" (Árdal 1966, p. 26); in 1968, John Valdimir Price takes the square as a "metaphor" indicating that no passion "can exist without being related to some other passion" and "be experienced or conceived as a distinct entity in the mind" (Price 1968, p. 49). Rarely do those scholars who discuss the subject resist the temptation to give their own representation of the square. Yet, like Quine's, Hayek's diagram is very simple and closer to Hume's language. Again, we can say that Hayek studied the *Treatise* closely indeed.

## THE "GREAT SCEPTIC"

Hume is a "great sceptic, with [a] profound conviction of the imperfection of all human reason and knowledge", Hayek writes 1963 (Hayek 1991, p. 117).

In the "Conclusion" to the first book of the *Treatise*, Hume shows his "sceptical disposition and principles", declares that "if we are philosophers, it ought only to be upon sceptical principles", and that "in all the incidents of life we ought still to preserve our scepticism" (Hume 2007, vol. I, pp. 175–176; SBN 269–270); finally, he pronounces himself a "true sceptic" (Hume 2007, vol. I,

p. 177; SBN 273). Since Hayek is a close reader of Book I, we would expect him to quote the "Conclusion of this Book". Yet, Hayek annotates nothing on Hume's Conclusion (not even a sign).

The Conclusion is the last section of the fourth part, entitled "Of the Sceptical and other systems of philosophy". Here, especially in the first two sections on scepticism with regard to reason (probable reasoning) and the senses (the external world), Hayek seems to be more interested in Hume's declaration that neither he nor any other person was "ever sincerely and constantly" of the opinion of "total scepticism" ("all is uncertain, and [...] our judgment is not in any thing possest of any measures of truth and falshood"). As Hume puts it (in italics), and Hayek underlines, belief is "*more properly an act of the sensitive, than of the cogitative part of our natures*" (Hume 2007, vol. I, p. 123; SBN 183).

Hayek follows (by a marginal vertical line) Hume's account of why Humean correct sceptical arguments do not produce "a total suspense of judgment" and the mind retains a degree of assurance and belief, "which is sufficient for our purpose, either in philosophy or common life" (Hume 2007, vol. I, p. 124; SBN 185). He repeats with Hume that "'tis in vain to ask, *Whether there be body or not?* That is a point, which we must take for granted in all our reasonings" (Hume 2007, vol. I, p. 125; SBN 187). Here too, Hayek's interest is attracted by Hume's account of the causes of our belief in the existence of bodies and the origin of philosophical opinion of a double existence of perceptions and objects. Yet he neglects the conclusive paragraph of "Of scepticism with regard to the senses", which anticipates the sceptical "Conclusion", and where Hume declares that the "sceptical doubt, both with respect to reason and the senses" is "a malady, which can never be radically cur'd", which "arises naturally from a profound and intense reflection on those subjects" and "must return upon us every moment, however we may chace it away, and sometimes may seem entirely free from it" (Hume 2007, vol. I, p. 125; SBN 187). This doubt, Hume says, "always encreases, the farther we carry our reflections, whether in opposition or conformity to it" and "Carelessness and in-attention alone can afford us any remedy" (Hume 2007, vol. I, p. 144; SBN 218).

Hume's great scepticism (according to Hayek) seems to lie in Hume's "profound conviction of the imperfection of all human reason" (Hayek 1991, p. 117), in Hume's limitation of the role of (modern philosophical) reason, which is typical of the *Treatise*. In every book, Hayek underlines (by marginal vertical lines) several passages where Hume asserts that our mental operations, like the inference from cause to effect—in Hayek's marginal words—are "said *not* to depend on reason". He puts a marginal line at Hume's famous and seemingly "somewhat extraordinary" adage "Reason is, and ought only to be the slave of the passions" (Hume 2007, vol. I, p. 266; SBN 415), and underlines those (Hutchesonian) passages in the section "Moral distinction not deriv'd from

Reason", where Hume maintains that "Reason of itself is utterly impotent" to excite passions, and produce or prevent actions, that "the rules of morality [...] are not conclusions of our reason", because "an active principle can never be founded on an inactive" (Hume 2007, vol. I, p. 294; SBN 457). The adage on the "rules of morality" is often quoted by Hayek to explain the gist of his thinking on spontaneous orders (as we said) and will be the epigraph (together with Ferguson and Menger) and "starting point" of his last book, *The Fatal Conceit* (Hayek 1988, epigraph and p. 8).

In 1963 Hayek also refers to Hume's "general philosophical conceptions, especially [...] his sceptical views on the 'narrow bounds of human understanding'" (Hayek 1991, p. 111). Hume's expression "narrow bounds of human understanding" occurs in the *Dialogues Concerning natural Religion* (Hume 1947, p. 162), where Hayek discovers the Darwinian Hume not only in the sphere of ethics (the evolution of institutions and biological organisms), even though in Hayek's copy of Hume's *Dialogues* the expression is not underlined. Hayek prefers to speak of "the weakness of men's minds [...] their inevitable ignorance" (Hayek 1991, p. 111). In the *Dialogues* Hume, like Hayek, often speaks of the "imperfections" (and "contradictions") of our reason, and insists on its "weakness, blindness, and narrow limits" (Hume 1947, p. 131); but Hayek doesn't note it.

In the Conclusion to the first book of the *Treatise*, total scepticism is the effect of the "intense view of these manifold contradictions and imperfections in human reason" (Hume 2007, p. 175; SBN 268); and Hume recalls the "weakness, and disorder of the faculties" and the "weakness of the mind" (Hume 2007, vol. I, pp. 172, 177; SBN 264, 272). According to the *Abstract* of the *Treatise*, a "very sceptical" philosophy "tends to give us a notion of the imperfections and narrow limits of human understanding" (Hume 2007, vol. I, pp. 403–417: p. 413; SBN 657). As we said, in 1938 Hayek published a short note on the *Abstract* reprinted by Keynes and Sraffa, but his own copy of the 1956 edition bears no signs (Hayek 1991, p. 118). Hayek never quotes the *Abstract* as well as he never quotes the Conclusion. Possibly his remark on the "great sceptic" depends on his reading of the *Dialogues* rather than the *Treatise*. However, in the 1742 essay *Of the Rise and Progress of the Arts and Sciences*, which Hayek used to read, Hume calls his idol Cicero "a great sceptic in matters of religion" (Hume 1742, p. 83; see also Hume 2021, p. 587).

## CONCLUSION

We do not know when Hayek's special affinity with Hume developed and when he met Hume and the *Treatise* first. Yet, we do know that between the end of the 1920s and the beginning of the 1930s he was already acquainted with Hume's economic-political *Discourses*. We do not even know exactly when Hayek studied the *Treatise* and made the abovementioned annotations. According to Hayek's wife, the only person able to read the minuscule handwriting of her husband was Kurt Leube. Leube reminds us that Hayek re-read his Hume during the mid-1960s in order to prepare his 1967 paper "The Results of Human Action but Not of Human Design", where he quotes the *Treatise* and refers to his own 1963 essay (Hayek 1967, p. 106), and suggests by this that some notes to the *Treatise* could have been made within that time frame.

We would be tempted to surmise that Hayek studied the *Treatise* between the end of the 1930s and the beginning of the 1940s, when he moved to Cambridge, if not in the early 1930s, when Plant suggested that he read the moral *Enquiry*. Hume could be considered a genuine inspiration for the "abuse of reason" project, which Hayek starts to ruminate about in 1939. By 1945, Hume stands solidly in Hayek's *pantheon*, though he will become a more central figure later in time.

Yet, in 1963 Hayek observes that, in the manuscript corrections of his printed works, Hume is "careful to substitute 'rules of justice' for 'laws of society'" (Hayek 1991, p. 115), and refers to a List of Variants published by Raymond Klibanski in 1951 (Hume 1947, p. 115 n. 53; Klibanski 1951, pp. 245–246). Since Hayek not only underlines Hume's sentence that men "put it out of their own power, as far as possible, to transgress the laws of society", but also cancels "laws of society" and replaces it with the marginal correction "rules of justice", we conclude that at least some of the notes were made after 1951 (Hume 2007, vol. I, p. 355; SBN 554).

Almost all the 27 quotations from the *Treatise* contained in the 1963 essay are passages entirely or partially underlined by Hayek in the book on *Morals* (only two are not underlined); even though no underlined passage of the books on the *Understanding* and the *Passions* is quoted in 1963. Since it seems improbable that Hayek read the *Treatise* after the composition of his own essay and underlined almost the same sentences, we can conclude that the *Treatise* has been studied before 1963. It seems also improbable that he read the moral *Enquiry* in 1931 and reviewed the *Abstract* in 1938 without knowing the *Treatise*.

If we consider Hayek's increasing interest in his "constant companion and sage guide" (Hayek 2011, p. 54 n. 10), his "great idol" (Hayek 2001, p. 35), and his relative reserve when confessing his own "idolatry" of "perhaps the greatest of all modern students of mind and society" (Hayek 1991, pp. 95–96), we may observe—recalling his own words—that Hayek's interpretation of Hume's legal philosophy remains "curiously neglected" (Hayek 1991, p. 104), especially with regard to the first two books of the *Treatise*. A detailed map of Hume's presence in Hayek's writings could be a useful instrument: not only all the explicit references to the different works, with their proper years (some of them have been added in the course of time), but also those silent or unaware references to them, and especially to the *Treatise*.

According to Hayek, Hume did not exert all the influence he should have, because of the "accusation" that his philosophy is "essentially negative". And Hayek acknowledges that this accusation has "often" been levelled "with some justice" (Hayek 1991, p. 117). Indeed, he argues, Hume "did not expect much positive good from political organisation. He knew that the greatest political goods, peace, liberty, and justice, were in their essence negative, a protection against injury rather than positive gifts" (Hayek 2001, p. 35). Why Hayek's interpretation of Hume did not exert all the influence it should have in the Hume literature? Was it too (liberal) conservative, evolutionary and anti-rationalist? Perhaps it didn't only because Hayek was at the same time less and more than a Hume scholar.[28] As he once observed, and some of us have learned by experience, "if you leave your proper subject, other people regard you as an amateur in what you are talking about" (Hayek 1983, p. 246).[29]

## NOTES

1. The essay "The Legal and Political Philosophy of David Hume" was first delivered as a lecture at the Faculty of Law and Political Science of the University of Freiburg on July 18, 1963. It was then published as Hayek (1963), together with its Italian translation by Rachele Corsico. It was later republished as Hayek (1966). This later version is better polished than the one published in *Il Politico*, the collection put together by important Humean scholars (Anthony Flew, T.E. Jessop, Ernest Campbell Mossner, James Noxon, Terence Penhelum, Richard H. Popkin, etc.), and somehow introduced Hayek to them. Hence, it would be proper to refer to this volume in the context of a work linking Hayek and Hume. Yet, one year later, Hayek included it as a chapter in Hayek (1967). We decided to refer to Hayek's *Collected Works* (1991), where the essays on Mandeville, Smith and the short note on Hume's *Abstract* of the *Treatise* are also included, assuming this later edition is the one more easily available to contemporary scholars. On Hayek's essay and its context, see Masala (2022); on Hayek and Hume, see Coventry, Sager (2013); Cubeddu (forthcoming).
2. It is unclear if the founder of the Austrian school, Carl Menger, would have approved of this project. Menger typically quotes disapprovingly Adam Smith, to whom he imputed confusions over the nature of value and an excessive emphasis on labour. Hayek thought that the Scots had exercised an indirect influence on Menger, through Savigny: "It would seem as if it had been largely by way of Savigny that those ideas of Mandeville and Hume eventually reached Carl Menger and thus returned to economic theory" (Hayek 1991, p. 96 n. 72). We can dare to assert that Menger knew Hume's work. Among his books conserved at Hitotsubashi University in Japan, there are copies of the *History of England*, the *Political Discourses* in the French 1754 translation,

"Banks and paper-money" and "Of public credit" in two collections edited by McCulloch (respectively *A select collection of scarce and valuable tracts on paper currency* and *A select collection of scarce tracts on the national debts and the sinking fund*), the 1760 edition of the *Essays and Treatises on Several Subjects; containing Essays Moral, Political and Literary,* the *Private Correspondence of David Hume with Several distinguished Persons between the years 1761 and 1776* (London, 1820), *The Life of David Hume, Esq. Written by Himself* (London, 1777) and a 1846 edition of *A Treatise of Human Nature.*

3. "Hayek's 1969 move to Salzburg was occasioned largely by financial considerations, as his earlier relocations to Chicago and Freiburg had been. Salzburg is also closer to Vienna than Freiburg is, and Helene's son's family live in Vienna. The University of Salzburg was willing to buy Hayek's library, and by moving there, Hayek would still be able to use it. He was not independent before he received the Nobel Prize" (Ebenstein 2003, p. 253).
4. The references are to Hume's editions owned by Hayek and now in the Law Department Library at Salzburg. We should point out that in his 1963 essay Hayek refers to the T.H. Green and T.H. Grose edition of Hume's *Works*: *A Treatise of Human Nature* (Hume 1874) and *Essays, Moral, Political, and Literary* (Hume 1875), and *History of England*, in six volumes (Hume 1762).
5. Hayek also had a copy of Hume's *Essays and Treatises*, in two volumes (Hume 1777).
6. In 1984, John Gray observes: "Hayek is alluding to his discussions with Sir Arnold in the early 1930s at the London School of Economics, where Hayek had migrated to take up the Tooke Professorship" (Gray 1998, p. 168 n. 3). Gray refers to Plant's testimony in his "Tribute to Hayek".
7. "Hayek was recruited to prepare a large volume on money and monetary theory for the great German Grundri der Sozialokonomik which had been started by Max Weber. Of this Hayek completed 'in something like final form' these four chapters on money and monetary theory from about 1650 to 1850. Before being able to complete the project, however, he was interrupted by his move from Vienna to London, and then 'before I could resume the work the publisher asked me, in view of Hitler's advent to power, to cancel the contract. But the book on which I got my 'licence to teach' (*Privatdozentur*), the test lecture on 'The Paradox of Savings' which I gave in the same connexion and which led to my invitation to London, and the lectures on *Prices and Production* which I delivered at the London School of Economics in January 1931 were all offshoots of this uncompleted task.' Later, Hayek gave his notes for the remainder of the projected book to his doctoral student at the LSE, Vera C. Smith (later Lutz)" (Hayek 1991, p. 127).
8. "Hume's analysis had such a decisive influence on all subsequent developments that it deserves to be considered one of the lasting landmarks in the history of monetary theory. [...] 'Of Money', 'Of Interest', and 'Of the Balance of Trade' [...] offer important contributions to all the major problems of monetary theory" (Hayek 1991, p. 151). On Hume, see Hayek (1991, pp. 150–154).

"His first major foray into the history of ideas was four chapters on the development of monetary theory and policy, 'Genesis of the Gold Standard in Response to English Coinage Policy in the 17th and 18th Centuries,' 'First Paper Money in 18th-Century France,' 'The Period of Restrictions, 1797–1821, and the Bullion Debate in England,' and 'The Dispute Between the Currency School and the Banking School, 1821–1848.' These chapters, completed in 1929 but not published until 1991, were originally foreseen, as was a considerable amount of his other early work, to be part of a larger treatise on money that he never completed. Somewhat like the later intended 'The Abuse and Decline of Reason', his intended work on money was to be introduced by a historical part before moving to theory. While the four chapters on monetary history remained unpublished at the time, his research was very beneficial, leading to *Monetary Theory and the Trade Cycle*, 'The 'Paradox' of Saving', *Prices and Production*, and ultimately his invitation to London. Among the early monetary theorists whom he discussed in these chapters is David Hume, whose doctrines, he wrote, 'undoubtedly constitute a first pinnacle in the development of monetary theory'" (Ebenstein 2003, p. 99).

9. "I will, however, first say a little about my brief but intense concern with the problems of physiological psychology, which took up a considerable part of my energies in 1919 and 1920. It had been caused mainly by my interest in the writings of Ernst Mach, then much in vogue among the generation just ahead of me. It was in reading his philosophical writings that I conceived the idea which I vainly tried to explain in a brief paper in 1920 and finally published thirty-two years later in *The Sensory Order*" (Hayek 1994, p. 62). "The main authors from which I derived my knowledge were still H. von Helmholtz and W. Wundt, W. James and G. E. Muller, and particularly Ernst Mach. I still vividly remember how in reading Mach, in an experience very similar to that which Mach himself describes with reference to Kant's concept of the *Ding an sich*, I suddenly realized how a consistent development of Mach's analysis of perceptual organization made his own concept of sensory elements superfluous and otiose, an idle construction in conflict with most of his acute psychological analysis" (Hayek 2017, p. 118).
10. While many have tried to "de-homogeneize" Mises and Hayek, the first was his mentor in the 1920s and was "unquestionably the personal contact from whom I profited the most, not only by the way of intellectual stimulation but also for his direct assistance in my career" (Hayek 1994, pp. 68–69).
11. For a rather humorous account of Popper's impinging on his friends in London, see Gombrich (1995).
12. "To begin with, I think it was Mises himself who made me familiar with utilitarianism, and in my early stages I studied them very much. In fact so much, that I discovered in studying the papers of Jeremy Bentham at University College that Bentham had been a very good economist, who had done very noticeable work on monetary theory. At that time I had started on the highly urgent work of organizing the Bentham papers, which were an awful mess. That broke down when the first Bentham committee at University College,

which I had started, broke up during the war, and the definite start of an edition was made only after I'd left London" (Hayek 1994, p. 140).

13. "Because Mises remained in the end himself a rationalist-utilitarian, and with a rationalist-utilitarianism, the rejection of socialism is irreconcilable [...]. But Mises's postulate – if we are strictly rational and decide all the bases, we can see that socialism is wrong – is a mistake. If we remain strict rationalists, utilitarians, that implies we can arrange everything according to our pleasure. So Mises never could free himself from that fundamental philosophy, in which we have all grown up, that reason can do everything better than mere habit. From this he could never loose himself. In this respect, although I accept nearly everything of his criticism of socialism, I now understand why it has not been fully effective, because in his case it's still based on the fundamental mistake of rationalism and socialism, that we have the intellectual power to arrange everything rationally, which is now in conflict with the assertion – In one place he says we can't do it, another place he argues, being rational people, we must try to do it" (Hayek 1994, pp. 72–73).
14. Cf. also Hume (1875) (Hayek's copy is the third printing of Oxford University Press World's Classics, March 1966).
15. Bibliothek Pro. Hayek. FB / H 178. 66.178 L3.3.1970 / Jurisdische Fakultätsbibliothek Universität Salzburg.
16. Menger does not, however, explicitly mention Hume.
17. According to Schneider, Hayek "has been greatly influenced by Menger's thought as set out in the *Untersuchungen*" (Schneider 1985, p. 2). Yet, here Menger, who mentions and discusses Mandeville and Smith, never mentions Hume.
18. The Hayek scholar who most pondered the issue is Shearmur (1996), especially pp. 88–101.
19. Hayek writes "in the second part of the *Treatise on Human Nature* which he published at the age of twenty-nine in 1740" (Hayek 1991, p. 103). He says the "second part" because *Of Morals*—unlike the 1739 *Of the Understanding* and *Of the Passions*, it was published in 1740—is contained in the second volume of Green's and Grose's edition.
20. In the 1963 version, Hayek writes "the *Treatise*, from which I have so far exclusively quoted [...]. But I shall continue to quote mainly from the *Treatise*" (Hayek 1963, pp. 698–699). In 1967 he turns "exclusively" into "mainly" (Hayek 1967, p. 114).
21. In 1963, 1967 and 1991, Hayek refers to the 1890 two volumes edition of the *Treatise*; in 1966, he refers to the 1874–1875 edition (Hayek 1963, p. 691 n.; 1966, p. 343 n. 11; 1967 p. 106 n.; 1991, p. 98 n. 1).
22. For example, where Hume says "I believe every one will readily agree with me, that the ideas of the memory are more *strong* and *lively* than those of the fancy" (Hume 2007, vol. I, p. 60; SBN 84), Hayek puts a question mark, then replies "not always", finally he asserts that the ideas of the imagination are "often" more vivid than those of memory. On the contrary, where Hume says "there can be no *demonstrative* arguments to prove, *that those*

*instances, of which we have had no experience, resemble those, of which we have had experience*" (Hume 2007, p. 62, emphasis added; SBN 89), and "Probability, as it discovers not the relations of ideas, consider'd as such, but only those of objects, must in some respects be founded on the impressions of our memory and senses, and in some respects on our ideas" (Hume 2007, pp. 62–63; SBN 89), Hayek asks himself: "Demonstration definition?" and "Probability definition?". In some cases, there are two question marks: both close to Hume's words. Hume observes: "According to this account of things, which is, I think, in every point unquestionable, probability is founded on the presumption of a resemblance betwixt those *objects*, of which we have had experience, and those, of which we have had *none*; and therefore 'tis impossible this presumption can arise from probability" (Hume 2007, p. 63; SBN 90). Hayek puts a marginal line, underlines "objects" and "none", puts one question mark at the level of object and one at the level of "none", and finally remarks: "Combination of objects: we must have had experience of the objects". In other cases, only one question mark that means Hume is wrong. Hume observes: "I therefore change the first impression into an idea; and observe, that tho' the customary transition to the correlative idea still remains, yet there is in reality no belief nor perswasion" (Hume 2007, p. 72; SBN 103). Hayek underlines in his personal copy of Hume's book the observation by a marginal vertical line and a question mark close to the line, the remarks or asks himself and Hume: "If belief arises by custom from constantly associated impressions, why can it not equally arise from similarly constantly associated ideas. The latter [i.e. ideas] are ex hypothesis: Simply fainter images of the former… belief in a lesser degree ought to arise".

23. Where Hume observes "Suppose an object perfectly simple and indivisible to be presented, along with another object, whose *co-existent* parts are connected together by a strong relation, 'tis evident the actions of the mind, in considering these two objects, are not very different" (Hume 2007, p. 146; SBN 221), Hayek, who has put a vertical marginal line, adds a question mark and remarks: "? Would any one confuse an object without parts with an object with parts however closely connected". Where Hume observes that the fundamental principle of modern philosophy is the opinion that colours, tastes, smells, heat and cold are "nothing but impressions in the mind, deriv'd from the operation of external objects, and without any resemblance to the qualities of the objects" (Hume 2007, p. 149; SBN 226), Hayek underlines "without any resemblance to the qualities of the objects", puts a question mark close to "any resemblance", and remarks: "What is meant by 'resemblance' / Impressions of the mind are surely exact copies of the qualities of the object so far as we are concerned or at any rate we have no other idea of them. Is in […] how […]?"
24. "What is meant by 'resemblance'?" (cf. Hume 2007, p. 149; SBN 226); "What is meant by thought here?" (cf. Hume 2007, p. 154; SBN 235); "What is meant by exist" (cf. Hume 2007, pp. 154–155; SBN 235–236); "What is meant by a 'motive'?" (cf. Hume 2007, p. 265; SBN 413).

25. Where Hume observes "In general we may observe, that in all the most establish'd and uniform conjunctions of causes and effects, such as those of gravity, impulse, solidity, *&c.* the mind *never carries its view expressly to consider any past experience*" (Hume 2007, p. 73, emphasis added; SBN 104), Hayek underlines "never carries its view expressly to consider any past experience" and ironically remarks: "Surely no principle can be more abstract than 'gravity'".
26. Hume observes: "All this, and every thing else, which I believe, are *nothing but ideas*; tho' by their *force* and settled order, arising from custom and the relation of cause and effect, they distinguish themselves from the other ideas, which are merely the offspring of the imagination" (Hume 2007, p. 75; SBN 108). Hayek put a marginal vertical line, then he underlines "are nothing but ideas" and "force". And remarks (a double but sentence): "But they are associated with no permanent impression. Where then does the vivacity & strength giving belief come from. But the force was said to be derived from the present impression." Hume observes: "As the relation of cause and effect is requisite to persuade us of any real existence, so is this persuasion requisite to give force to these other relations" (Hume 2007, p. 76; SBN 109). Hayek put a marginal vertical line, then a question mark and remarks: "Existence & real existence are the same thing: but existence is said to be no different from the same imagination which has a relation of…".
27. "I recall his excitement when I called his attention to the profound discussion of these matters [the scope and functions of property and ownership, both private and public, the economic significance of the ramifications of property law] in David Hume's Inquiry concerning the Principles of Morals: section III, 'Of Justice'" (Plant 1970, p. 5). "My own attention was first drawn to Hume in this respect many years ago by professor Sir Arnold Plant, whose development of the Humean theory of property we are stizz [sic] cagerly awaiting" (Hayek 1963, p. 693 n. 3a); "My attention was first directed to these parts of Hume's works many years ago by Professor Sir Arnold Plant, whose development of the Humean theory of property we are still eagerly awaiting" (Hayek 1966, p. 339 n. 5; 1967, p. 109 n. 5); "My attention was first directed to these parts of Hume's works many years ago by Professor Sir Arnold Plant" (Hayek 1991, p. 101 n. 10).
28. Perhaps Hayek's reading of Hume was neglected for the same reason that, according to him, explains the general reaction to *The Constitution of Liberty*: "It was a book on political science by somebody who was not recognized as a political scientist. It was on that ground very largely neglected by the professionals; it was too philosophical for the non-philosophers. When I say I was disappointed, I was disappointed with regard to the *range* of effect. It was received exceedingly friendly by the people whom I really respect, but that's a very small crowd" (Hayek 1983, p. 230).
29. At the beginning of his essay on Hume, Hayek admonishes his reader: "it is always *misleading* to label an age by a name which suggests that it was ruled by a common set of ideas" (Hayek 1991, p. 101). We should be careful not to

make the same mistake and label (with Hayek) Hume's philosophy as "anti-rationalism". He who cultivates the "gardener" does not necessarily eradicate the knowledge that the "craftsman" misuses in order to shape his handiwork. Hayek himself was aware of the danger. Three years afterwards, in the essay on Mandeville, he acknowledges that "anti-rationalism" is a "*misleading* term which has been widely used for Mandeville and Hume, and which we had now better drop in favour of Sir Karl Popper's 'critical rationalism'" (Hayek 1991, p. 94). Elsewhere Hayek confesses: "I just accepted the Popperian philosophy for spelling out what I had always felt [...] I agree with him more than with anybody else on philosophical matters" (Hayek 1994, p. 43). In *Conjectures and Refutations*, where he logically criticizes Hume's psychological theory and his sceptical despair of reason, and attacks his irrationalism (an "unintended consequence"), Popper will celebrate Hume as a "calm analyst", "one of the greatest thinkers" in the theory of knowledge (Popper 2002, p. 270).

## REFERENCES

Árdal P. (1966). *Passion and Value in Hume's Treatise*. Edinburgh: Edinburgh University Press.

Caldwell B. (2004). *Hayek's Challenge: An Intellectual Biography of F. A. Hayek*. Chicago, IL: University of Chicago Press.

Caldwell B. (2010). Introduction, in Hayek F. von (ed.), *Studies on the Abuse and Decline of Reason*. Chicago, IL: University of Chicago Press, pp. 1–5.

Caldwell B. (2014). Introduction, in Hayek F. von (ed.), *The Market and Other Orders. The Collected Works of F.A. Hayek. Volume XV*. Edited by B. Caldwell. Chicago, IL: University of Chicago Press, pp. 1–35.

Coventry A., Sager A. (2013). Hume and Contemporary Political Philosophy. *The European Legacy*, 18(5), pp. 588–602.

Cubeddu R. (forthcoming). Hayek and Hume's Epicureanism, in Mazza E., Mingardi A. (eds.), *Hayek and Hume*. London: Bloomsbury, forthcoming.

Ebenstein A. (2003). *Hayek's Journey: The Mind of Friedrich Hayek*. London: Palgrave Macmillan.

Ferguson A. (1767). *An Essay on the History of Civil Society*. London: A. Millar and T. Caddel.

Gamble A. (2006). Hayek on Knowledge, Economics, and Society, in Feser E. (ed.), *The Cambridge Companion to Hayek*. Cambridge, UK: Cambridge University Press, pp. 111–131.

Gombrich E. (1995). The Open Society and its enemies: Remembering its publication fifty years ago. http://www.the-rathouse.com/2010/Gombrich-OSE.html [Accessed 27.06.2025].

Gray J. (1998). *Hayek on Liberty*. Oxford, UK: Oxford University Press.

Green T. H., Grose T. H. (1874). Preface, in Hume D., *The Philosophical Works of David Hume*. Edited by T. H. Green and T. H. Grose; 4 vols. London: Longmans, Green, and Co., vols. 1–2., pp. iii–vii.

Hayek F. von (1938). Review of *An Abstract of a Treatise of Human Nature*, by J. M. Keynes & P. Sraffa. *Economica*, 5(19), pp. 364–365.

Hayek F. von (1948). Individualism: True and False, in Hayek F. von (ed.), *Individualism and Economic Order*. Chicago, IL: University of Chicago Press, pp. 3–22.

Hayek F. von (1951). *John Stuart Mill and Harriet Taylor: Their Friendship and Subsequent Marriage*. New York, NY: Kelley.
Hayek F. von (1963). The legal and political philosophy of David Hume. *Il Politico*, 28(4), 691–704. Italian translation by Corsico, R. (1963) on pp. 705–720.
Hayek F. von (1966). The legal and political philosophy of David Hume, in Chappell V. C. (ed.), *Hume: A Collection of Critical Essays*. New York, NY: Anchor Books, pp. 335–360.
Hayek F. von (1967). The Legal and Political Philosophy of David Hume, in Hayek, F. von (ed.), *Studies in Philosophy, Politics, and Economics*. London: Routledge & Kegan Paul, pp. 106–121.
Hayek F. von (1982). *Law, Legislation and Liberty*. Volumes 1–3. London: Routledge & Kegan Paul.
Hayek F. von (1983). *Nobel Prize-Winning Economist: Friedrich A. von Hayek*. Los Angeles: The Regents of the University of California.
Hayek F. von (1988). *The Fatal Conceit: The Errors of Socialism*. Edited by W. W. Bartley III. London: Routledge and Chicago, IL: University of Chicago Press.
Hayek F. von (1989). The pretence of knowledge. Nobel Memorial Lecture, December 11, 1974. *The American Economic Review* 79(6), 3–7.
Hayek F. von (1991). *The Trend of Economic Thinking. Essays on Political Economists and Economic History. The Collected Works of F. A. Hayek. Volume III*. Edited by W. W. Bartley III and S. Kresge. Chicago, IL: University of Chicago Press.
Hayek F. von (1994). *Hayek on Hayek: An Autobiographical Dialogue*. Edited by S. Kresge and L. Wenar. Chicago, IL: University of Chicago Press.
Hayek F. von (2001). Individual and Collective Aims, in Mendus S., Edwards D. (eds.), *On Toleration*. Oxford, UK: Clarendon Press, pp. 35–54.
Hayek F. von (2011). *The Constitution of Liberty. The Collected Works of F. A. Hayek. Volume XVII*. Edited by R. Hamowy. Chicago, IL: University of Chicago Press.
Hayek F. von (2017). Preface (1952) to *The Sensory Order*, in Vanberg V. (ed.), *The Sensory Order and Other Writings on the Foundations of Theoretical Psychology. The Collected Works of F.A. Hayek, Volume XIV*. Chicago, IL: University of Chicago Press, pp. 115–122.
Hume D. (1742). Of the Rise and Progress of the Arts and Sciences, in *Essays, Moral and Political, Volume II*. Edinburgh: A. Kincaid by R. Fleming and A. Alison, pp. 53–100.
Hume D. (1762). *The History of England, from The Invasion of Julius Cæsar to The Accession of Henry VII*, 6 vols. London: A. Millar.
Hume D. (1777). Essays, Moral, Political, and Literary, in *Essays and Treatises on Several Subjects*, 2 vols. London: T. Cadell / Edinburgh: A. Donaldson and W. Creech, vol. 1.
Hume D. (1874). A Treatise of Human Nature: Being an Attempt to Introduce the Experiment Method of Reasoning into Moral Subjects, in *The Philosophical Works of David Hume*. Edited by T. H. Green and T. H. Grose; 4 vols. London: Longmans, Green, and Co., vol. 1.
Hume D. (1874a). *The Philosophical Works of David Hume*. Edited by T. H. Green and T. H. Grose; 4 vols. London: Longmans, Green, and Co., vol. 2.
Hume D. (1875). *The Philosophical Works of David Hume*. Edited by T. H. Green and T. H. Grose; 4 vols. London: Longmans, Green, and Co., vol. 3.
Hume D. (1875a). *The Philosophical Works of David Hume*. Edited by T. H. Green and T. H. Grose; 4 vols. London: Longmans, Green, and Co., vol. 4.

Hume D. (1890). *A Treatise of Human Nature: Being an attempt to introduce the experimental method of reasoning into moral subjects and Dialogues Concerning Natural Religion*. Edited by T. H. Green and T. H. Grose; 2 vols. London: Longmans, Green, and Co.

Hume D. (1932). *The Letters of David Hume*. Edited by J. Y. T Greig; 2 vols. Oxford: Clarendon Press.

Hume D. (1938). *An Abstract of A Treatise of Human Nature 1740. A Pamphlet hitherto unknown by David Hume*. Edited by J. M. Keynes and P. Sraffa. Cambridge: University Press.

Hume D. (1947). *Dialogues Concerning Natural Religion*. Edited by N. K. Smith. London: T. Nelson.

Hume D. (1954). *The New Letters of David Hume*. Edited by R. Klibansky and E. C. Mossner. Oxford: Clarendon Press.

Hume D. (1956). *The Natural History of Religion*. Edited by H. E. Root. London: A. and C. Black.

Hume D. (2007). *A Treatise of Human Nature*. Edited by D. F. Norton and M. J. Norton; 2 vols. London: Clarendon Press.

Hume D. (2010). *An Enquiry Concerning the Principles of Morals*. Edited by T. Beauchamp. London: Clarendon Press.

Hume D. (2021). *Essays, Moral, Political, and Literary. A Critical Edition*. Edited by T. Beauchamp and M. A. Box; 2 vols. Oxford: Clarendon Press.

Klibanski, R. (1951). Appendix, in Watkins F. (ed.), *Hume: Theory of Politics*. London, UK; Toronto, ON: T. Nelson and Sons, pp. 245–246.

Laird J. (1932). *Hume's Philosophy of Human Nature*. London: Methuen & Co.

Leoni B. (1961). *Freedom and the Law*. New York, NY: Van Nostrand.

Letwin S. (1976). The Achievements of Hayek, in Machlup F. (ed.), *Essays on Hayek*. New York, NY: New York University Press, pp. 153–170.

Masala A. (2022). Leoni, Hayek and Il Politico. *Il Politico*, 87(2), 5–22.

McArthur, N. (2005). David Hume and the common law of England. *Journal of Scottish Philosophy*, 3(1), 67–82.

McArthur, N. (2018). Hume and the philosophy of law, in Coventry A., Sager A. (eds.), *The Humean Mind*. London: Routledge, pp. 349–358.

Menger C. (1985). *Investigations into the Method of Social Sciences with Special Reference to Economics*. Translated by F. J. Nock. New York and London: New York University Press.

Menger C. (2007). *Principles of Economics*. Translated by J. Dingwall, B. Hoselitz. New York, NY: New York University Press.

Mises L. von. (2005). *Liberalism*. Translated by B. Bien-Greaves. Indianapolis, IN: Liberty Fund.

Mises L. von. (2007). *Human Action: A Treatise on Economics*. Indianapolis, IN: Liberty Fund.

Popper K. (1935). *Logik der Forschung: Zur Erkenntnistheorie der modernen Naturwissenschaft*. Wien: Springer-Verlag.

Popper K. (2002). *Conjectures and Refutations: The Growth of Scientific Knowledge*. London: Routledge.

Plant A. (1970). A tribute to Hayek – the rational persuader. *Economic Age*, 2(2), pp. 4–8.

Price J. (1968). *David Hume*. Boston, MA: Twayne Publishers.

Quine W. V. O. (2003). 1946 Lectures on David Hume's Philosophy, in Buickerood, J. G. (ed.), *Eighteenth-Century Thought. Volume 1.* New York, NY: AMS Press, pp. 171–254.

Quine W. V. O. (2008). Lectures on David Hume's Philosophy 1946, in Føllesdal D., Quine D. B. (eds.), *Confessions of a Confirmed Extensionalist and Other Essays.* Boston, MA: Harvard University Press, pp. 36–136.

Radnitzky G. (1994). Hayek's Contributions to Epistemology, Ethics and Politics, in Frei C., Nef R. (eds.), *Contending with Hayek.* Bern, CH: Peter Lang, pp. 65–85.

Rotwein E. (1955). Introduction, in Hume D. (ed.), *Writings on Economics.* Edited by E. Rotwein. London: Nelson, pp. ix–cxi.

Schneider L. (1967). Introduction, in Schneider, L. (ed.), *The Scottish Moralists on Human Nature and Society.* Chicago and London: The University of Chicago Press, pp. xi–lxxviii.

Schneider L. (1985). Introduction, in Menger C., *Investigations into the Method of Social Sciences with Special Reference to Economics.* Translated by F. J. Nock. New York and London: New York University Press, pp. 1–21.

Shearmur J. (1996). *Hayek and After: Hayekian Liberalism as a Research Programme.* London: Routledge.

Shearmur J. (2011). Editor's Introduction, in Hayek F. von (ed.), *Law, Legislation and Liberty: A New Statement of the Liberal Principles of Justice and Political Economy* (Volumes I–III). Chicago, IL: University of Chicago Press, pp. xxi–xlvii.

Stringham E., Zywicki T. (2011). Hayekian anarchism. *Journal of Economic Behavior & Organization,* 78(3), pp. 290–301.

# 7. Hayek and Friedman: two counterrevolutions in monetary theory

**Hansjörg Klausinger**

The Keynesian revolution, initiated by Keynes's *General Theory* in 1936 (Keynes 1973) and implemented in Keynesian policies in the postwar decades, was challenged and eventually superseded by what has been described as the "counter-revolution in monetary theory" (Johnson 1971). Gradually, then, Keynesianism was replaced by "monetarism" as the mainstream approach in macroeconomics, and the latter's success was imputed to its main protagonist Milton Friedman. Yet, at a somewhat more subliminal level, the writings of Friedrich A. Hayek had also contributed to the demise of Keynesianism. It has been perhaps no coincidence that both were awarded the Nobel Prize in economics in the 1970s, Hayek in 1974 and Friedman in 1976.[1]

However, although they concurred in rejecting Keynesianism, Hayek and Friedman differed in major respects, methodologically and substantially, in their monetary economics. These differences will be the subject of this chapter, though this investigation will be restricted to the period when both argued and presented their advice, with more or less conviction, within the traditional confines of monetary policy, that is, a government monopoly in money entrusted to the management of a central bank. Only in the 1970s and 1980s did both lose their faith in what could be eventually accomplished within this traditional framework and propagated more radical approaches – Hayek introduced the idea of competing (private) currencies and Friedman advocated a mandated policy of base money freeze (see, e.g., Hayek 1976, 1978b, and Friedman 1987). Yet, even if in this regard some may liken investigating Hayek without *Denationalisation of Money* to playing Hamlet without the prince, we will content ourselves here to this modest task and leave the examination of the more far-reaching proposals of both Hayek and Friedman to a future effort.[2]

While we presuppose some familiarity with the approaches of Hayek and Friedman, the chapter is introduced by two short sections summarizing the key elements of Hayek's and Friedman's views on money and inflation. The core of the chapter will then investigate the commonalities and differences in these two counterrevolutions, in particular focusing on the diagnoses and therapies of the inflation experienced in the 1970s, the respective frameworks proposed for monetary stability and their setting within the international monetary system.

## HAYEK ON THE MONETARY FRAMEWORK

Hayek's blueprint for a liberal society, *The Constitution of Liberty* (*COL*, Hayek 2011 [1960]), contained a chapter on "The Monetary Framework," which presented a systematic summary of his position and to which he stuck until he resumed his "campaign" in the 1970s. It integrated the novel insights from the postwar period with his earlier writings on money and the trade cycle into a general perspective.[3] The starting point is the identification of inflation as the main problem and government's role in money as its main cause. The inflationary pressure derives from the governments' (and public's) pursuit of "welfare state-ism,"[4] manifest in full-employment policies combined with trade union wage pressure, the state provision for old age pensions, and generally the incentive to get rid of the burden of public debt through inflation. Hayek also points out the cumulative nature of inflation and government interventions: in the face of the detrimental effects of inflation, even if fully anticipated, the introduction of controls and rigidities appears politically expedient, yet eventually produces the kind of frictions to be cured by another dose of inflation, and so on. Notably, the seemingly beneficial effects of inflation, either in bringing about full employment or in overcoming ever more stringent controls and rigidities, are restricted to the short run, just as long as inflation has not been fully anticipated, that is, as long as the new money injected into the circuit of money displays its stimulating effect on the economy. Yet, after every new round of inflation this stimulation can only be maintained by increasing inflation. This process can ultimately result only either in the advent of hyperinflation and its complete disruption of the economy or, if inflation is stopped or reversed, in a severe, if only temporary, depression. Hayek also pointed to the asymmetry between inflation and deflation; in contrast to that usually emphasized which attributed to deflation the severer economic harms, he focused on the political asymmetry that, as the short-run effects of inflation appear pleasant while those of deflation are painful, governments have a much greater incentive to acquiesce in inflationary policies (Hayek 2011, 457–458).

Then, how to solve this problem? In *COL*, Hayek does not present one grand solution, but follows a pragmatic approach where in the end his recommendations are driven by practical considerations – and do not yet transcend the boundaries of the tradition.

First, and perhaps surprisingly, Hayek sees no viable alternative to the state control of money. This is so because on the one hand money is an important disturbing element in the market economy – "a kind of loose joint in the otherwise self-steering mechanism of the market" (ibid., 452), and on the other hand, due to the interaction of money and credit within the modern system of banking, the supply of money may fluctuate spontaneously and not adequately adjust to changes in money demand (ibid., 453). This makes a completely private system of money not only "politically impracticable," but also "undesirable" (ibid., 451), yet government-regulated money need not be a monopoly; rather, competition with other media of exchange need not be prohibited (ibid., 452n2).

If then a government-controlled central bank is accepted as the institution to which the task of monetary policy is assigned, how could its discretion be effectively limited in order to prevent it from complying with the government's inclination towards inflation? Should it be bound by rules or granted (some measure of) discretion? Hayek argues against strict rules because of the inescapable tension between the actions prescribed by such a rule and the bank's role as a lender of last resort indispensable in a modern banking system (ibid., 463). It is noteworthy that Hayek's reference for the advocacy of a rule-based monetary policy is still Henry Simons (1936), and not yet Milton Friedman. This leads Hayek in the end to his (somewhat anticlimactic) recommendation: the establishment of an independent central bank committed to the principle of monetary stability to which, if in conflict, the pursuit of employment goals must be subordinated. Of course, there is no obvious reason why a government susceptible to capture easy short-run gains should ever commit to such an act of self-restraint. Yet, when written, *COL* was not thought of as a textbook for immediate political action but as part of the wider intellectual discourse destined to win support for the liberal cause.

## THE MONETARIST COUNTERREVOLUTION

In the following, eschewing a detailed historical account, we concentrate on the crucial elements of the monetarist position, and implicitly the state of the art of (mainstream) macroeconomics, as it evolved in the 1970s. Although it was by far not the accomplishment of a single person, the focus will be on Milton Friedman and his specific variety of monetarism, and his writings throughout two decades will be used as the primary sources of reference.[5]

Up to the 1970s, monetarism evolved in opposition to the Keynesian mainstream, and following Modigliani (1977) three contentious issues, even though intertwined, may be distinguished: first, the quantity theory as an alternative framework to the income–expenditure approach, or monetarism versus fiscalism; second, stability versus instability of the market system; and third, the desirability or not of countercyclical stabilization policies. While the early debate, for example, the (in)famous controversy on "cost push" versus "demand pull," was led within "static" models of aggregate demand and supply, later on "dynamic" versions centered on the investigation of the properties of the "Phillips curve."

To cut a long story short, the discussion of empirical "interest elasticities" (of the demand for money and for goods) pointed towards a confirmation of the monetarist position. In addition, the low interest elasticity of money demand also appeared to confirm that in the case of effective demand failures[6] the interest rate mechanism could act as a stabilizing mechanism so that only minor adjustments in the general wage and price level were called for. Therefore, although the notion of a "destabilizing deflation" could not be refuted in principle, such deflations should not be a major phenomenon, as long as the quantity of money were kept constant. However, this assumption did not apply to the major example presented for the market system's purported instability, the Great Depression of the 1930s. In their magisterial study of the monetary history of the United States, Friedman jointly with Anna J. Schwartz (1963, chap. 7) had shown that instead the Great Depression was accompanied by a "Great Contraction" of the money supply. This was ascribed to the inept policies of the Fed, partly because it adhered to a sort of "real bills doctrine," partly because the ease of monetary policy was misjudged by looking at a too narrowly defined monetary indicator – in present terminology, the monetary base instead of a broader monetary aggregate. Another constraint that severely reduced its room for maneuver was the Fed's obeisance to the gold standard. Thus, it was the errors of policy and not the malfunctioning of the market system that had caused this economic catastrophe.

If it is money rather than fiscal variables that drive aggregate demand, then the quantity theory can be used for determining output and prices. Here Friedman (1971) utilized a theoretical framework according to which in the long run money affects only the price level. This is the traditional idea of the "neutrality of money"[7] and gave rise to Friedman's (1970, 24) famous dictum that (persistent) "inflation is always and everywhere a monetary phenomenon." In contrast, in the short run (over the business cycle) the effects of money are split between prices and output, producing the temporary output effects of monetary expansions and contractions. This appears to offer the possibility for countercyclical monetary policy to improve upon the short-run stabilizing mechanism of the market system. However, Friedman denied even this restricted role for stabilization policy. On the one hand, although powerful, the effects of monetary policy are unpredictable because its lags are "long and variable" (Friedman 1961). On the other hand, due to this difficult timing problem and perhaps also because of the imperfect wisdom of policymakers, in the real world such attempts to stabilize may indeed prove destabilizing, when the monetary instrument is used "too much too late" (Friedman 1970, 19). In addition, monetarists (like classical liberals in general) might hesitate to entrust such a powerful instrument like monetary policy to fallible and possibly not completely benevolent human beings.

Then, in conclusion, what is the monetarists', and in particular Friedman's, prescription for the conduct of monetary policy? The classic answer is in Friedman's *A Program for Monetary Stability* (1959): let the (appropriately chosen) quantity of money grow at a predetermined constant rate k, that is, Friedman's "k%-rule," and as a consequence abstain from any attempts at countercyclical policy. Of course, this rule is not as simple as it might look at first glance. To begin with, Friedman proposed a magnitude for k that should take account of the increases in money demand due to economic growth and some decline in velocity, yet on average would mean some, even if low inflation.[8] While the possibly negative effects of such a low inflation might be minor, it would ease the problem of the zero lower bound of the nominal rate of interest in case of a severe decline in economic activity where the equilibrium (or natural) real rate would become negative. In addition, Friedman's rule is conceived as a strategy, in Hayek's words, of "monetary nationalism," that is, designed to work for a single country. In this regard, then, the autonomy of monetary policy must be safeguarded by a regime of flexible exchange rates – incompatible with the fixed exchange rates in principle prescribed by the then still ruling system of Bretton Woods. Furthermore, if the choice of "k" is nontrivial, the selection of the proper monetary aggregate to which to apply this k is still more so. Beyond that, the choice would depend on which aggregate could offer the best statistical "fit" with nominal income, a venture prone soon to prove as chasing a will-o'-the-wisp.

Most of the above discussions were conducted within a theoretical framework derived from the simple Keynesian macro model, with an exogenous nominal wage. Yet, it had always been evident that wages would react when the labor market was approaching full employment. This common-sensical notion was eventually formalized when A. W. H. Phillips (1958) discovered the "Phillips curve," in its original version just a negative statistical relation between the rate of unemployment and changes in money wages. Taking into account that wage changes fed into prices, the Phillips curve was eventually transformed (see, e.g., Samuelson and Solow 1960) into a negative relation between unemployment and inflation. This offered the interpretation that there were different "equilibrium" (or steady state) rates of unemployment associated with different rates of inflation, or in some sense that full employment did not define a unique rate of unemployment but rather a range of such rates. Thus, from the point of view of policymaking, there appeared to exist a "menu of choice" (Rees 1970) exhibiting a "trade-off," for example, a higher rate of inflation buying a lower rate of unemployment.

However, this trade-off and the existence of a range of equilibria owed their existence to an incomplete adjustment of money wages to changes in the price level.[9] This was made explicit in Friedman's famous Presidential Address (Friedman 1968), where he pointed out that in the end it was not money but real wages that were to react to the labor market situation. Consequently, in order to represent the reaction of (expected) real wages, the Phillips curve had to be augmented by the inclusion of inflation expectations. This gave rise to two different versions of the Phillips curve: with correct expectations, there is a unique "equilibrium" rate of unemployment, called the "natural rate" (in analogy to Wicksell's "natural rate" of interest). The corresponding "long-run" Phillips curve is thus vertical and the trade-off vanishes. In contrast, the "short-run" Phillips curve, with given expectations of inflation, still exhibits a trade-off, which is due to that part of inflation that is unexpected.

At the time, economists tried to explain this awkward property of the Phillips curve by providing "microeconomic foundations" of the mechanism that produced it. These ranged from Friedman's (1968) notion of workers' misperception of the actual real wage that led them to unwarranted changes in labor supply, with Lucas and Rapping's (1970) variant that emphasized the intertemporal substitution of leisure, Phelps's (1970) sophisticated analysis of search unemployment with imperfect information, to the straightforward introduction of long-term wage contracts that could not instantaneously adjust to actual inflation (Fischer 1977). Notably, all these stories exhibited a short-run–long-run dichotomy so that short-run deviations would disappear in the long run. In addition, although simpler than those imagined by Hayek, these short-run deviations resulted from "distortions," mainly located in the labor market, brought about by (unexpected) inflation.

There remained, then, the problem of how to link the short with the long run. As these differed just in the existence or not of errors in inflation expectations, the link hinged on the adjustment of expectations. At the time, the most common mechanism proposed was that of "adaptive expectations" where expectations reacted (partly) to perceived past errors.[10] For a variety of, but not all conceivable (stochastic) processes followed by inflation, such a mechanism would eventually lead to a convergence of expected to actual rates of inflation, and thus grant the stability of the long-run equilibrium. However, expected inflation would (until the ultimate convergence) lag behind actual rates, and thus with a suitably chosen path of accelerating rates of inflation, unexpected inflation and thereby deviations from the natural rate of unemployment could prevail for an indefinite period of time.

In his address, Friedman identified two corollaries for stabilization policies. First, with his k%-rule, the stability of the system appeared granted in the dynamic version, too. And second, stabilization policies targeting an unemployment rate different from the natural rate would in the end prove destabilizing, pushing the economy into a spiral of either deflation or (more probably) inflation. As the natural rate was not directly observable and prone to shift over time, Friedman regarded this as a serious danger.

## HAYEK'S CAMPAIGN AND FRIEDMAN'S MONETARISM: UNEASY COMRADES-IN-ARMS

After having summarized both Hayek's and Friedman's writings that gave rise to a "counterrevolution in monetary theory," it appears appropriate to investigate the relationship between their approaches. This is not an easy task: while Friedman's monetary writings represented the core area of his research and by 1970 existed as a coherent body of thought, Hayek's "Campaign" (1978a) consisted just of a collection of manuscripts for various speeches. In addition, the protagonists only rarely discussed the existing differences directly with each other, in their correspondence or in their writings, so that the exchange of arguments did not happen in a dialogue but rather resembled mutual monologues addressed at an absent partner.[11] It may also be noted that neither Friedman (before *Denationalisation*) nor Hayek provided specific references to published writings of the other; in particular for Hayek's case, it might even be conjectured that he knew Friedman's position rather from the lectures and discussions at the MPS meetings than from published sources.

### Methodology

As will be seen, methodological matters made up the vital conflict between the approaches of Hayek and Friedman, and the disputes on money just provided a case in point. In his reminiscences, Hayek was quite explicit in his criticism:

> Milton and I agree on almost everything except monetary policy. ... They [the economists of the Chicago School] believe economic phenomena can be explained as macrophenomena, that you can ascertain cause and effects from aggregates and averages. But although in a sense it seems to be true, there is no necessary connection. In fact, I should have preferred to demonstrate historically that every period of inflation ends with a crash. But the historical demonstration is no proof that this must be so. The reason why it happens cannot be accounted for by macroeconomic analysis. (Hayek 1994, 144–145)[12]

Similarly, in a letter to Arthur Seldon (May 13, 1985, FAHP 27:6):

> I do indeed regard the abandonment of the whole macroeconomics nonsense as very important, but it is for me a very delicate matter and I have for some time avoided stating my views too bluntly ... The source of the difficulty is the constant danger that the Mont Pèlerin Society might split into a Friedmanite and a Hayekian wing. I have long regretted my failure to take time to criticize Friedman's

> *Positive Economics* almost as much as my failure to return to the critique of Keynes *General Theory* ...

It was therefore the – in Hayek's view: questionable – methodological status of such "macroeconomic theories" that represented the crucial point of contention. However, the only documented dispute between Hayek and Friedman was not sparked by criticism of the quantity theory of money but by Hayek pointing to the contrast between his own and the Keynesian explanation of unemployment. In *Full Employment at Any Price?* Hayek referred to his own theory as "true, though untestable," and he explained:

> Briefly, we find the curious situation that the (Keynesian) theory which is comparatively best confirmed by statistics because it happens to be the only one which can be tested quantitatively, is nevertheless false. Yet it is widely accepted only because the explanation earlier regarded as true, and which I still regard as true, cannot *by its very nature* be tested by statistics. (Hayek 1975a, 19)[13]

Indeed, according to Hayek's "true theory" the cause of unemployment is to be ascribed to the deviation of current from equilibrium prices, yet as equilibrium prices cannot be known beforehand, this deviation cannot be measured and thus a statistical correlation with the amount of unemployment cannot be established (Hayek 1975a, 19–20, 2022 [1978a], 351).

Friedman (in a letter of Sept 11, 1975) told Hayek that this passage had been among those intensely discussed at the Hillsdale MPS meeting in Hayek's honor at which Hayek was not present.[14] His crucial counterargument was then how to decide between two competing claims that theories are true but untestable. Rather than settling them by conversation or by force, Friedman proposed in a Popperian spirit agreeing on what set of facts, if observed, would confirm or disconfirm either theory.[15] Unfortunately, Hayek's response (if there ever was one) has not been preserved so that there is no clue about the conclusion of this singular debate.

In any case, Hayek extended his criticism to the quantity theory of money, a key point of Friedman's monetarism. He disavowed its methodological soundness because it dealt with statistical aggregates and because it was justified by the mere observation of empirical regularities, and he also attacked its preoccupation with the effects of money on the general price level instead of on the structure of relative prices and of production.

Anyway, Hayek had conceded in the 1930s and repeated now, four decades later, that the quantity theory could serve as "a useful rough approximation to a really adequate explanation" (Hayek 1999 [1978b], 183), and in particular that "from a practical point of view, it would be one of the worst things which could befall us if the general public should ever again cease to believe in the elementary propositions of the quantity theory" (Hayek 2012a [1931], 195, quoted in 2022 [1980, Mar 5], 505). In addition, he pledged to its "irrefutable chief content … that inflation is always and everywhere the effect of an excessive supply of money and that it can be cured only by a restriction of its supply" (ibid.). And though Hayek would not content himself with an analysis of the monetary phenomena of inflation that stopped at its effects on the general price level – as one of those over-simplifications to which Friedman's approach was prone to fall prey – for all practical purposes, putting aside differences in fine points of abstract theory, he was ready to join Friedman's side and to consider himself "a monetarist" in this narrow sense.[16]

## Causes and Consequences of Inflation

As regarded the diagnosis of the current situation in the 1970s, both Hayek and Friedman agreed on taking as the point of departure a position of equilibrium of the economy that can be sustained with a stable price level or, that is, without an accelerating (or decelerating) rate of inflation. This corresponds to what Friedman famously termed the "natural rate of unemployment" where the labor market is characterized by an "equilibrium structure of real wages."[17] Both were also aware of the evil effects of stabilization policies attempting to target a rate of unemployment different from the equilibrium rate by an accommodating monetary policy that just secures the level of aggregate demand required for accomplishing this employment goal.[18] Notably, Friedman emphasized that any kind of pegging a rate of unemployment will lead to instability, while Hayek was more concrete in the description of the crucial constellation: he envisaged the problem as the opposition between governments committed to the goal of "full employment" and trade unions which in setting their money wages are determined to achieve real wages incompatible with full employment. In any case, the full employment goal can only be realized temporarily by inflation, that is, by (that part of) inflation that is not anticipated, and consequently persistent attempts to secure full employment will only end up in accelerating inflation.

In this sense, in the view of Hayek and Friedman, the economy's short-run position at full employment, as a deviation from equilibrium due to monetary expansion, is characterized by "distortions."

Yet, there are differences in emphasis. Friedman focuses on the labor market, where unexpected inflation tricks workers into employment above the natural level, by at once raising the expected real wage that determines workers' labor supply and lowering the actual real wage that determines firms' labor demand. At the same time, as Friedman acknowledged, the market rate of interest is driven below its natural level, without however elaborating on this source of distortion. In any case, all these distortionary effects are to vanish at the moment that the expectational errors are eliminated.

Hayek was less concrete on the specific nature of distortions. As long as, before the advent of Keynesian full-employment policies, inflation had been the result of excessive credit creation, the main distortion was in the structure of capital due to malinvestment or overinvestment. However, in the postwar period, full employment policies had used a full array of instruments, besides monetary, also fiscal policies and other interventions, so that although the existence of such distortions was beyond doubt, Hayek felt it had become much more difficult to locate them. It is perhaps legitimate to interpret him such that the combined use of policies generated changes in the structure of production in a way that would not simply vanish if inflation stopped, but the aftereffects of which would persist for some time.[19]

To reiterate, to keep the economy away from its equilibrium position, the mere continuance of inflation at a stable rate will not suffice. Rather, when the errors of expectations are realized – either after the money injected has moved through the whole circuit and affected all prices (Hayek) or after wage contracts have expired and new ones are negotiated (Friedman and Fischer) – the actually experienced inflation is built into inflation expectations. Thus, to accomplish the same effects as before in the next round, another increase of inflation is needed, to keep the lead of inflation in advance of expectations, and so on. Thus, the "accelerationist hypothesis" is part of both Hayek's and Friedman's approach, and it may be noted that Hayek was aware of this issue already in the 1930s (see, e.g., Hayek 2012b [1934], 198).

Although there appeared to be agreement on the fundamentals, Hayek and Friedman diverged on the role attributed to trade unions as a "cause" of inflation. In particular, in the British debate some participants even went so far as to distinguish "Hayekians" from "Friedmanites" in this regard.[20]

According to Friedman, there is no specific role assigned to trade unions. As long as the government is committed to a policy of monetary stability, there cannot be inflation (at least, in the longer run). While if the government (erroneously) tries to target an unemployment rate incompatible with (that is, lower than) equilibrium, this will give rise to inflation irrespective of trade union behavior. In the end, if trade unions were rigidly committed to a fixed level of the real wage, then equilibrium with monetary stability would be reached just at the rate of unemployment (below "full employment") compatible with this real wage.

Hayek's more politico-economic approach would concede Friedman's theses as far as they went, but for him did not go far enough. For he took into account that, due to the rule of Keynesian full employment policies, government was not (or felt not) free in its decisions: "... politically it is unfortunately true that by pushing up wages the trade unions can make it 'politically necessary' to increase the quantity of money, i.e., create a condition in which government believes it must do so" (Hayek 2022 [1980, June 13], 511).[21] In this situation, then, the bargaining power or belligerency of trade unions does indeed matter. On this, Hayek could even have drawn on some indirect support from Friedman as both concurred that trade union behavior would influence the level of the natural (or equilibrium) rate. Thus, stronger trade unions would mean a higher natural rate, and thus a wider gap to the full employment goal. This also meant that a greater sacrifice would have to be accepted for the sake of monetary stability, and thus put governments in a position still less inclined to resist a policy of monetary accommodation. In any case, trade unions occupied a much more prominent place on Hayek's agenda for reform than on Friedman's, and Hayek went so far as to proclaim his conviction "that trade union reform must precede monetary reform" (Hayek 2022 [1980, June 13], 512).

It may also be noted that Hayek's analysis of the strategic options of government and trade unions, the interactions of which determine the outcome in terms of employment and inflation, intuitively described a constellation that was only later rigorously reformulated in terms of game theory, that is, as a non-cooperative (dynamic) game.[22] In this sense, if the government announces its commitment to monetary stability, it becomes a dominant player, and there is only one (that is, Friedman's) equilibrium where all expectations are fulfilled: zero inflation at the natural rate. In contrast, if the government commits to a full employment goal incompatible with the real wages demanded by trade unions, there will be no equilibrium because both actors' expectations cannot be simultaneously fulfilled. As a consequence, this gives rise to the instability of ever-increasing inflation. We may add that if the government's target function permits a trade-off between deviations from full employment and the height of inflation, the economy will end up at the natural rate with stable, but positive inflation – the famous idea of the "inflationary bias" (Barro & Gordon 1983) of an activist stabilization policy. Without doubt, this conclusion has a Hayekian ring to it.

## How to Fight Inflation

Turning from diagnosis to therapy, there is at first again broad agreement on how to stop an ongoing or accelerating inflation like that of the 1970s. The answer agreed upon is, of course, monetary restraint and the recognition of the inevitability of a stabilization crisis with a temporary increase in unemployment.

As has been pointed out above, the stabilization crisis is the compound result of three effects of monetary restraint. Starting at a short-run position of "full employment," such restraint will bring about, first, a fall in the aggregate demand in goods markets, which will lead to a decline in overall output and thereby to a reduction of actual inflation towards and then below its anticipated level. Second, the drop in actual inflation must eventually bring down expectations of inflation; barring announcement effects resulting from credible regime changes, this meant that until expectations had arrived at a level conducive to monetary stability, the pressure on output and inflation in the goods markets, and therefore the source of crisis, had to persist. Third, when the errors in expectations have gone, a viable structure of production must be rebuilt – Hayek, who was almost alone in stressing this aspect, may have pointed to complications in this process of readjustment due to specific properties of the capital structure, and this would justify his view that the longer the inflation had gone on, the more difficult it would be to get rid of these distortions.[23] Summing up, the only controversial point where Hayek challenged the monetarists' view was with regard to this last effect, the neglect of which might have led them to underestimate the obstacles of the path towards a sustainable equilibrium.

Even the agreement on the theoretical fundamentals left open the practical policy problem of how to spread the process of disinflation over time. The issue became known as "gradualism" versus "shock therapy," and overall monetarists, with due regard to special circumstances, favored the former while Hayek favored the latter. For the gradualist position, the problem consisted just in finding the optimal intertemporal distribution of the sacrifices coupled with the restoration of monetary stability – in this regard, "gradualists" were ready to accept a longer period until low rates of inflation were reached in exchange for containing unemployment at moderate levels.[24] Only when the process had degenerated into the range of hyperinflation, rather than gradualism, the remedy was to convince the public of a complete system change that would eliminate inflationary expectations once and for all.[25] In contrast, Hayek adhered to shock therapy. (In some sense, he preferred the stabilization crisis to be nasty and brutish, but short.) He rested his view not on economic, but on political grounds, that is, on the political impossibility of the gradualist strategy: "No inflation has yet been terminated without a 'stabilization crisis'. To believe that it can be slowed down gradually over a period of years means accepting a prolonged misery. No government could stand such a course of prolonged depression. If we want to stop inflation, we must do it here and now" (Hayek 2022 [1980, Mar 5], 506).[26]

## A Framework for Monetary Stability

The still more important task was finding a solution to safeguard the preservation of monetary stability jointly with the prevention of crises and depressions like those experienced in the 1930s. Friedman believed that both problems could be solved by his k%-rule. As we have seen, the rule consists of the choice of a broader monetary aggregate, including at least cash and demand deposits,[27] and the fixing of an annual rate of change k. Based on the tenets of the monetarist approach, the stability of the market system and the unreliability of political control, such a rule should guarantee fairly low rates of inflation and only minor aberrations from natural rate equilibrium. It would also prove superior to any attempts at countercyclical stabilization, let alone "fine tuning" the economy, and prevent policymakers from the venture of pegging some rate of unemployment (or, that is, some rate of interest).

Just as Hayek regarded Friedman's endorsement of the quantity theory of money as too simplistic, although practically useful, he agreed with Friedman's attempt at depriving "the monetary authorities, in order to prevent the abuse of their powers for political purposes, of all discretionary powers" by introducing "some more or less automatic system for regulating the quantity of money" (Hayek 2022 [1978a], 370), yet was critical of the specifics of Friedman's proposal.

Drawing on his discussions of neutral money in the 1930s, Hayek's main contention was that the value of money did not only depend on the supply but also on the demand for money and that identifying a statistical magnitude that could serve as an adequate measure of the quantity of money would prove almost impossible. In particular, as there is no "sharp distinction between what is to be regarded as money and what is not," the targeting of a specific monetary aggregate for control might be vitiated by the public's attempts to substitute near monies for real money (or vice versa) (Hayek ibid., 370; see also 1980, Mar 5). Hayek was not alone in voicing these warnings, but Friedman may have felt confident that he could ward them off by his empirical studies on the stability of money demand.

However, as the British experience was to demonstrate in the 1980s, the link between money (or, that is, a monetary aggregate, like M1, chosen for control) and inflation proved less reliable than a mechanical application of Friedman's rule would have presupposed. Indeed, inspired by this experience, the British economist Charles Goodhart formulated what came to be known as "Goodhart's law," that "any observed statistical regularity will tend to collapse once pressure is placed upon it for control purposes" (Goodhart 1981, 116, see also Goodhart 1989). Thus, towards the end of the century, in a sort of vindication of Hayek's criticism, the evolving literature on the optimal monetary instrument, as well as the practices of central banks, recognized the variability in the demand for money and turned away from money to interest rate or exchange rate targeting.[28]

Even conceding that adherence to a Friedman-type rule could achieve, by and large, the goal of monetary stability, the question remained if it was also the proper device to prevent crisis and depression. At the time of the discussion, this was a most crucial point because of widespread anxieties that the stabilization crisis accepted as the by-product of combating inflation might degenerate into depression, with unemployment of an extent comparable to the Great Depression of the 1930s. Thus, once again the debate on the causes of the Great Depression came to the fore, and the differences in the interpretations between Friedman on the one side and the evolving view of Hayek on the other, in the end proved significant for evaluating the Friedman rule even in the changed circumstances of the 1970s.

We may start by shortly recapitulating Hayek's contemporary interpretation of the 1930s which distinguished a primary and a secondary phase or type of the depression.[29] Hayek traced the origins of the primary depression back to distortions, such as malinvestments, created by inflationary credit creation; when inflation stops, the distorted structure of production cannot be upheld any longer and the necessary adjustment, due to frictions, will generate a crisis. This is when the secondary phase of the depression may set in. Its ultimate source is "the instability of credit," a process of credit destruction and of banks and private actors rushing for cash and reserves, thus giving rise to an automatic (secondary) deflation, in the sense of a shrinking circulation of money. While in the 1930s Hayek would have preferred to let the deflation run its course, he had recanted his former position and now pleaded for a monetary policy that would credibly counteract any such deflationary tendencies.[30]

However, that did not mean that Hayek now fully concurred with Friedman; in particular, he doubted if the Friedman rule of stabilizing the quantity of money would suffice in any circumstances. Drawing once more on the substitutability of near monies for real money, Hayek questioned if Friedman's plan would exhibit enough flexibility to cope with emergency situations. Rather, he believed "that in order to ensure the convertibility of all kinds of near-money into real money, which is necessary if we are to avoid severe liquidity crises or panics, the monetary authorities must be given some discretion" (Hayek 2022 [1978a], 370). "Fixing by law the rate at which the quantity of money may and should increase," as required by the Friedman rule, "would probably produce the greatest financial panic of history" (Hayek 2022 [1980, Mar 5], 506). Thus, regretfully and in accordance with the views expressed in *COL*, Hayek believed that – under the existing regime of government monopoly of money – some amount of discretion was indispensable.

Turning to Friedman, he had always been a harsh critic of the early Hayek (and others) who treated the ills of the secondary deflation with benign neglect. Without naming names,[31] he had castigated in his "Restatement" "the atrophied and rigid caricature [of the quantity theory]" (Friedman 1969 [1956], 51), which, he later explained (in Gordon 1974 [1972], 162–163), referred to

> the London School of Economics, where the dominant view was that the depression was an inevitable result of the prior boom, that it was deepened by the attempts to prevent prices and wages from falling and firms from going bankrupt, that the

> monetary authorities had brought on the depression by inflationary policies before the crash and had prolonged it by "easy money" policies thereafter; that the only sound policy was to let the depression run its course, bring down money costs, and eliminate weak and unsound firms.

In fact, Friedman never (neither in his retrospect of the Great Depression nor in his current views in the 1970s) placed any emphasis on the problems of structural adjustment as the result of distortions that played such a prominent role in Hayek's explanation of the crisis. In contrast, Friedman's main if not sole concern was with secondary deflation or what had been described as the "Great Contraction."[32] Accordingly, the Great Depression in the US had been driven by a shrinkage in the quantity of money that the Fed had not only failed to counteract but even exacerbated by its wrong-headed policies. In Friedman's view, the evidence presented was so incontrovertible that he speculated had contemporaries like Keynes and Simons only known those facts they would have eschewed their ill-conceived beliefs in the impotency of monetary policy. The crucial shock to the market system had not originated in some built-in "instability of credit" but in the unfortunate policy of the monetary authorities.[33]

Before this background Friedman appears to have been able to refute two main points of Hayek's criticism: first, rather than exacerbate, a stable quantity of money, defined inclusive of bank deposits, would absorb the deflationary effect of attempts to convert near into real money, that is, for example, of demand deposits into cash. As long as this conversion was among types of money within the monetary aggregate to be stabilized, as would have been the case for money defined as M1, such an increase in the demand for cash (or base money) under Friedman's rule would have generated an increase in the supply of base money as an automatic response of the central bank and thus would have nipped the panic in the bud.[34] Second, contrary to contemporary opinion of the 1930s, faced with a process of automatic deflation as Hayek and others had sketched, the Fed could have prevented the contraction in the quantity of money had it been ready to do so. The reason for its failure was not innate deficiencies in the monetary or financial system but simply what in retrospect appear as egregious errors in the conduct of monetary policy. And of course, Friedman's proposal was just designed to avoid repeating this kind of errors.

There is, however, an irrefutable kernel of truth in Hayek's criticism insofar as the stabilizing effects of the Friedman rule apply only to shifts within the monetary aggregate to which the rule is applied, not to shifts of the demand for near monies that cross this boundary. Of course, this is just a reformulation of the problems inherent in Goodhart's law which in the end forced central banks to abandon the monetarist strategy of money targeting.

## The International Monetary System

There remained still the question of how to fit a policy geared to monetary stability at a national level into the international monetary system. Here, too, the opinions of Hayek and Friedman differed.

At first glance, the dispute appears as a simple example of what has become widely known as the open economy trilemma or "impossible trinity."[35] Accordingly, of the three goals, the autonomy of national monetary policy, fixed exchange rates and unrestricted capital mobility, only two can be simultaneously realized. Thus, given capital mobility, the pursuit of fixed exchange rates implies abandoning an autonomous monetary policy, and vice versa. Notably, this is similar to the problem of "monetary nationalism" versus "international stability" that Hayek (1937) had investigated decades before. Again, facing this choice, Hayek opted for a system of fixed exchange rates while Friedman advocated flexible rates.

Hayek rejected the idea of flexible (or floating) exchange rates that were introduced into the theoretical debate throughout the 1960s[36] and became current practice in the 1970s after the breakdown of the Bretton Woods system. His main reason was his belief that short-sighted governments need to be constrained by some institution that forces (monetary) discipline upon them. After the demise of the gold standard, its restoration had proved politically impossible. The Bretton Woods system had imposed some monetary discipline due to the fixity of exchange rates but, in the end, imploded because of its faulty design that put the burden of adjustment asymmetrically only on surplus and not on deficit countries. Both systems could have worked, but both required that deviations from their rules, for example, devaluations of the currency, would impose some cost on the government in the form of a loss of reputation. When the corresponding "convictions" were lost, there was no chance to revive them, and Hayek was skeptical of the attempt to reinstate their complements at a merely national level. In any case, the floating of exchange rates would just confirm to policymakers that another brake against inflation had gone and they had no more to care for the movement of the exchange rate.[37]

Friedman's investigations had from the beginning concentrated on the working of a monetary system at a national level or, that is, of a single country like the US. This was also the subject to which his k%-rule applied, and it could only be realized if the required autonomy of the country's monetary policy could be taken for granted, which implied the introduction of floating rates. Otherwise, the economy would be exposed either "to the vagaries … of an impersonal and automatic gold standard [or] of the politics – deliberate or accidental – of other monetary authorities" (Friedman 1969 [1968], 107). Friedman, in correspondence with Hayek (Sept 11, 1975), also pointed out that

Hayek was misled in identifying the supporters of floating rates with economists in favor of inflation or full-employment policies.

Then, taking into account that these proposals were discussed at a time when the global economy experienced the disintegration of the international monetary system and the advent of inflation at levels unprecedented in the postwar period, it may be concluded that the differences between Hayek and Friedman owed more to conflicting appraisals of political expediency than to disputes in economic theory. As it were, at the time, both approaches, Friedman's and Hayek's, had a Utopian ring in them. Friedman put priority on the task of realizing monetary stability in one country and then to protect it – by introducing flexible exchange rates – from the disturbances due to inflation elsewhere. The experiences of Germany and Switzerland at the final phase of the Bretton Woods system provided examples of how monetary stability in a country could be impaired in a system of fixed rates. Hayek was more ambitious but less concrete than Friedman when he pointed to the necessity of a global solution, an international monetary system to replace the failed one and to reestablish monetary stability such that thereby – in combination with fixed rates – discipline could again be enforced on national monetary policies.[38]

***

Then, ultimately, the crucial problem was not the intellectual challenge to construct model monetary constitutions that would guarantee stability, at the national or international level, but the ways and means to realize them in practice. The aporia such ventures face is well known as "the paradox of government."[39] If such rules (or monetary constitutions) prove necessary because otherwise policymakers would misuse discretion for inflationary purposes, why in the first instance should they enact a rule that would enforce monetary restraint on them and secondly what should deter them from breaking the rule if it appeared expedient? Indeed, in the 1970s and 1980s, some fortuitous moments would offer opportunities, with mixed success, to put the monetarist program into practice in various countries, while ever since the international monetary system did not experience any attempts to reconstruct it along the lines Hayek would have proposed.

## NOTES

1. For biographical accounts see, respectively, Caldwell and Klausinger (2022) and Burns (2023).
2. See Klausinger (2024), a first version of a chapter for the forthcoming second volume of Caldwell and Klausinger (2022).

3. For a summary of Hayek's prewar theories, see Caldwell and Klausinger (2022, 258–267); for their adaptation to the novel experience of Keynesian policies see Hayek (1944, Apr 30), (1946, July 18), (1950) and (1958).
4. See the title of Hayek (1959, Mar 19), a preprint of excerpts from the monetary chapter of *COL*.
5. Many of his important writings are collected in Friedman (1969), see also (1971) and (1972). On the counterrevolutionary aspect of monetarism, see Friedman (1970) and Johnson (1971); for a contemporary account of the monetarist controversy from a Keynesian point of view see Modigliani (1977). For an overview of the early development of Friedman's monetarism see Tavlas (2023).
6. For later reference, it should be noted that here Keynesians and monetarists discuss the crisis phenomena of, in Hayekian terms, a "secondary deflation" with, in this sense, "hoarding" which keeps the money above the natural rate of interest.
7. That is, that in the long run output is invariant to changes in the quantity of money, which is related to but different from Hayek's notion of "neutral money."
8. Originally Friedman proposed a range between 2% and 4%; however, see Friedman (1969) for a more intricate discussion of the optimal value of k.
9. Note that in his chapter on the "theory of prices," Keynes (1973 [1936], 298–306) stipulated that full employment is only reached when an increase in effective demand leads to prices and wages rising at the same rate (called "true inflation," ibid., 303), while at lower levels of employment wages rise less than prices.
10. The classical source of the adaptive expectations hypothesis is Cagan (1956).
11. Friedman referred to Hayek mostly in the context of the causes of the Great Depression, implicitly as a member of LSE and the Austrian School (in Friedman 1969 [1956], 51, and Gordon 1974 [1972], 162), and explicitly in his "Simons lecture" (Friedman 1969 [1967], 88n7). Hayek's dispersed references are mainly to Friedman as an exponent of the quantity theory and of his monetary rule. Apart from the various reminiscences and interviews, there are some passages in "Campaign" (2022 [1978a], e.g., 345, 346 and 370; see also 1975a, 19–20, and 1975b, 16, 17), a "note on monetarism" added in the second edition of *Denationalisation* (1978b, chap. 14), and commentaries on monetarism and Friedman in his letters to the editor of *The Times* (see, e.g., 1980, Mar 5, Mar 27 and June 13). From the correspondence on monetary matters, only two substantial documents have been preserved: Friedman to Hayek, Sept 2, 1967, and Sept 11, 1975 (in FAHP 20:19); apparently, these have been part of a larger exchange that has been lost.
12. Taken from an interview with Bartley, 1984–1988. It is in the same place that Hayek calls Friedman's *Essays in Positive Economics* (1953) a "dangerous book."
13. We refer here to the 1975a version and not to the reprint in 1978a, because this is the one with which Friedman took issue. Notably, this version was heavily

edited by Arthur Seldon so that the reprint is probably closer to Hayek's original text. In particular, while Seldon's version speaks of "the true, though untestable, explanation," the reprint has just "the older, and to me convincing, explanation" (Hayek 2022 [1978a], 351). However, the gist of the paragraph quoted above is the same in both versions.

14. The papers presented at Hillsdale have been published in Machlup (ed.) (1976); for some qualifications of Hayek's verdict on macroeconomics see Shenfield (1976, 68–71).
15. Friedman also provided an example of a potential disconfirmation of Hayek's theory: Would it not imply that the larger the prior inflation, the larger the depression that follows? This, when Friedman tested it, came out as false. See his "plucking model" (Friedman 1993).
16. See Hayek (1983 [1978], 99) (I have substituted "abstract" for the obviously erroneous "abstruse").
17. Or in a more elaborate definition, the natural rate of unemployment is the level that "would be ground out by the Walrasian system of general equilibrium equations, provided there is imbedded in them the actual structural characteristics of the labor and commodity markets, including market imperfections, stochastic variability in demands and supplies, the cost of gathering information … the costs of mobility, and so on" (Friedman 1969 [1968], 102). Of course, it is highly questionable if the "uniqueness" of such an equilibrium could be proven.
18. The same would have been true of monetary policy pegging, in Wicksellian terms, the money rate of interest at a level different from the "natural" rate.
19. For example, fiscal policy measures targeted at the construction sector would leave excess capacities even after the policy had been reversed.
20. See the contributions and the discussion in Institute of Economic Affairs (IEA) (1974), in particular Jay (1974).
21. See also Hayek (2022 [1978a], 345).
22. Early applications of game theory to this problem have been Kydland and Prescott (1977) and Barro and Gordon (1983).
23. In particular, Hayek pointed to the specificity and complementarity of capital as obstacles to a swift redeployment of existing capital goods for alternative uses.
24. See Friedman (1974), and Friedman to Hayek, Sept 11, 1975; for Britain see Laidler (1974, 56).
25. Friedman (1974, 80–81) cited the Brazilian stabilization of 1964–1966 as an example; see on this also Boianovsky (2020). The end of the German hyperinflation of the 1920s may also have been a case in point.
26. We may shortly note that Friedman and Hayek clashed on the issue of indexation, too. Friedman advocated it first for eliminating some of the incentives for the governments' pursuit of inflation from the system, e.g., indexing the tax system and introducing indexed government bonds, and second for easing the adjustment process of disinflation. Hayek criticized that inasmuch as indexation facilitated living with inflation it undermined at the same time

the incentives to combat it. See Friedman (1974), and Hayek (2022 [1978a], 345–346, 353), (1999 [1978b], 184–186).

27. In particular, the main candidates were the aggregates M1 (cash and demand deposits), M2 (M1 plus time deposits), or M3 (M2 plus savings deposits). Friedman (1969 [1968], 109) maintained that it was important to choose a definite monetary target but was rather agnostic on which one to prefer.
28. See Poole (1970) as the classical piece on the optimal monetary instrument.
29. See the summary in Caldwell and Klausinger (2022, 264–267).
30. In his "recantation" Hayek (2022 [1978a], 356) stated that he "would certainly endeavour to prevent a threatening actual deflation … with all suitable means, and would announce that I intend to do so."
31. Apart from Hayek, Mises and Robbins might have been the targets of Friedman's criticism.
32. See the reference above to Friedman and Schwartz (1963, chap. 7).
33. See Friedman (1969 [1967]), in particular, 89–93, and his reference to a letter from Hayek, 88n7.
34. Hayek (1975b, 16) offered as an example the historical experience with Britain's Banking Act of 1844, which limited the amount of bank notes issued; soon after its enactment it became necessary to break the rigid limits in order to prevent a financial panic. Friedman (in a letter to Hayek, Sept 11, 1975) responded that in this case the choice of the aggregate (that did *not* include deposits), not the rule itself, had been wrong.
35. See, e.g., Obstfeld and Taylor (1998).
36. At the Bellagio group meetings, Gottfried Haberler and Fritz Machlup, two Austrian-born economists with strong liberal credentials, were pivotal in furthering the idea of flexible exchange rates. See Triffin (1978).
37. This draws on Hayek's statements on international monetary systems (2022 [1978a], 351–352, 358, 363–364, 372–373), and (1999 [1978b], 207–209).
38. Of course, in the end, Hayek saw the introduction of competing currencies as the preferable alternative to a reconstruction of the international monetary system.
39. See, e.g., Boettke (2021, 19–21).

# REFERENCES

## Writings by Friedrich August Hayek

*CW-FAH*: *The Collected Works of F. A. Hayek*. Series edited by W. W. Bartley, Stephen Kresge, and Bruce Caldwell. Chicago, IL: University of Chicago Press; London: Routledge.

1931. *Prices and Production*. London: Routledge. Reprinted in Hayek 2012a, pp. 167–283.

1934. Capital and Industrial Fluctuations: A Reply to a Criticism. *Econometrica* 2, pp. 152–167. Reprinted in Hayek 2012b, pp. 186–205.

1937. *Monetary Nationalism and International Stability*. London: Longmans, Green (The Graduate Institute of International Studies, Geneva). Reprinted in Hayek 1999, pp. 37–99.

1944, Apr 30. Good and Bad Unemployment Policies. *The Sunday Times*, p. 4. Reprinted in Hayek 2022, pp. 465–468.

1946, July 18. Full Employment Illusions. *The Commercial and Financial Chronicle*, 164(4508), p. 372.

1950. Full Employment, Planning and Inflation. *Institute of Public Affairs Review*, 4, pp. 174–184. Reprinted in Hayek 2022, pp. 200–209.

1958. Inflation resulting from the downward inflexibility of wages, in Committee for Economic Development (ed.), *Problems of United States Economic Development*. New York: Committee for Economic Development, vol. 1, pp. 147–152. Reprinted in Hayek 2022, pp. 210–214.

1959, Mar 19. Inflation and Welfare State-ism. *The Commercial and Financial Chronicle,* 189(5830): pp. 5, 31.

1960. *The Constitution of Liberty*. Chicago, IL: University of Chicago Press. Reprinted in Hayek 2011.

1975a. *Full Employment at any Price?* IEA Occasional Paper, Volume 45. London: Institute of Economic Affairs.

1975b. *A Discussion with Friedrich von Hayek: Held at the American Enterprise Institute*. AEI Domestic Affairs Studies, Volume 39. Washington, DC: American Enterprise Institute for Public Policy Research.

1976. *The Denationalisation of Money: An Analysis of the Theory and Practice of Concurrent Currencies*. IEA Hobart Paper Special, volume 70, 1st edition. London: Institute of Economic Affairs.

1978a. The campaign against Keynesian inflation, in *New Studies in Philosophy, Politics, Economics and the History of Ideas*. London: Routledge & Kegan Paul, pp. 191–231. Reprinted in Hayek 2022, pp. 341–382.

1978b. *The Denationalisation of Money – The Argument Refined: An Analysis of the Theory and Practice of Concurrent Currencies* IEA Hobart Paper Special, volume 70, 2nd edition. London: Institute of Economic Affairs. Reprinted in Hayek 1999, chap. 4.

1980, Mar 5. Monetarism and Hyper-inflation. *The Times*, p. 17. Reprinted in Hayek 2022, chap. 31, pt. 31.

1980, Mar 27. How to Deal with Inflation. *The Times*, p. 16. Reprinted in Hayek 2022, chap. 31, pt. 32.

1980, June 13. A Testing Time for Monetarism. *The Times*, p. 13. Reprinted in Hayek 2022, chap. 31, pt. 34.

1983. Nobel Prize-Winning Economist. Edited by Armen Alchian. Transcript of an interview conducted in 1978 under the auspices of the Oral History Program, University Library, UCLA, 1983. Oral History transcript no. 300/224, Department of Special Collections, Charles E. Young Research Library, UCLA.

1994. *Hayek on Hayek: An Autobiographical Dialogue*. Edited by Stephen Kresge and Leif Wenar. London: Routledge.

1999. *Good Money, Part II: The Standard*. Edited by Stephen Kresge. *CW-FAH*, 6.

2011. *The Constitution of Liberty: The Definitive Edition*. Edited by Ronald Hamowy. *CW-FAH*, 17.

2012a. *Business Cycles, Part I*. Edited by Hansjoerg Klausinger. *CW-FAH, 7.*

2012b. *Business Cycles, Part II*. Edited by Hansjoerg Klausinger. *CW-FAH*, 8.

2022. *Essays on Liberalism and the Economy*. Edited by Paul Lewis. *CW-FAH*, 18.

## Writings by Other Authors


Barro R. J., Gordon D. B. (1983). A Positive Theory of Monetary Policy in a Natural Rate Model. *Journal of Political Economy*, 91, pp. 589–610.

Boettke P. (2021). The battle of ideas: Economics and the struggle for a better world, in Boettke P. (ed.), *The Struggle for a Better World*. Arlington, VA: Mercatus Center, pp. 19–40.

Boianovsky M. (2020). The Brazilian Connection in Milton Friedman's 1967 Presidential Address and 1976 Nobel Lecture. *History of Political Economy,* 52, pp. 367–396.

Burns J. (2023). *Milton Friedman: The Last Conservative*. New York, NY: Farra, Straus and Girou.

Cagan P. (1956). The monetary dynamics of hyperinflation, in Friedman M. (ed.), *Studies in the Quantity Theory of Money*. Chicago, IL: University of Chicago Press, pp. 25–117.

Caldwell B., Klausinger H. (2022). *Hayek: A Life, 1899–1950*. Chicago, IL: University of Chicago Press.

Fischer S. (1977). Long-Term Contracts, Rational Expectations, and the Optimal Money Supply Rule. *Journal of Political Economy* 95, pp. 191–205.

Friedman M. (1953). *Essays in Positive Economics*. Chicago, IL: University of Chicago Press.

Friedman M. (1956). The quantity theory of money – a restatement, in Friedman M. (ed.), *Studies in the Quantity Theory of Money*. Chicago, IL: University of Chicago Press, pp. 3–24. Reprinted in Friedman 1969, pp. 51–68.

Friedman M. (1959). *A Program for Monetary Stability*. New York, NY: Fordham University Press.

Friedman M. (1961). The Lag in Effect of Monetary Policy. *Journal of Political Economy,* 69, pp. 447–466. Reprinted in Friedman 1969, pp. 237–260.

Friedman M. (1967). The Monetary Theory and Policy of Henry Simons. *Journal of Law and Economics,* 10, pp. 1–13. Reprinted in Friedman 1969, pp. 81–94.

Friedman M. (1968). The Role of Monetary Theory. *American Economic Review* 58, pp. 1–17. Reprinted in Friedman 1969, pp. 95–110.

Friedman M. (1969). *The Optimum Quantity of Money and Other Essays*. Chicago, IL: University of Chicago Press.

Friedman M. (1970). *The Counter-Revolution in Monetary Theory*. First Wincott Memorial Lecture. London: Institute of Economic Affairs.

Friedman M. (1971). *A Theoretical Framework for Monetary Analysis*. New York, NY: Columbia University Press. Reprinted in Gordon R. J. (ed.) 1974, pp. 1–62.

Friedman M. (1972). Comments on the Critics. *Journal of Political Economy* 80, pp. 906–950. Reprinted in Gordon R. J. (ed.) 1974, pp. 132–177.

Friedman M. (1974). *Monetary Correction: A Proposal for Escalator Clauses to Reduce the Costs of Ending Inflation*. IEA Occasional Paper, Volume 41. London: Institute of Economic Affairs.

Friedman M. (1987). Monetary policy: Tactics versus strategy, in Dorn J. A., Schwartz A. J. (eds.), *The Search for Stable Money*. Chicago, IL: University of Chicago Press, pp. 361–382.

Friedman M. (1993). The 'Plucking Model' of Business Cycles Revisited. *Economic Inquiry,* 31, pp. 171–177.

Friedman M., Schwartz A. J. (1963). *A Monetary History of the United States, 1867–1960*. Chicago, IL: University of Chicago Press.

Goodhart C. (1981). Problems of monetary management: The U.K. experience, in Courakis A. (ed.), *Inflation, Depression, and Economic Policy in the West.* London: Mansell, and Oxford: Alexandrine Press, pp. 111–143.

Goodhart C. (1989). The Conduct of Monetary Policy. *Economic Journal,* 99, pp. 293–346.

Gordon R. J. (ed.) (1974). *Milton Friedman's Monetary Framework: A Debate with His Critics.* Chicago, IL: University of Chicago Press.

Institute of Economic Affairs (IEA) (ed.) (1974). *Inflation: Causes, Conseqences, Cures. Discourses on the Debate between the Monetary and the Trade Union Interpretations.* London: Institute of Economic Affairs.

Jay P. (1974). Do trade unions matter? in Institute of Economic Affairs (ed.), 1974, London: Institute of Economic Affairs. pp. 25–50.

Johnson H. G. (1971). The Keynesian Revolution and the Monetarist Counter-Revolution. *American Economic Review,* 61, pp. 1–14.

Keynes J. M. (1973). *The General Theory of Employment, Interest and Money (The Collected Writings of John Maynard Keynes),* Volume 7. Cambridge, MA: Cambridge University Press; London: Macmillan for the Royal Economic Society.

Klausinger H. (2024). Currency Competition: Hayek's Campaign for Good Money. Typescript.

Kydland F. E., Prescott E. C. (1977). Rules Rather Than Discretion: The Inconsistency of Optimal Plans. *Journal of Political Economy,* 85, pp. 473–491.

Laidler D. (1974). The crisis – when and why did it start? in Institute of Economic Affairs (ed.), *Inflation: Causes, Conseqences, Cures. Discourses on the Debate between the Monetary and the Trade Union Interpretations.* London: Institute of Economic Affairs, pp. 51–70.

Lucas R. E., Rapping L. E. (1970). Real wages, employment and inflation, in Phelps E. S. (ed.), *Microeconomic Foundations of Inflation and Employment Theory.* New York, NY: Norton, pp. 257–305.

Machlup F. (ed.) (1976). *Essays on Hayek.* New York, NY: New York University Press.

Modigliani F. (1977). The Monetarist Controversy or, Should We Forsake Stabilization Policies? *American Economic Review,* 67(2), pp. 1–19.

Obstfeld M., Taylor A. M. (1998). The great depression as a watershed: International capital mobility over the long run, in Bordo M., Goldin C., White E. (eds.), *The Defining Moment. The Great Depression and the American Economy in the Twentieth Century.* Chicago, IL: University of Chicago Press, pp. 353–402.

Phelps E. S. (1970). Money wage dynamics and labor market equilibrium, in Phelps E. S. (ed.), *Microeconomic Foundations of Inflation and Employment Theory.* New York, NY: Norton, pp. 124–166.

Phillips A. W. H. (1958). The Relation between Unemployment and the Rate of Change of Money Wage Rates in the United Kingdom, 1861–1957. *Economica,* 25, pp. 283–299.

Poole W. (1970). Optimal Choice of Monetary Policy Instruments in a Simple Stochastic Macro Model. *Quarterly Journal of Economics,* 84, pp. 197–216.

Rees A. (1970). The Phillips Curve as a Menu for Policy Choice. *Economica,* 37, pp. 227–238.

Samuelson P. A., Solow R. M. (1960). Analytical Aspects of Anti-inflation Policy. *American Economic Review,* 50, pp. 177–194.

Shenfield A. (1976). Scientism and the study of society, in Machlup 1976, pp. 61–72.

Simons H. C. (1936). Rules versus Authorities in Monetary Policy. *Journal of Political Economy,* 44, pp. 1–30.

Tavlas G. S. (2023) *The Monetarists: The Making of the Chicago Monetary Tradition, 1927–1960.* Chicago, IL and London: University of Chicago Press.
Triffin R. (1978). The impact of the Bellagio Group on world monetary reform, in Dreyer J. (ed.), *Breadth and Depth of Economics: Fritz Machlup – the Man and His Ideas*. Toronto: Lexington Books, pp. 145–158.

## Archival Source

FAHP = Friedrich A. von Hayek Papers, Hoover Institution Archives, Stanford University, CA.

# 8. In search of Hayek's theory of entrepreneurship?[1]

**Per L. Bylund**

## INTRODUCTION

Entrepreneurship plays a central role in Austrian economic theory (Bylund, 2019, 2020b; see also Klein and Bylund, 2014) and Austrian economists have theorized on the entrepreneurship function for as long as there has been an Austrian approach. In his *Principles of Economics* (2007), the founding document of the Austrian School, Carl Menger places the entrepreneur at the center of market production and notes that the "functions [that] are included in this so-called entrepreneurial activity" include "obtaining *information*," "economic *calculation*," "the *act of will*," and "*supervision* of ... the production plan" (Menger, 2007, p. 160, emphases in original). Second-generation Austrian economist Friedrich von Wieser, who recognized entrepreneurs for their leadership ability (e.g., Wieser, 1927), frequently references entrepreneurship in his works (McCaffrey et al., 2024). Similarly, Ludwig von Mises (e.g., 1998) frequently comments on entrepreneurship, both as a general category of action (uncertainty-bearing) and as the driving force of the market (Bylund, 2020a) in his *magnum opus* and beyond. Ludwig Lachmann (e.g., 1978) places the entrepreneur at the core of capital theory as the cause of the "ever changing" capital combinations (cf. Bylund, 2015). These are only a selection of noteworthy examples of how entrepreneurship has been (and continues to be) an important component of Austrian economic theorizing. However, despite this, there were no separate treatments of entrepreneurship theory *per se* until Israel Kirzner's *Competition and Entrepreneurship* (1973), published over a century after Menger's treatise.

Conspicuously, Friedrich von Hayek, by far the most well-known of Austrian economists both within the economics discipline and among the general public,[2] placed comparatively little emphasis on the economic role of the entrepreneur.[3] He also did not publish separately on entrepreneurship theory. Despite making many important contributions to production and capital theory (e.g.,

Hayek, 1931, 1941), unlike Lachmann, Hayek did not explicitly place the entrepreneur at the center of the market's productive dynamic. In his groundbreaking work on knowledge and the market as a spontaneous order (e.g., Hayek, 1945, 1978), Hayek appears to treat entrepreneurs as businessmen (or even firms) that respond to rather than cause change (cf. Garrison and Kirzner, 1987). Yet, as an economist in the Austrian tradition, Hayek must certainly, like those before and after him, have considered the entrepreneur's key role in the market process. Thus, should he not have had some entrepreneurial function in mind – a *theory* of entrepreneurship, albeit implicit – when developing and contributing to other parts of economic theory?[4]

It is easy to assume that the answer is "yes," but surprisingly little ink has been spilled on attempting to uncover Hayek's implied economic theory of entrepreneurship. A notable exception, Ebner (2005) argues that there is such a Hayekian theory, but that it is not explicit because Hayek's system did not require it to be explicated further than its "outline" as "a potential":

> Hayek does not present a distinct theory of entrepreneurship with an elaborate apparatus of behavioural arguments. Instead, both his theory of the market process and the theory of cultural evolution focus on the coordinative impact of rules, which derive their functional importance from the subjectivity of knowledge as well as from the related complexity of evolving socio-economic systems. All of this is outlined in a mode of reasoning that approaches entrepreneurship in terms of a potential which does not require further analytical efforts. (Ebner, 2005, p. 146)

Ebner continues:

> Still, entrepreneurship plays a major role in Hayek's approach, highlighting search, experimentation and discovery as crucial factors in the stimulation of economic change – which is identified as the constitutive problem of economic theory. Accordingly, entrepreneurship is viewed as the decisive force in the growth of civilisation, interpreted as a historical process that coincides with cultural evolution. (Ebner, 2005, p. 146)

Unfortunately, Ebner offers little evidence in support of those "crucial factors" of Hayek's implicit entrepreneurship theory and is unsuccessful in explicating Hayek's theory as it relates to the market process. He focuses instead on the role entrepreneurship plays in cultural evolution and relies predominantly on what Hayek wrote in works outside the bounds of economics like *Law, Legislation, and Liberty* (Hayek, 1973, 1976a) and *The Fatal Conceit* (Hayek, 1988), neither of which is a work primarily on economics or market process.

Hayek's scholarly contributions are vast and in several different disciplines: economics, psychology (Hayek, 1976b), legal theory, and so on. His work also suggests that Hayek continued to develop his views on science overall, including the appropriate methodology for social sciences (Hutchison, 1981). We are here interested only in his contributions to economic theory, on which there is voluminous scholarship attempting to interpret and extend Hayek's legacy. But it stops short of discovering or uncovering his theory of entrepreneurship and at best relates Hayek's contributions to or pairs it with other entrepreneurship theories (primarily Kirzner's) (e.g., Garello, 2002; Horwitz, 2010; Minniti and Koppl, 1999). As such, Hayek's economic entrepreneurship theory, if any, remains implicit.

This chapter constitutes a first attempt to identify and uncover Hayek's entrepreneurship theory based on his contributions to economic theory. Rather than surveying the full extent of Hayek's work, a massive undertaking that will be left for future scholarship, or even all of his work on a specific specialization within economics, we here present preliminary findings using several of Hayek's main and seemingly most relevant works on economics and market process. The works largely address Hayek's contributions relating to production, capital theory, and competition, economic phenomena in which entrepreneurship is typically recognized as a main function. Specifically, we consider in chronological order the following works:

- *Prices and Production* (Hayek, 1931)
- "Economics and Knowledge" published in *Economica* (Hayek, 1937)
- *The Pure Theory of Capital* (Hayek, 1941)
- "The Use of Knowledge in Society" published in the *American Economic Review* (Hayek, 1945)
- "The Meaning of Competition" published in *Individualism and Economic Order* (Hayek, 1948)
- "Competition as a Discovery Procedure" published in *New Studies in Philosophy, Politics, Economics, and the History of Ideas* (Hayek, 1978).

Each of the aforementioned works will be discussed separately in chronological order. The respective sections below use block quotes accompanied by brief commentary on how those quotes relate to entrepreneurship and how they may, therefore, be indicative of Hayek's implicit entrepreneurship theory. It is expected that these discussions can serve as a starting point for future work aiming to reconstruct Hayek's entrepreneurship theory in greater detail.

## PRICES AND PRODUCTION

Hayek's *Prices and Production* (1931) collects his series of lectures presented at the London School of Economics in 1931. Invited by Lionel Robbins on Mises's recommendation (Hülsmann, 2007), the lectures focused on and elaborated on Hayek's prior work on the trade cycle. Below are quoted the sections from the book that are most related to entrepreneurship.

Hayek makes clear that entrepreneurs in the market economy are responsible for generating and determining how the market's capital structure changes over time. Acting within specific stages of the production structure, entrepreneurs decide whether and to what degree they reinvest in the production capital to maintain productive capability in pursuit of profits:

> ...whether the structure of production remains the same depends entirely upon whether entrepreneurs find it profitable to re-invest the usual proportion of the return from the sale of the product of their respective stages of production in turning out intermediate goods of the same sort. Whether this is profitable, again, depends upon the prices obtained for the product of this particular stage of production on the one hand and on the prices paid for the original means of production and for the intermediate products taken from the preceding stage of production on the other. (Hayek, 1931, pp. 48–49)

As credit expansion lowers interest rates and sets in motion the trade cycle, the additional money available allows entrepreneurs to shift investments toward earlier production stages even though consumers do not refrain from consumption. This causes prices of higher-order goods to rise:

> The reason why forced saving will always lead to a subsequent increase in the money available for the purchase of consumers' goods, is fairly obvious and will probably not be contested. Entrepreneurs are in this case enabled to attract factors of production from later to earlier stages, not by a corresponding transfer of funds from consumers' to producers' goods, but by additional money handed to them. This means that they will bid up the prices of these factors without there being a corresponding fall in the prices of other factors. (Hayek, 1931, p. 146)

The rising prices in higher-order goods make it impossible for entrepreneurs to reinvest in their productive capital to the degree necessary to maintain production at the present level. Whereas their reported profits increase, this is a result of prices increasing rapidly and not increased real value production:

> Once this stage [of rapidly rising prices] is reached, such a policy will soon begin to defeat its own ends. While the mechanism of forced saving continues to operate, the general rise in prices will make it increasingly more difficult, and finally practically impossible, for entrepreneurs to maintain their existing capital intact. Paper profits will be computed and consumed, the failure to reproduce the existing capital will become quantitatively more and more important, and will finally exceed the additions made by forced saving.
>
> It is important in this connection to remember that the entrepreneur necessarily and inevitably thinks of his capital in terms of money, and that, under changing conditions, he has no other way of thinking of its quantity than in value terms, which practically means in terms of money. But even if, for a time, he resists the temptation of paper profits (and experience teaches us that this is extremely unlikely) and computes his costs in terms of some index number, the rate of depreciation has only

> to become fast enough, and such an expedient will be ineffective. (Hayek, 1931, pp. 151–152)

Whereas the entrepreneur is discussed in *Prices and Production* and has a central role in the progression of the trade cycle, Hayek does not specify this function further than necessary for his purposes. Consequently, we learn that entrepreneurs make decisions about their productive capital in pursuit of profits. During the trade cycle, the market's time-structure of production changes in a predictable fashion because entrepreneurs respond to prices when they make their (re)investment decisions.

## ECONOMICS AND KNOWLEDGE

In his article "Economics and Knowledge," published in 1937 in the London School of Economics' in-house journal *Economica*, Hayek explores the role of knowledge in economic processes.

Production is here discussed in terms of producers' (or, as he put it in *Prices and Production*, entrepreneurs') production *plans*, which are based on available market data. Hayek points out that the data on which any one plan is based are in fact the production plans of others – the expectations that other producers will behave in some specific way. For this reason, markets tend to consist of numerous compatible production plans:

> ...since some of the "data" on which any one person will base his plans will be the expectation that other people will act in a particular way, it is essential for the compatibility of the different plans that the plans of the one contain exactly those actions which form the data for the plans of the other since some of the "data" on which any one person will base his plans will be the expectation that other people will act in a particular way, it is essential for the compatibility of the different plans that the plans of the one contain exactly those actions which form the data for the plans of the other since some of the "data" on which any one person will base his plans will be the expectation that other people will act in a particular way, it is essential for the compatibility of the different plans that the plans of the one contain exactly those actions which form the data for the plans of the other. (Hayek, 1937, p. 38)

Equilibrium, Hayek notes, must be understood as all producers (entrepreneurs) having formed correct expectations about each other's production plans:

> ...the concept of equilibrium merely means that the foresight of the different members of the society is in a special sense correct. It must be correct in the sense that every person's plan is based on the expectation of just those actions of other people which those other people intend to perform, and that all these plans are based on the expectation of the same set of external facts, so that under certain conditions nobody will have any reason to change his plans. (Hayek, 1937, p. 41)

Consequently, a tendency toward equilibrium is established because producers (entrepreneurs) learn and thus their production plans become "more and more into agreement":

> ...the assertion that a tendency towards equilibrium exists [...] can hardly mean anything but that under certain conditions the knowledge and intentions of the different members of society are supposed to come more and more into agreement, or, to put the same thing in less general and less exact but more concrete terms, that the expectations of the people and particularly of the entrepreneurs will become more and more correct. (Hayek, 1937, p. 44)

The problem of knowledge, which keeps the market process from quickly closing in on equilibrium, is in part embodied in prices, but the more important knowledge problem lies in understanding the value of goods and under what circumstances they have such value:

> ...price expectations and even the knowledge of current prices are only a very small section of the problem of knowledge as I see it. The wider aspect of the problem of knowledge with which I am concerned is the knowledge of the basic fact of how the different commodities can be obtained and used, and under what conditions they are actually obtained and used, that is, the general question of why the subjective data to the different persons correspond to the objective facts. Our problem of knowledge here is just the existence of this correspondence which in much of current equilibrium analysis is simply assumed to exist. (Hayek, 1937, p. 50)

Hayek here introduces two issues important for understanding the market process. First, that the market's production apparatus consists of entrepreneurs' production plans that must be compatible with other production plans in order to be successful and profitable. Entrepreneurs are expected to attempt to adjust their production plans as they acquire more data, by which is meant that they learn about the plans of other entrepreneurs, and the market equilibrates to the degree production plans become inter-compatible. Second, every production plan suffers from the problem of knowledge, that is, why there is correspondence between subjective data of different persons and objective facts.

## THE PURE THEORY OF CAPITAL

In *The Pure Theory of Capital* (1941), Hayek analyzes in detail the dynamics of the capital structure and thus elaborates on and contributes to Austrian capital theory. Capital theory constitutes an important basis for the Austrian response to and rejection of Keynesian theory. Hayek's detailed discussion also provides a more elaborated basis for understanding the trade cycle per the Austrian Business Cycle Theory (ABCT).

We noted above that Hayek sees the entrepreneur as a core player in determining the market's capital structure, which suggests that the dynamics in capital theory, much as Lachmann asserted, are fundamentally entrepreneurial. Consequently, we should expect to find discussions on what the entrepreneur does, in response to what events, and with what intentions.

Again explaining the market's overall production structure in terms of production plans and equilibrium as the complete compatibility of entrepreneurs' plans, the role of the entrepreneur is to revise production plans when conditions "compel" him to do so. When an entrepreneur learns that factors are different than expected, he revises his production plan in response to this new knowledge:

> ...if we want to predict at all, it must be on the basis of the plans which entrepreneurs are likely to make in the light of their present knowledge, and of an analysis of the factors which in the course of time will determine whether they will be able to carry out these plans or whether they will have to alter them. It seems natural to begin by constructing, as an intellectual tool, a fictitious state under which these plans are in complete correspondence without, however, asking whether this state will ever, or can ever, come about. For it is only by contrast with this imaginary state, which serves as a kind of foil, that we are able to predict what will happen if entrepreneurs attempt to carry out any given set of plans. The description of the equilibrium position in this sense is at the same time a description of the mutual interdependence of the decisions of different entrepreneurs.
>
> The direction in which an entrepreneur will have to revise his plans will depend on the direction in which events prove to differ from his expectations. The statement of the conditions under which individual plans will be compatible is therefore implicitly a statement of what will happen if they are not compatible.
>
> It will be seen that this extension of the equilibrium concept provides the bridge from equilibrium analysis to the explanation in terms of causal sequences, since it is designed to elucidate the factors which will compel entrepreneurs to change their plans analysis and to help us to understand the way in which their plans will have to be changed. (Hayek, 1941, pp. 22–23)

Hayek reiterates what we learned above about equilibrium, stating that equilibrium can be understood as the full "harmonization" of production plans:

> In any given situation there will be one (and in most instances only one) way in which the plans of the various entrepreneurs can be made to harmonise with one another and with the preferences of the consumers. The use of the equilibrium method here then means constructing an imaginary state in which the plans of the different people (entrepreneurs and consumers generally) are so adjusted to one another that each individual will be able to sell or buy exactly those quantities of commodities which he has been planning to sell or buy. (Hayek, 1941, p. 26)

Entrepreneurs make production plans in great detail and for "fairly long periods." These plans are made in real rather than monetary terms. Assuming no changes will be necessary, entrepreneurs have little use for money. However, as entrepreneurs learn that their expectations may be incorrect, they are compelled to revise their plans. At this point, they also have a need to hold money in order to effect the necessary revisions:

> The analysis of the relations between the production plans of different entrepreneurs must necessarily proceed in what is known as "real terms". If we assume – as we must if we are to investigate the compatibility of the different plans – that the entrepreneurs make definite and detailed plans for fairly long periods, there is indeed little room for money in the picture at all, except as "mere counters" which stand for definite quantities of particular commodities. In fact, so long as we assume entrepreneurs to decide every detail in advance in the certain expectation that they will be able to adhere to all their plans, the need for holding money almost vanishes. (Hayek, 1941, p. 29)

In a capitalist economy, circumstances may compel the entrepreneur to not only revise the production plan but also to reconsider investing in it:

> Sooner or later in the course of the process some entrepreneur will find that in consequence of this change in circumstances it is no longer profitable either to invest the same amount in equipment of the kind he already possesses or to invest anything at all in equipment of that same kind. Wherever under the changed conditions the return obtainable from a given type of equipment, which he can buy at a price which only covers the prime cost of its production, is lower than the returns which could be obtained elsewhere, the owner of the existing equipment of this sort will find it in his interest to re-invest in capital goods of a different sort. (Hayek, 1941, p. 263)

In response to increased savings, entrepreneurs are compelled to shift their investments away from the production of consumption goods to higher-order goods, which causes a reduction in present consumption goods production but increases future consumption goods production:

> Let us consider what kinds of investments will appear most advantageous to entrepreneurs if they expect that in the near future there will for some time be a shift of demand away from consumers' goods and towards capital goods generally. We shall assume that the entrepreneurs regard a present increase of saving as an indication that, for a considerable time to come, saving and investing will continue at the same rate as present. I am deliberately speaking here of entrepreneurs in general, and not merely of savers or of those people who have the newly saved funds to invest, because, as we shall see, the decisions of all entrepreneurs will be affected by the expectation of future savings. Since it is assumed that the shift of demand is foreseen and that there is in consequence time to adjust supplies, there is no reason to conclude that there will immediately be a corresponding change in relative prices. And it will be less question-begging if we describe the general situation by saying that the expected demand curves for consumers' goods and capital goods in general are being shifted, the former to the left and the latter to the right.

> The main question which arises is the following: Towards what kind of capital goods will the new demand be directed, and how will the relative prices of the different resources, and the quantities produced, be affected by this change in demand? In abstract terms the situation can be described by saying that a greater potential command over consumers' goods available in the comparatively near future is offered in exchange for means to obtain consumers' goods in the more distant future. And it is reasonable to expect this to induce an expansion of production for that more distant future. (Hayek, 1941, pp. 280–281)

In *The Pure Theory of Capital*, Hayek finds that the entrepreneur acts in the economy through production plans that are revised in response to learning that conditions are different than previously expected. As such conditions primarily consist of other entrepreneurs' plans, the result of such revisions is increased plan compatibility and thus equilibration. When consumer behavior changes (or is expected to change), entrepreneurs must revise their plans accordingly and therefore bring about an overall redirection of the market's capital structure and production.

## THE USE OF KNOWLEDGE IN SOCIETY

Hayek's "The Use of Knowledge in Society" (1945), published in the *American Economic Review*, is one of his most influential works in economics.[5] The article addresses the fundamental problem of how to utilize dispersed knowledge to make efficient economic decisions and includes the oft-quoted phrase "the knowledge of the particular circumstances of time and place" (Hayek, 1945, p. 521) to denote the non-scientific, unorganized knowledge that must nevertheless be included in rational, economizing decision-making.

Hayek here further develops the "knowledge problem" that he discussed in prior writings (see especially the discussion on "Economics and Knowledge" above) as based on dispersed and non-aggregable knowledge. The economic problem is stated as overcoming this lack of knowledge so that the economy overall can find in what ways resources can be used in the most economizing manner possible:

> The peculiar character of the problem of a rational economic order is determined precisely by the fact that the knowledge of the circumstances of which we must make use never exists in concentrated or integrated form, but solely as the dispersed bits of incomplete and frequently contradictory knowledge which all the separate individuals possess. The economic problem of society is thus not merely a problem of how to allocate "given" resources – if "given" is taken to mean given to a single mind which deliberately solves the problem set by these "data." It is rather a problem of how to secure the best use of resources known to any of the members of society, for ends whose relative importance only these individuals know. (Hayek, 1945, pp. 519–20)

Hayek explains how the price mechanism communicates relevant information that allows entrepreneurs to use resources in an economizing way. In fact, Hayek argues, entrepreneurs need not know more than what the prices communicate in order to make accurate, economizing decisions regarding resource uses:

> Assume that somewhere in the world a new opportunity for the use of some raw material, say tin, has arisen, or that one of the sources of supply of tin has been eliminated. It does not matter for our purpose – and it is very significant that it does not matter which of these two causes has made tin more scarce. All that the users of tin need to know is that some of the tin they used to consume is now more profitably employed elsewhere, and that in consequence they must economize tin. (Hayek, 1945, p. 526)

Hayek emphasizes that the lack of specific knowledge does not hamper the ability of the market process to appropriately assign resources to productive uses. In fact, as prices increase (fall) they instruct entrepreneurs to use less (more) of a resource, thereby pushing market production toward a more economizing use of resources. This allows the market to adjust to new knowledge long before it could possibly have been codified, collected, and aggregated:

> The marvel is that in a case like that of a scarcity of one raw material, without an order being issued, without more than perhaps a handful of people knowing the cause, tens of thousands of people whose identity could not be ascertained by months of investigation, are made to use the material or its products more sparingly; i.e., they move in the right direction. This is enough of a marvel even if, in a constantly changing world, not all will hit it off so perfectly that their profit rates will always be maintained at the same constant or "normal" level. (Hayek, 1945, p. 527)

The market's ability to correctly adjust to knowledge before it is widely available is based on and due to the price mechanism, which through price signals directs and effectuates production. Entrepreneurs, seeking to earn (if not maximize) profits, respond to changes in market prices by economizing more on higher-priced and less on lower-priced resources, which without central direction, as if directed by an "invisible hand" (to use Adam Smith's well-known phrase), brings about overall market coordination of production plans.

## THE MEANING OF COMPETITION

The core of the essay "The Meaning of Competition" (Hayek, 1948), published in *Individualism and Economic Order*, was originally delivered as the Stafford Little Lecture at Princeton University in May 1946. The essay elaborates on Hayek's knowledge perspective of the market and argues that competition, acting under free market prices, is a mechanism for uncovering information about costs.

The market process is here understood as the result of individuals learning about changing circumstances and therefore making adjustments to their production plans:

> ...a process which necessarily involves continuous changes in the data for the different individuals ... the causal factor enters here in the form of the acquisition of new knowledge by the different individuals or of changes in their data brought about by the contacts between them. (Hayek, 1948, p. 94)

The main issue that competition within the market process solves is to figure out how to most cheaply produce to satisfy consumers' wants. To do this requires adapting production plans to new knowledge, that is, circumstances that were not accurately predicted:

> The real problem in all this is not whether we will get given commodities or services at given marginal costs but mainly by what commodities and services the needs of the people can be most cheaply satisfied. The solution of the economic problem of society is in this respect always a voyage of exploration into the unknown, an attempt to discover new ways of doing things better than they have been done before. This must always remain so as long as there are any economic problems to be solved at all, because all economic problems are created by unforeseen changes which require adaptation. Only what we have not foreseen and provided for requires new decisions. If no such adaptations were required, if at any moment we knew that all change had stopped and things would forever go on exactly as they are now, there would be no more questions of the use of resources to be solved. (Hayek, 1948, pp. 100–101)

It is not required of entrepreneurs that they cut prices to the extent that they reduce their production costs. In fact, by adjusting their production to the new cost situation, entrepreneurs set in motion a process toward overall adaptation of market production enacted by competition:

> A person, who possesses the exclusive knowledge or skill which enables him to reduce the cost of production of a commodity by 50 per cent still renders an enormous service to society if he enters its production and reduces its price by only 25 per cent-not only through that price reduction but also through his additional saving of cost. But it is only through competition that we can assume that these possible savings of cost will be achieved. (Hayek, 1948, p. 101)

Market adaptation to new knowledge happens so quickly, thanks to the profit motive of competing entrepreneurs, that we as observers often disregard what takes place during this process:

> The best ways of producing the commodity, its character and uses, are most of the time known to nearly the same degree to all members of the market. The knowledge of any important change spreads so rapidly and the adaptation to it is so soon effected that we usually simply disregard what happens during these short transition periods and confine ourselves to comparing the two states of near-equilibrium which exist before and after them. But it is during this short and neglected interval that the forces of competition operate and become visible. (Hayek, 1948, p. 103)

Only when the adaptation process is slow compared to learning new knowledge, as may be the case in regulated markets, will the market experience continuous competition:

> It is only in a market where adaptation is slow compared with the rate of change that the process of competition is in continuous operation. And though the reason why adaptation is slow may be that competition is weak, e.g., because there are special obstacles to entry into the trade, or because of some other factors of the character of natural monopolies, slow adaptation does by no means necessarily mean weak competition. (Hayek, 1948, p. 103)

Competition is the adaptation process from one state of the market to the next. This is brought about by entrepreneurs acting on new knowledge, which allows them to take advantage of lower costs of production. Their doing so, and thus gaining competitive advantage and earning higher profits, incentivizes other entrepreneurs to make similar adjustments to their production plans. As a result, market production is quickly adjusted to new knowledge. This process is typically swift and leads to the market finding a new near-equilibrium state. However, it is the process and not the states that matter for understanding the market.

## COMPETITION AS A DISCOVERY PROCEDURE

Originally a 1968 lecture to the Philadelphia Society and later at the University of Kiel and published in German in the *Kieler Vorträge*, a translation to English with the title "Competition as a Discovery Procedure" (Hayek, 1978) was published as a chapter in Hayek's *New Studies in Philosophy, Politics, Economics, and the History of Ideas*. The essay was later published in the *Quarterly Journal of Austrian Economics* in a new translation by Marcellus S. Snow (Hayek, 2002). The quotes below are from this more recent translation.

Hayek here argues that competition is specifically a procedure for discovering facts, which are not readily available to actors and that become known through economic action:

> ...it is useful to recall that *wherever* we make use of competition, this can only be justified by our *not* knowing the essential circumstances that determine the

> behavior of the competitors. [...] I wish now to consider competition systematically as a procedure for discovering facts which, if the procedure did not exist, would remain unknown or at least would not be used. (Hayek, 2002, p. 9)

The specifics of scarcity are unknown until they are discovered through competition between entrepreneurs seeking to produce for consumers:

> ...market theory often prevents access to a true understanding of competition by proceeding from the assumption of a "given" quantity of scarce goods. Which goods are scarce, however, or which things are goods, or how scarce or valuable they are, is precisely one of the conditions that competition should discover: in each case it is the preliminary outcomes of the market process that inform individuals where it is worthwhile to search. Utilizing the widely diffused knowledge in a society with an advanced division of labor cannot be based on the condition that individuals know all the concrete uses that can be made of the objects in their environment. Their attention will be directed by the prices the market offers for various goods and services. (Hayek, 2002, p. 13)

The market does more than coordinate entrepreneurs' production plans, as Hayek discussed in previous works. It also directs production of goods into the hands of those entrepreneurs who can produce them most cheaply:

> ...the market's accomplishments are not exhausted in bringing about a mutual adjustment of individual plans. It also provides that every product is produced by those who can produce it more cheaply (or at least as cheaply) as anyone who does not in fact produce it, and that goods are sold at prices that are lower than those at which anyone could offer the goods who does not offer them. (Hayek, 2002, p. 15)

It is the lack of ability to perfectly forecast the future, which implies discovery of new and previously unknown facts, that necessitates adaptation of production. But it is not the fault of the one entrepreneur that their production plan appears poorly adjusted as new facts are discovered:

> ...all economic decisions are made necessary by unanticipated changes, and that the justification for using the price mechanism is solely that it shows individuals that what they have previously done, or can do now, has become more or less important, for reasons with which they have nothing to do. The adaptation of the total order of human action to changing circumstances is based on the fact that the compensation of the various services changes without taking into account of the merits or defects of those involved. (Hayek, 2002, p. 17)

Whereas prices compel entrepreneurs to adjust their production plans with respect to *what* they produce, they do not provide information about *quantities*. This information is made available only as producers' compensations (i.e., their profits) change:

> The most important function of prices, however, is that they tell us *what* we should accomplish, *not how much*. In a constantly changing world, merely maintaining a given level of welfare requires constant adjustments in how the efforts of many individuals are directed; and these will only occur when the relative compensation of these activities changes. (Hayek, 2002, p. 17)

Competition is important in developed economies in order to discover what should be produced, but it should be even more important in "underdeveloped societies" where less information about production possibilities is available:

> If even in highly developed economies competition is important primarily as a discovery procedure whereby entrepreneurs constantly search for unexploited opportunities that can also be taken advantage of by others, then this is true of course to an even greater extent as far as underdeveloped societies are concerned. I have intentionally begun by considering the problems of maintaining an order in societies in which most techniques and productive forces are generally known, but also an order that requires continuous adjustment of activities to unavoidable small changes simply to maintain the previously attained level. (Hayek, 2002, p. 18)

Whereas this essay repeats some core insights from Hayek's previous work, it also expands the scope of his discussion on knowledge in the market process in important ways. For example, he here distinguishes between the discovery of unforeseen facts that allows entrepreneurs to adapt and thus coordinate their production plans and the knowledge of appropriate production quantities as discoverable in the compensations to entrepreneurs. He also distinguishes between economies at different levels of development, suggesting that the comparatively limited knowledge available in less developed economies makes the competitive process more important. Hayek thereby suggests that the knowledge available correlates with the level of development and, possibly, that the more developed economies are better able to deal with restrictions to competition.

## HAYEK'S ENTREPRENEURSHIP

We started this chapter by discussing how core the entrepreneurship function is within Austrian economic theory and that Austrian economists have commonly discussed entrepreneurship and its implications. The previous sections show that Hayek did as well, which should be expected. However, he did so less explicitly than other leading Austrian economists.

In the block quotes provided, we can easily identify themes of Hayek's understanding of entrepreneurship. Specifically, we find the entrepreneur to be the main (or only) cause of the market's continuous coordination of production plans through adjustments made in response to unexpected changes. The entrepreneur is also both the creator and supervisor, as Menger (2007,

p. 160) would put it, of the production plans in the economy. Entrepreneurs consequently reallocate resources, primarily in response to changing information – whether in the form of objective market data like prices or subjectively understood "local" information – that require adaptation. Hayek also sees in competition an entrepreneurial process of a leader, making adjustments in accordance with new knowledge, and followers, making adjustments in part in response to the information discovered through the former's actions – responding to the changes made in the former's production plan(s). Some questions remain, however, specifically regarding entrepreneurs' new value creation and uncertainty-bearing, both of which are only indirectly addressed in Hayek's work. We will discuss each below.

## Production Plans and Responsiveness

It should be clear from what was discussed above that Hayek's main interest is the dynamics of the production structure in a market economy, specifically how it adjusts to changing circumstances. He asserts that the role of entrepreneurs is primarily in the revising of their production plans in pursuit of profits. In several of the block quotes above, Hayek notes that entrepreneurs respond to changes in prices, which "compel" them to revise their plans both regarding what is produced and how much is produced.

This description appears to comply with Menger's functions of entrepreneurial activity as "obtaining *information*," "economic *calculation*" of opportunities, "the *act of will*" to bring it about, and "*supervision* of … the production plan" (Menger, 2007, p. 160, emphasis in original). It should appear reasonable to assume that the entrepreneurial revising of a production plan may include all of these functions, especially considering how Hayek explicitly mentions how entrepreneurs in their revisions in fact respond to changes in price and other relevant information. However, Hayek only discusses the revision of production plans already in place and does not address their original creation (see further in the next section). And there may be reason to believe that Menger's entrepreneurial functions referred to the full lifecycle of the production plan as organized within a business firm. To Menger:

> The firm is an organization entrepreneurs use to design and execute time consuming production plans. It is a way for entrepreneurs to organize decisions about how to plan for an uncertain future. (McCaffrey et al., 2024, p. 9)

It is not clear that Menger by entrepreneurial activity was referring to the firm's ongoing operations. In fact, those functions imply capital ownership: the "entrepreneurial activity … can only be performed if the economizing individuals in question have at their disposal the services of large amounts of capital" (Menger, 2007, p. 172) and thus residual control.[6] Writes Menger:

> The process of transforming goods of higher order into goods of lower or first order, provided it is economic in other respects, must also always be planned and conducted, with some economic purpose in view, by an economizing individual. This individual must carry through the economic computations …, and he must actually bring the goods of higher order, including technical labor services, together (or cause them to be brought together) for the purpose of production. (Menger, 2007, pp. 159–160)

This suggests that the function of revising existing production plans may be a better fit within Menger's fourth function: the "*supervision* of the execution of the production plan so that it may be carried through as economically as possible" (Menger, 2007, p. 160). Supervision is inert unless it allows for making changes where necessary, including revising the quantities produced, the means by which production is carried out, and perhaps also the overall structure of the plan. This would then be more in line with the role of the manager, which Mises refers to as the entrepreneur's "junior partner" (Mises, 1998, p. 301) instructed to run the business within specified boundaries with a focus on earning profits (Bylund, 2018).

The evidence at hand does not allow us to draw any specific conclusions, but Hayek's consistent reference to revisions in response to new information, whether or not in the form of prices, suggests that the Hayekian entrepreneur may be more akin to a manager than an uncertainty-bearing creator of new production. In Mises's conception of (market-level) economic calculation, entrepreneurs do not merely respond to price changes but collectively *determine* them. They do this through competitive bidding for resources based on their anticipated value creation:

> The entrepreneurs, eager to earn profits, appear as bidders at an auction, as it were, in which the owners of the factors of production put up for sale land, capital goods, and labor. The entrepreneurs are eager to outdo one another by bidding higher prices than their rivals. Their offers are limited on the one hand by their anticipation of future prices of the products and on the other hand by the necessity to snatch the factors of production away from the hands of other entrepreneurs competing with them. (Mises, 1998, pp. 332–333)

This leads us to another important finding regarding Hayek's entrepreneur, which we will turn to now: new value creation under uncertainty.

## New Value Creation and Uncertainty-Bearing

Market entrepreneurship is often understood as "the intentional pursuit of new *economic* value" (Packard, 2017, p. 537; emphasis in original), which implies uncertainty-bearing. As I have put it elsewhere, "Entrepreneurship is the economic function of bearing the uncertainty of creating future goods" (Bylund, 2022b, p. 62). Among Austrian economists, Mises's conceptualization of the entrepreneur, primarily the "entrepreneur-promoter" (Bylund, 2020a), is perhaps the one most closely related to this view (Bylund, 2022a, 2024). Uncertainty and new value creation are two sides of the same coin, as one cannot attempt to produce new value (new goods) for consumers without risking failing because consumers in the future, when the good is offered for sale, may not consider the goods sufficiently valuable.

Hayek's conceptualization differs from Mises's in that the Hayekian entrepreneur is primarily described as a responsive agent – they revise their production plans *in response to new information*. This suggests that those plans are already in place rather than, as with the entrepreneur-promoter, novel production attempts with unknown outcomes. Also, whereas revisions to existing production plans may imply some uncertainty, primarily regarding the correctness (and interpretation) of the new information, this is different from the uncertainty-bearing implied in most entrepreneurship theories since Richard Cantillon (Cantillon, 1931; cf. Thornton, 2020): that the costs are known (and incurred) in the present but the revenues are not (until later). In contrast, Hayek's entrepreneur appears to respond to new or changing *knowledge* of (or *information* about) conditions that force a change in expectations, and therefore "compel" revisions.

We also saw Hayek emphasize that entrepreneurs revise their production plans in response to – and *in order to* – increase their plans' compatibility with other entrepreneurs' plans. These revisions cause plans overall to become "more and more into agreement," which suggests a trend toward equilibrium (full harmonization). Two important implications of this reasoning stand out: first, that this process toward general plan compatibility, as Hayek describes it, appears to leave no room for disruptive, innovative new value creative entrepreneurship (as with e.g., Mises, 1998; Schumpeter, 1934); and second, that there appears to be no room for (creating new) errors as incompatibilities, both cross-plan and with market data, are consistently *corrected* by entrepreneurs' revisions (cf. Kirzner, 1978). This suggests that there is kinship between Hayek's entrepreneur and Kirzner's "alert" entrepreneur (e.g., Kirzner, 1973, 1979, 1997).

### Future Directions

As noted in the introduction, the findings presented and discussed here are preliminary and need further analysis and elaboration. We cannot, based on the discussion above, draw any firm conclusions regarding Hayek's implied economic entrepreneurship theory – we could only identify themes and, for illumination, relate them to works by other Austrian economists. We have, however, found that there is enough commentary in Hayek's economic works to begin formulating what Hayek's theory of entrepreneurship may have been.

Future research can further explicate Hayek's theory by including a broader selection of Hayek's many works on economics. Of interest would also be elaborating on Hayek's specific views on the entrepreneur – the role and function – within his production theory, capital theory, and competition, respectively. We addressed all three in a limited fashion above, but each should warrant a separate "deep dive" to clarify what specifically the entrepreneurial role is with respect to the dynamic of and evolution within each economic phenomenon.

It would also be of scholarly interest, both within Austrian economics and the study of entrepreneurship, to further relate Hayek's theory of entrepreneurship, after it has been formulated and understood, to other entrepreneurship theory – both within and beyond Austrian economics proper. For example, how does Hayek's view of the entrepreneurial function in the market process relate to Mises's or Kirzner's? How are they similar or different?

## NOTES

1. The author has benefited from constructive feedback from Ryan Turnipseed as well as comments on the subject matter for this chapter from Bruce Caldwell and Mark Pennington.
2. In addition to Hayek's voluminous contributions to economic theory, he won the Sveriges Riksbank Prize in Economic Sciences in Memory of Alfred Nobel in 1974, and his *The Road to Serfdom* (1944) is an international bestseller that was also published by Reader's Digest and thus available to millions of subscribers (Caldwell, 2020).
3. For example, the entry on Hayek in the *Palgrave Dictionary of Economics* (Garrison and Kirzner, 1987) mentions entrepreneurship only as actions in response to price changes and Kirzner's (1992) obituary does not once mention the term entrepreneur.
4. This is not a necessary conclusion, but this chapter is written under the assumption that this is so.
5. Per September 15, 2024, Google Scholar reports that the article has been cited by 23,620 works.
6. See McCaffrey et al. (2024, pp. 7–12) for an elaboration.

## REFERENCES


Bylund P. (2015). The realm of entrepreneurship in the market: Capital theory, production, and change, in Bylund P., Howden D. (eds.), *The Next Generation of Austrian Economics: Essays in Honor of Joseph T. Salerno*. Auburn, AL: Ludwig von Mises Institute, pp. 89–104.

Bylund P. (2018). Management is what's wrong with socialism: Cost at the expense of value, in McCaffrey M. (ed.), *The Economic Theory of Costs: Foundations and New Directions*. London: Routledge, pp. 225–241.

Bylund P. (2019). Entrepreneurship and Austrian Economics: Theory, History, and Future. *MISES Journal*, 7(3), pp. 517–521.

Bylund P. (2020a). Finding the Entrepreneur-Promoter: A Praxeological Inquiry. *Quarterly Journal of Austrian Economics*, 23(3–4), pp. 355–389.

Bylund P. (2020b). Introduction to the Entrepreneurship Special Issue. *Quarterly Journal of Austrian Economics*, 23(3–4), pp. 255–264.

Bylund P. (2022a). Entrepreneurship and the market process, in Bylund P. (ed.), *A Modern Guide to Austrian Economics*. Cheltenham, UK: Edward Elgar Publishing, pp. 84–102.

Bylund P. (2022b). *How to Think about the Economy: A Primer*. Auburn, AL: Ludwig von Mises Institute.

Bylund P. (2024). Beyond Dynamic Efficiency: Entrepreneurship and the Progressing Economy. *Cosmos+Taxis*, 12(11+12), pp. 107–116.

Caldwell, B. (2020). The Road to Serfdom after 75 Years. *Journal of Economic Literature*, 58(3), pp. 720–748.

Cantillon R. (1931). *Essai sur la nature du commerce en général*. Translated by H. Higgs. London: Macmillan & Co.

Ebner A. (2005). Hayek on entrepreneurship: Competition, market process and cultural evolution, in Backhaus J. (ed.), *Entrepreneurship, Money and Coordination*. Cheltenham, UK: Edward Elgar Publishing, pp. 131–149.

Garello P. (2002). Entrepreneurship and Progress: The Need for a Greater Integration of Kirzner's and Hayek's Insights. *Journal Des Économistes et Des Études Humaines*, 12(2), pp. 213–228.

Garrison, R., Kirzner, I. (1987). Friedrich August von Hayek, in Eatwell J., Milgate M., Newman P. (eds.), *The New Palgrave: A Dictionary of Economics*, volume 2. London: Macmillan, pp. 609–614.

Hayek F. von (1931). *Prices and Production*. London: Routledge and Sons.

Hayek F. von (1937). Economics and Knowledge. *Economica*, 4(13), pp. 33–54.

Hayek F. von (1941). *The Pure Theory of Capital*. London: Routledge and Kegan Paul.

Hayek F. von (1944). *The Road to Serfdom*. London: Routledge and Kegan Paul.

Hayek F. von (1945). The Use of Knowledge in Society. *American Economic Review*, 35(4), pp. 519–530.

Hayek F. von (1948). The meaning of competition, in Hayek F. von (ed.), *Individualism and Economic Order*. Chicago: The University of Chicago Press, pp. 92–106.

Hayek F. von (1973). *Law, Legislation and Liberty, Volume 1: Rules and Order*. Chicago: The University of Chicago Press.

Hayek F. von (1976a). *Law, Legislation and Liberty, Volume 2: The Mirage of Social Justice*. Chicago: The University of Chicago Press.

Hayek F. von (1976b). *The Sensory Order: An Inquiry into the Foundations of Theoretical Psychology*. Chicago: The University of Chicago Press.

Hayek F. von (1978). Competition as a Discovery Procedure, in *New Studies in Philosophy, Politics, Economics, and the History of Ideas.* Chicago, IL: The University of Chicago Press, pp. 179–190.

Hayek F. von (1988). *The Fatal Conceit: The Errors of Socialism.* Chicago: University of Chicago Press.

Hayek F. von (2002). Competition as a Discovery Procedure. *Quarterly Journal of Austrian Economics*, 5(3), pp. 9–23.

Horwitz S. (2010). Kirznerian Entrepreneurship as a Misesian Solution to a Hayekian Problem. *Journal of Private Enterprise*, 25(2), pp. 97–103.

Hülsmann J. G. (2007). *Mises: The Last Knight of Liberalism.* Auburn. AL: Ludwig von Mises Institute.

Hutchison T. (1981). *The Politics and Philosophy of Economics: Marxians, Keynesians and Austrians.* Oxford, UK: Basil Blackwell.

Kirzner I. (1973). *Competition and Entrepreneurship.* Chicago: The University of Chicago Press.

Kirzner I. (1978). Economics and error, in Spadaro L. (ed.), *New Directions in Austrian Economics.* Kansas City, MO: Sheed, Andrews and McMeel, pp. 57–76.

Kirzner I. (1979). *Perception, Opportunity, and Profit: Studies in the Theory of Entrepreneurship.* Chicago: The University of Chicago Press.

Kirzner I. (1992). Friedrich A. Hayek 1899–1992. *Critical Review*, 5(4), pp. 585–592.

Kirzner I. (1997). Entrepreneurial Discovery and the Competitive Market Process: An Austrian Approach. *Journal of Economic Literature*, 35(1), pp. 60–85.

Klein P., Bylund P. (2014). The Place of Austrian Economics in Contemporary Entrepreneurship Research. *The Review of Austrian Economics*, 27(3), pp. 259–279.

Lachmann L. (1978). *Capital and Its Structure.* Kansas City, MO: Sheed, Andrews and McMeel.

McCaffrey M., Bylund P., Klein P. (2024). Austrian Economics and Entrepreneurship. *Foundations and Trends in Entrepreneurship*, 20(1), pp. 1–108.

Menger C. (2007). *Principles of Economics.* Translated by J. Dingwall, B. Hoselitz. Auburn, AL: Ludwig von Mises Institute.

Minniti M., Koppl R. (1999). The Unintended Consequences of Entrepreneurship. *Journal Des Économistes et Des Études Humaines*, 9(4), pp. 567–586.

Mises L. von. (1998). *Human Action: A Treatise on Economics. The Scholar's Edition.* Auburn, AL: Ludwig von Mises Institute.

Packard M. (2017). Where did Interpretivism go in the Theory of Entrepreneurship? *Journal of Business Venturing*, *32*(5), pp. 536–549.

Schumpeter J. (1934). *The Theory of Economic Development: An Inquiry into Profits, Capital, Credit, Interest, and the Business Cycle.* Cambridge, MA: Harvard University Press.

Thornton M. (2020). Turning the Word Upside Down: How Cantillon Redefined the Entrepreneur. *Quarterly Journal of Austrian Economics*, 23(3–4), pp. 265–280.

Wieser F. von. (1927). *Social Economics.* Translated by A. F. Hinrichs. London: George Allen and Unwin.

# 9. Of triangles and trapezoids: Hayek, Rothbard, and Hülsmann on the structure of production

**Kristoffer Mousten Hansen**

## INTRODUCTION

One of the mainstays of Austrian capital theory is the depiction of the relationship between consumption, investment, and the rate of interest in the form of a triangle (Hayek 1935; Rothbard 2009; Garrison 2001). This "Hayekian investment figure" shows the monetary value of all services of capital goods used per year across the structure of production. At the final stage are consumer goods bought by final consumers, and the services of all the capital goods in the higher stages are valued at a discount to final consumers' goods. This yields a triangular shape, as the higher stages become narrower and narrower, until all factor payments in the highest stage furthest from consumption go to original factors.

In recent years, a debate has developed on the proper shape of the Hayekian investment figure, with Hülsmann arguing that rather than a triangle, it is really a trapezoid (Hülsmann 2008; 2011). This debate is not only about matters of presentation, but touches on essential elements of capital theory. According to the standard theory, net saving leads to a lengthening and narrowing of the structure of production and a shift of productive factors into the higher stages of production, eventually yielding a higher output of consumer goods. This follows necessarily if the investment figure has a triangular shape; if instead it is trapezoidal, a lengthening of the structure of production does not necessarily follow, it is just one of several possible outcomes (Fillieule 2007; Hülsmann 2011). The orthodox Austrian understanding of the relationship between time preference, the rate of interest, and the proportion of investment to consumption has also been criticized, especially the way Rothbard presented the time market (Rothbard 2009, chap. 6), since his proof for the causal role of time preference in setting the rate of interest and the amount of saving in the economy is flawed (Hülsmann 2008).

Defenders of the classic conception have criticized Hülsmann (Méra 2011; Newman 2014) and others have tried to expand on this new approach (Machaj 2015; Granot 2019). At the same time, recent literature on money and capital uses the trapezoid as a better depiction of the capital structure (Davidson 2014; Hansen 2023), a position that, as Hülsmann pointed out, can be traced back to Rothbard's own exposition (Rothbard 2009, 407).

In the present note, our goal is to re-examine the issue of the relationship between the rate of interest, the amount of investment, and the length and shape of the structure of production. We here follow Newman (2014) in his defence of Rothbard, but go beyond his focus on Rothbard's time market. Specifically, we argue that when we analyse the process of capital formation in detail, a rise in the supply of present money (net saving) can, in some circumstances, call forth a rise in the demand for money from original factors. This induces first a fall and then a rise in the rate of interest, but it does not mean that the amount of savings and the rate of interest are unconnected. Hülsmann is thus correct in introducing the trapezoid, but the classic understanding of capital and interest, correctly developed, still holds true.

## ROTHBARD'S THEORY AND HÜLSMANN'S CRITIQUE

According to Rothbard, in order to invest in capital goods, an economic actor has to restrict current consumption (Rothbard 2009, 49). Capital goods are future goods that eventually mature into consumer goods. As such, they are always valued at a discount to present goods. What determines the height of this discount as well as the amount invested in capital is time preference, for each individual and in the aggregate for the economy as a whole. Higher time preference yields a higher rate of interest and a smaller amount of investment, and lower time preferences lead to a lower rate of interest and a larger amount of investment (Rothbard 2009, 400). The rate of interest is determined in the time market, where capital goods and claims to future money trade against present money. In a progressing economy, social time preference falls leading to increased saving. This increased saving enters the time market as present money offered against future money (claims and capital goods), leading to a fall in the rate of interest and an extension of the structure of production, since the lower rate of interest makes investment projects in the higher stages or in wholly new stages of production even more remote in time from consumption possible. The result of saving is thus a lower rate of interest, a higher amount of saving relative to consumption, and a longer, narrower structure of production.

Hülsmann (2008) argues that Rothbard overlooks a fundamental point: time preference explains both the supply of and the demand for present goods. When time-preference schedules rise, this implies reduced supply and increased demand for present goods at any given interest rate, so all we can conclude is that the rate of interest goes up with no systematic implication for aggregate investment (Hülsmann 2008, 17–19). The rate of interest does, however, determine the shape of the structure of production, as the slope of the triangle is steeper and the production structure shorter the higher the rate of interest. Additional saving, however, has no systematic impact. Net saving may be invested in lengthening the structure of production, which is the classic case of economic growth in Austrian theory. Net saving can, however, also be invested to "widen" the structure of production, adding processes of similar length to the already existing ones (Hülsmann 2008, 24). This is similar to Garrison's (2001) concept of secular growth, but with two crucial differences. First, Hülsmann is discussing one possible scenario of net saving, whereas Garrison is arguing for the possibility of growth in the absence of net saving; second, in Garrison's case the structure of production grows proportionally, lengthening and widening, whereas in Hülsmann's scenario it only widens. Hülsmann is therefore led to the trapezoidal shape by his argument: if savings increase, and if they are invested in such a way that the structure of production widens, then the Hayekian investment triangle central to Rothbard's exposition does not describe all possible production structures. Hence, various investment and growth scenarios become possible (Hülsmann 2011; cf. Fillieule 2007).

Newman (2014) provides so far the main counterargument to Hülsmann's critique. He argues that Rothbard's time market does not lead to Hülsmann's conclusion. Since capitalists are net suppliers of present goods across the capital structure, lower time preferences yield more investment. Newman is, however, focused on a specific numerical example rather than on the general logic of the argument. In the following, we will therefore proceed on similar lines to attempt a more general critique of Hülsmann's argument.

## TIME PREFERENCE, SAVING, AND CAPITAL FORMATION

The connection between saving and capital building and the causal role of time preference was laid out by Mises (1998). In order to direct action to temporally more remote ends, it is first necessary to save, that is, to consume less than current production. More time-consuming production processes are technologically superior, but even if this were not the case, there would be some saving. What restricts the amount of saving is always time preference, the premium of present over future goods inherent in all valuation (Mises 1998, 487). Whether for the individual in isolation or under the division of labour in society, it is necessary to accumulate consumer goods in order to undertake longer production processes. Only thus can acting man satisfy those wants that are more urgent, that is, higher ranked than the product of the longer process of production which he wants to undertake. The decision to save or consume is thus completely a matter of valuation, specifically of comparing temporally closer to more remote goods. Only if the capitalist is willing to forego some present enjoyment will there be any investment in longer processes of production. The amount of saving and investment is therefore always limited by time preference, by the fact that some consumption in the present is always ranked higher than future consumption.

This preference for present over future goods is for Mises also the source of interest. "Time preference manifests itself in the phenomenon of originary interest, that is, the discount of future goods as against present goods" (Mises 1998, 521). If time preferences fall, this means that the value of future goods as against present goods rises, and a higher number of more remote ends will be pursued. And so the rate of originary interest falls, as consumer goods are set free for longer-term processes. The rate of interest directs investment activity across the structure of production, determining the length of production processes, and a lower rate of interest will direct more investment to the higher stages of production more remote from consumption. It might then seem that there is a direct connection between the supply of capital goods and the rate of interest, since both are based in time preference. Mises, however, ends his discussion somewhat enigmatically by both affirming this and denying a clear quantitative connection:

> Changes in the originary rates of interest and in the amount of saving are … two aspects of the same phenomenon… The quantity of the available supply of capital goods influences neither the rate of originary interest nor the amount of further saving. (Mises 1998, 530)

This statement points both towards Rothbard's development of capital theory and to Hülsmann's critique of this development. In the following, we will try to spell out the meaning of Mises's statement, since, enigmatic though it may be, it points the way to a correct understanding of the issue.

## CAPITALISTS IN THE TIME MARKET

In order to see the dynamics of the time market, we need to disaggregate it into the original factor owners (landowners and labourers) and capitalists. We turn first to the capitalists.

Capitalists are the suppliers of present money across all stages of production. Capitalists in a lower stage of production purchase factor services from original factors and from capitalists in the higher stages. The capitalists in the highest stage, furthest from consumption, only supply present money to original factors. At one point in time, therefore, capitalists supply present money, while at a later point, when the product of their stage is finished, they demand present money, which in turn is supplied by the next-lower stage capitalists. The role of the capitalists in the time market must therefore be understood over two stages, over two sets of exchanges (Newman 2014). However, they are, in the aggregate, net suppliers of present money. Their demand for present money is, by definition, less than their income, whereas the demand of the original factors is equal to or higher than their incomes.[1]

When there is a fall in time preference, either for a few individuals or systematically across the economy, the valuation of future as against present money changes. Future money rises on the value scales of some capitalists, so they are willing to give up more present money in exchange for it. Their supply of present money offered increases while their demand for present money falls. The rate of interest, the spread between the prices of factors in different stages, therefore falls. This must necessarily be the case, since there are no new supplies of factors of production (no new demand for present money) forthcoming in the short term. The overall supply of present money in the time market also increases, which is again clear when we look narrowly at the capitalists. Since their time preferences have fallen, they prefer to invest out of their net income rather than consuming all of it. A fall in time preference therefore simultaneously leads to a fall in the rate of interest and a rise in the amount of saving.

There is now more money capital available and capitalists bid up the prices of factors of production and especially so in the higher stages. Since the rate of discount has fallen, longer processes of production are now possible, and it is profitable to employ more factors in the higher stages of production. The product of these stages is now discounted to a lesser extent than before, so the prices paid to factors in these stages rise, inducing a shift of (non-specific) factors backwards or up the structure of production (Hayek 1935, 77, 80–83). New stages may open up if capitalists employ original factors in the creation of capital goods in stages above the previous highest stage.

Looking narrowly at the role of capitalists in the time market, the standard Austrian account of the progressing economy thus appears correct. So far we have only discussed the changes in value and allocation of factors resulting from a fall in time preferences. In the long run, as more capital goods are produced and the longer processes of production come to fruition, the result will be an increase in the production of consumer goods. Looking at the Hayekian triangle, this is not immediately apparent, since it only depicts the value of capital in the different stages of production.

In order to fully understand the dynamics of the time market, however, we need to look more closely at the original factors of production. Labour and land only demand present money in exchange for future goods. Labourers and landowners can, of course, save and be the source of net saving in the economy, but insofar as they do this, they exercise the capitalist function. Original factors of production *qua* original factors always demand present money (cf. Rothbard 2009, 410–416).

## ORIGINAL FACTORS IN THE TIME MARKET

An increase in the supply of present money raises income to original factors. Let us first look at how this affects labour.

A fall in the rate of interest means that labour receives higher wages, since the discount on their product falls. In the short term, some labourers in the lower stages may see declining wages since capitalists are shifting their demand for labour services to the higher stages. In the aggregate, income to labour increases. Since there is a higher money demand for all productive factors, wages overall rise. In the long run, as new capital goods are produced, the productivity of labour increases, increasing real wages as well as money wages (Rothbard 2009, chap. 7). The effect of this increase is, however, indeterminate. It can induce a greater labour supply, as higher wages induce more people to work or to work longer hours, which on the time market would take the form of an increase in the demand for present money. Then, the rate of interest would rise again. But an increase in wages can also lead to more leisure consumption and a fall in the supply of labour on the market. This fall in labour supply is also a fall in the demand for present money on the part of labourers, and it thus reinforces the fall in the rate of interest. Whichever effect dominates will depend on the preferences of labourers for leisure as against money income.

Turning to land, the supply of land factors is usually considered inelastic, but this is only true in the short term (Hansen 2021, 47–50). When the rate of interest falls, the margin determining what is profitably employable land shifts. Submarginal land becomes supramarginal. These plots of land had been left out of productive activity because the complementary factors of production could be better, more profitably, employed elsewhere. With a lower rate of interest, returns on investment throughout the economy narrow, and it becomes profitable to cultivate some new land as the expected discounted marginal revenue product of these land factors exceeds the returns on alternative investments. At the same time, since net saving induces the formation of more capital goods, the supplies of the complementary factors of production increase. Indeed, the prospect of creating new land factors may guide investment into producing capital goods specific to cultivating new lands. Production of new land factors is an ongoing activity in the changing economy, although it can be impeded by institutional barriers that make it impossible to claim and bring into production unused land areas.

An increase in the supply of land factors thus follows from net saving. This extra supply can in principle be employed at any stage in the structure of production, dependent on its own specificities. The lower rate of discount will, as in the case of labour, tend to make employment in higher stages more profitable, but additional land may also substitute for labourers in lower stages such as agriculture. The additional land, wherever it is employed in the structure of production, constitutes an extra demand for present money. In the long term, therefore, when the new land factors have been developed, the rate of interest may rise again after initially falling in response to the increase in saving. It cannot, of course, rise so far that the land factors become submarginal again. If this happens, we are dealing with a case of malinvestment, since capitalists invested in the formation of factors of production which ultimately proved unprofitable. What rate of interest would make the new land factors submarginal is not determinate, however. It may well be different from the initial rate of interest before saving and investment occurred. The accumulation of capital, the increase in productivity and the greater supplies of the different capital goods and land factors all contribute to make the new economic situation different from the old. The increase in the supplies of other factors of production leads to a rise in the marginal value product of land factors (Rothbard 2009, chap. 7), which may compensate the return to the initial or an even higher rate of discount. If net saving has induced a greater labour supply, this will especially tend to be the case.

Interestingly, when net saving finances the formation of land factors, we have a situation where the structure of production first lengthens and narrows, as the discount rate falls, and then widens and shortens once the land factors are completed and "detach" from the Hayekian investment figure. There are thus more productive factors available in the economy than the capital structure would suggest once the process is complete. How important this process is in the real economy is hard to judge, especially since institutional barriers likely limit the formation of land factors much below what would be the case. However, it is clear that a fall in time preference can lead to both an increased supply of present money from capitalists (in the short term) and an increased demand for present money from landowners (in the long term). This is the case because it induces a rise in the supply of land factors beyond what would otherwise have been the case. This process is largely hidden in the classic Hayekian triangle, however, where all new capital is invested in the formation of capital goods "within" the triangle, so to speak. Thus, the trapezoidal shape, for this reason alone, appears more correct.

## THE TRAPEZOID

While the classic Austrian account of the role of time preference in determining the amount of savings and the rate of interest is correct, the structure of production does not necessarily have the classic triangular shape. The structure of production depicts the value of the services of producer goods per unit of time. By abstracting from the durability of capital goods, it yields an elegant depiction of the yearly value of producer goods services and its distribution across the different stages of production and between capitalists and original factors. It is clear that the higher stages must be "smaller", that is, receive lower cumulative revenues, since time preference means there is always some positive discount on future goods. While the structure will therefore tend to slope, it does not follow that it will be triangular, as we have seen. It is more realistic to conceive of it as a trapezoid. In the highest stage of production, that is, the first stage where capitalists hire factor services to work on a product, which they then sell on down the structure, they exclusively hire land and labour services. Thus, a trapezoid is a much more logical shape, since there is no reason to suppose that investment takes place in ever smaller amounts of capital goods higher in the structure before finally resolving into original factors.

While aggregate savings rise and the rate of interest tends to fall as social time preference falls, it does not necessarily follow that the structure of production lengthens. If the amount of net saving is small relative to the change in the rate of interest, then a shorter structure of production will result, but still one where more capital is invested than before. In other words, when the supply of present money is inelastic this scenario will follow. However, only over certain ranges of the supply schedule is the rate of interest likely to be inelastic. This will especially be the case when some quantity has already been supplied, since the utility of present money to the actor will then tend to greatly rise (Rothbard 2009, 386). In a progressing economy, this is unlikely to be the case and the case of shortened, but more capital-intensive structure of production therefore appears to be of little interest. In analyses of the impact of money and finance on the capital structure, however, the trapezoidal shape has proven helpful. Davidson (2014) shows how loan maturity mismatching leads to a shorter, broader structure of production using Hülsmann's trapezoid, and Hansen (2023) uses it to show the impact of money creation and financialization on the structure of production.

One shortcoming of this approach to the structure of production is that it only shows the value of the periodic services of producer goods; the capital values of capital goods and land factors are hidden from view. The process of land formation described above thus appears as an increase in the demand for present money and supply of future money, but we do not see how big the increase in the supply of land is. The case is obviously very different whether capitalists invest in a capital good that will yield its service worth $x$ monetary units once or in a land factor that will permanently yield a service worth $x$ monetary units per year. In the former case, capital worth $x$ discounted to the present (when its product is sold) has been created; in the latter case, capital worth $x/i$ has been created. The case is similar for durable capital goods.

We could try to depict the whole capital value of the structure of production. Then we would show the discounted value of the various durable capital goods and land factors extending backwards in time from the point in the structure of production where they yield their services. Such a capital structure would be much longer and closer to the triangular shape. It would be an attempt to show the total capital accumulated in society, the social capital fund, rather than the value of yearly production. If we consider such a capital structure (mindful of the fact that "social capital" per Mises (1998, 264) is not really a meaningful concept), then we would see that accumulation of capital always leads to a lengthening of the capital structure. Alternatively, a three-dimensional depiction could show the location of durable capital goods and land factors in the structure of production.

## CONCLUSION

The Austrian capital theory as developed by Rothbard is essentially correct. The easy inference, that capital accumulation and a reduction in the rate of interest go hand in hand since both spring from time preference, however, needs to be qualified. It may be that in the long run the rate of interest is more stable and less responsive to an increase in net saving and an increase in the supply of present money on the time market. The formation of new land factors, which naturally takes place in a progressing economy, constitutes an additional demand for present money and thus tends to push the interest rate upwards.

Hülsmann's critique is therefore partly justified, and his proposal of depicting the structure of production as a trapezoid rather than as a triangle is sound. Fundamentally, these issues in capital theory point to the problems of any graphic depiction of social capital and the structure of production. These are heuristic devices that help explain the concepts of capital theory and the processes of saving and capital accumulation, but they are no substitute for logical analysis.

## NOTE

1. We here as always deal with functional distinctions in the economy.

## REFERENCES

Davidson L. (2014). The Economic Consequences of Loan Maturity Mismatching in the Unhampered Economy. *Quarterly Journal of Austrian Economics*, 17(1), pp. 67–91.

Fillieule R. (2007). A Formal Model in Hayekian Macroeconomics: The Proportional Goods-in-Process Structure of Production. *Quarterly Journal of Austrian* Economics, 10(3), pp. 193–208.

Garrison R. (2001). *Time and Money: The Macroeconomics of Capital Structure.* London and New York: Routledge.

Granot E. (2019). An Overlooked Scenario of "Reswitching" in the Austrian Structure of Production. *Quarterly Journal of Austrian Economics*, 22(4), pp. 509–532.

Hansen K. M. (2021). *Monetary Systems and Industrial Organization: The Case of Agriculture.* Doctoral thesis. Angers: Université d'Angers.

Hansen K. M. (2023). The Myth of the Price Premium. *Quarterly Journal of Austrian Economics* 26(3), pp. 325–362.

Hayek F. von (1935). *Prices and Production*, 2nd revised edition. New York, NY: Augustus M. Kelley Publishers.

Hülsmann J. G. (2008). Time Preference and Investment Expenditure. *Procesos de Mercado: Revista Europea de Economía Política*, 5(2), pp. 13–33.

Hülsmann J. G. (2011). The Structure of Production Reconsidered. Working paper 2011-09-034. Angers: GRANEM, Université d'Angers. http://granem.univ-angers.fr/_resources/Cahiers/2011/DT_GRANEM_08_034.pdf [Accessed 21.06.2025].

Machaj M. (2015). The Interest Rate and the Length of Production: An Attempt at Reformulation. *Quarterly Journal of Austrian Economics*, 18(3), pp. 272–293.

Méra X. (2011). Time Preference and Investment Expenditure: Comment on Hülsmann. *Procesos de Mercado: Revista Europea de Economía Política*, 8(2), pp. 291–304.

Mises L. von (1998). *Human Action: A Treatise on Economics.* Scholar's edition. Auburn, AL: Ludwig von Mises Institute.

Newman P. (2014). Rothbard's Time Market and the Demand for Present Goods. *Quarterly Journal of Austrian Economics*, 17(1), pp. 46–66.

Rothbard M. (2009). *Man, Economy, and State with Power and Market.* Scholar's edition, 2nd edition. Auburn, AL: Ludwig von Mises Institute.

# 10. Investment dynamics in a Hayekian framework

**Przemysław Rapka**

## INTRODUCTION

Friedrich August von Hayek as a macroeconomist is known for broad and diverse contributions to economic theory – theory of capital, economic calculation, interventionism and business cycle theory. His theory of economic fluctuations reemerged on the horizon of mainstream economists after the Great Recession of 2008. Economists such as Claudio Borio (e.g. 2014) or Guillermo Calvo (2013) pointed out, that Hayek's business cycle theory was among the first theories to explain how credit expansion causes business cycles. Ricardo Caballero warned of the potential pretence of knowledge which could arise from contemporary economic models (2010). Axel Leijonhufvud, known mostly as a Keynesian economist, wrote favourably on Austrian business cycle theory in the context of the recession of 2008:

> Operating an interest targeting regime keying on the CPI, the Fed was lured into keeping interest rates far too low far too long. The result was inflation of asset prices combined with a general deterioration of credit quality. This, of course, does not make a Keynesian story. It is rather a variation on the Austrian overinvestment theme. (Leijonhufvud 2008)

In his theory of business cycles, Hayek showed how relative prices and the intersectoral allocation of resources change over time under the influence of credit expansion and the artificial lowering of the interest rate below its natural level. He also sought to explain why, because of the scarcity and specificity of factors of production, recessions lead to unemployment and idle capacity that cannot be quickly redeployed when demand rises. Workers are gradually hired as the economy grows, just as capacity utilization gradually increases after a recession (Hayek 1935, 1939).

However, one aspect of Hayek's business cycle theory remains little known even among Austrian School economists, namely the theory of macroeconomic investment dynamics.[1] Hayek shows that while there is a systematic relationship between the interest rate and investment, this does not mean that an increase in the interest rate will lead to a quick decline in investment and economic activity. This is because initial investment started under the influence of a lower interest rate requires complementary investment. Initial investments started under the influence of a lower interest rate create additional demand for capital in physical form, but also for funds. For this reason, a rise in interest rates after a period of time does not mean that companies will quickly reduce the scale of their investments. When the investment demand is higher, not every rise in interest rates will lead to a rapid fall in investment spending.

Changes in interest rates also affect the relative profitability of production for individual companies. An increase in interest rates makes it relatively more profitable to produce less durable and non-durable capital goods and consumer goods. For this reason, an increase in interest rates does not just lead to a weakening of economic activity in the short term. It also encourages increased production of less durable goods for shorter periods of time and an increase in inventories. Since an increase in interest rates increases the relative profitability of producing less durable goods, this effect helps to delay the slowdown in economic activity of the whole economy in response to an increase in interest rates.

This is a very different approach to that found in advanced macroeconomics textbooks. In mainstream economics, the basic relationship between investment and the interest rate is simple. The most common assumption is that of a representative firm whose output is determined by the Cobb–Douglas production function. A fall in the interest rate makes it profitable for the firm to increase the amount of capital it uses, because the cost of using capital falls. There is a windfall profit from the use of an additional unit of capital, which leads firms to increase their capital stock in order to maximize profit. For this reason, the marginal product of capital falls as a result of the fall in the interest rate (Romer 2019, pp. 421–422). In Hayek's case, on the other hand, the relationship is more complicated, since for him the heterogeneity and complementarity of factors of production are crucial. Initial investment creates demand for complementary factors of production, so that not every increase in the interest rate leads entrepreneurs to abandon investment or to abandon investments already under way.

It is important to bear in mind that investment in Hayek's case does not only mean expenditure on durable capital goods. In Hayek's terminology, investment consists of all expenditures by firms related to the production of goods. He distinguishes between different types of investment and different capital goods. The expansion of the economic structure requires investment not only in the expansion of the stock of durable capital goods, but also in the stock of various non-durable factors of production, such as materials or semi-finished goods. In examining the dynamics of investment, Hayek considered the effect of changes in the interest rate not only on expenditure on durable capital goods, but also on investment in less durable and non-durable factors of production.

Hayek's theory of macroeconomic investment dynamics has important implications for business cycle analysis and economic theory. In terms of business cycle analysis, firms react differently to changes in interest rates depending on the type of goods they sell. Therefore, over the course of a business cycle, changes in interest rates will affect different industries in different ways, which can explain the time lag between the start of the interest rate hike cycle and the economic downturn. Therefore, the theory of investment dynamics contained in Hayek's work allows us to explain why economic activity is not immediately stifled by central banks when they raise interest rates, but with some delay.

Regarding theory, according to Hayek, an increase in the supply of capital goods is not necessarily associated with a decrease in the interest rate, which is in stark contrast to the standard neoclassical approach to investment theory. In other words, the supply of capital goods does not determine the rate of interest, nor is there a monotonic relationship between the amount of physical capital and the rate of profit.

This chapter presents an outline of a theory of macroeconomic investment dynamics based on Hayek's work from the 1930s. This chapter is theoretical in nature, as a theory of the impact of interest rate changes on macroeconomic investment dynamics, as found in the macroeconomic theoretical framework developed by Hayek, will be synthesized on the basis of Hayek's work and papers on his theory of business cycles.

The following section discusses the literature on the effects of interest rate changes on business investment and economic activity. The third section is devoted to a discussion of Hayek's macroeconomic theoretical framework, in particular the structure of production. The fourth section is the body of the chapter and discusses the effects of a change in interest rates on economic activity and investment in the economy. The fifth section is devoted to the importance of changes in savings for the ability to complete and maintain a developed production structure. The final section concludes the chapter.

## INTEREST RATE, INVESTMENT AND ECONOMIC ACTIVITY – A LITERATURE REVIEW

Some studies show that the interest rate has no significant effect on firms' investment decisions. Baddeley (2017) or Shackle (1946) argue that companies usually set a hurdle rate several times higher than the interest rate and rarely change the hurdle rate – it doesn't always change with a change in the weighted average cost of capital. Using Australian firms as an example, Lane and Rosewall (2015) and Edwards and Lane (2021) show that firms' investment decisions show little sensitivity to changes in interest rates.

Sharpe and Suarez (2021) conducted a survey of Chief Financial Officers of companies with revenues between $25 million and $10 billion. They asked them how a fall or rise in interest rates would affect their companies' investment decisions. The researchers found that only 8% of companies would increase investment in response to a 100 basis point decline in interest rates, while a 100–200 basis point decline in interest rates would cause 16% of companies to initiate additional investment.

Businesses are expected to be more sensitive to interest rate hikes. 16% of firms are expected to refrain from making an investment if the interest rate rises by 100 basis points, and if the interest rate rises by between 100 and 200 basis points, 31% of firms will refrain from making an investment (Sharpe and Suarez 2021, p. 721). According to the authors, these results suggest that interest rates have a weak effect on firms' investment decisions. While it is hard to provide an objective measure of what percentage of companies should be considered large, it is hard to agree that it is a small percentage. More than one in ten companies are willing to start additional investment if interest rates fall by two percentage points, and almost one in three companies are willing to reduce investment if interest rates rise by two percentage points.

Peersman and Smets (2005) examined the impact of interest rate changes on the financial characteristics of firms. The change in interest rates had the strongest impact on firms' investment, especially in durable capital goods.

Theoretically, the basic relationship between interest rates and the investment rate should be clear – an increase in interest rates should have a negative effect on the investment rate. Conclusions consistent with the theory are reached by Farooq et al. (2021), who find that changes in the interest rate significantly affect investment in durable capital goods.

Using Australian firm-level data, Hambur and La Cava (2018) also find that interest rates affect firms' investment decisions. However, firms differ in the interest rate they are offered. Therefore, a decline in interest rates does not affect all firms' decisions to the same extent. Cloyne et al. (2018) came to similar conclusions by studying the reactions of companies to changes in central bank interest rates in the UK and the US. According to this research, small firms react strongly to changes in interest rates, while the reaction of large companies is much weaker. Durante et al. (2022) came to the same conclusion by studying companies from Germany, France, Italy and Spain. They also found that a change in interest rates has a particularly significant effect on firms producing durable capital goods.

Givens and Reed (2018) examined with a VAR model changes in the volume of output and prices of various types of capital goods (and residential real estate) in the United States in response to changes in the interest rate. Their calculations show that investment responds with a lag to changes in interest rates. Under the influence of the decline in the interest rate, first of all, the output of residential real estate (about one quarter after the monetary shock) and durable capital goods, such as machinery (about four quarters after the monetary shock) grew first. Prices rose to a lesser extent and with a lag to the increase in sales (after about four and ten quarters, respectively). Production of real estate for business (non-residential structures) grew after about ten quarters, and their prices after eight quarters.

The dynamics of investment from an Austrian School perspective have been addressed by Montgomery. In his work, he shows that a nominal demand shock precedes an increase in the procurement of capital goods, the construction of new real estate for economic activity and spending on capital improvements (1995b). He also shows that the observed lag in incremental construction starts can be explained by the Austrian theory of complementary investment – primary investment entails complementary investment (2006).

A study by Givens and Reed (2018) shows that there is a lag in the response of economic activity to changes in interest rates, but this is not the only study to point this out. The lags in the impact of monetary policy on economic activity are well known. Cloyne and Hürtgen (2016), using a VAR model and data for the UK, conclude that a one percentage point increase in the central bank interest rate leads to a 0.5% reduction in GDP and industrial production after two to three years. Coibion (2012), studying the impact of interest rate changes on the US economy, concludes that an increase in interest rates has a significant impact on the level of industrial production and real GDP, but the effects are delayed.

Based on the literature review, it can be concluded that: (1) the impact of a change in interest rates is heterogeneous; (2) the real estate sector reacts most strongly to changes in interest rates, followed by the durable capital goods sector; (3) the effect of an increase in interest rates affects the economy with a lag.

## HAYEK'S MACROECONOMIC FRAMEWORK – STRUCTURE OF PRODUCTION

Hayek's theoretical framework allows us to understand certain observed regularities in the economy's response to changes in interest rates. This is mainly due to the approach he developed for analysing macroeconomic stability. Hayek did not focus exclusively on broad aggregates such as investment or consumption. He was interested in the interrelationships between individual firms or industries, which together make up the complex structure of production. All these firms together make up the production process.[2] These production processes form the structure of production, which Hayek illustrated with a characteristic diagram (Figure 10.1).

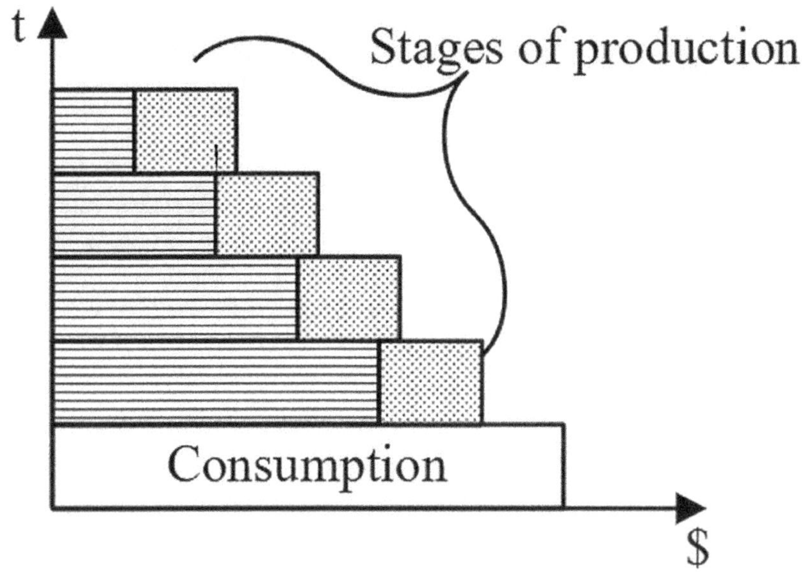


*Source:* Own exposition based on Hayek (1935).

*Figure 10.1 Macroeconomic structure of production*

Figure 10.1 provides a simplified view of all the production processes currently taking place in the economy. On the vertical axis is time, according to which the stages of production are ordered. On the horizontal axis is the monetary value. The horizontally shaded part of each rectangle is the value of the capital goods produced at that stage of production, and the dotted part of the rectangle is the primary factors of production (labour and unprocessed natural resources).[3] Each of the rectangles represents a different stage of production.

The lowest rectangle shows consumer spending. The rectangles above it are the stages of production. Each rectangle represents one stage in the production process, where factors of production are gradually produced and transformed into finished consumer goods. The difference in width between the stages of production represents the income earned by the higher stage from the sale of its manufactured goods to firms in the lower stage or to consumers. The rate of profit (i.e. the interest earned) at each stage of production in equilibrium is the same.[4]

Before originary factors of production can be used in the production of a consumer good, they have to pass through a series of production stages. In successive stages, different firms produce other factors of production by combining existing factors of production with other originary factors of production. At each stage, new complementary factors of production are created and then sold to firms in the next stage of production. In this way, the originary factors of production are recycled until, finally, consumer goods are produced from them.

What do the areas of stages and number of stages in the production structure mean specifically? This can be briefly described.

First, they show the value of capital used in production. Second, the amount of time and capital used in all production processes in the economy. Third, the more stages of production structure there are, the more advanced technologies are used. Fourth, a higher number of stages shows a greater division of labour between firms within the production structure (Cachanosky and Lewin 2014, pp. 650–652).

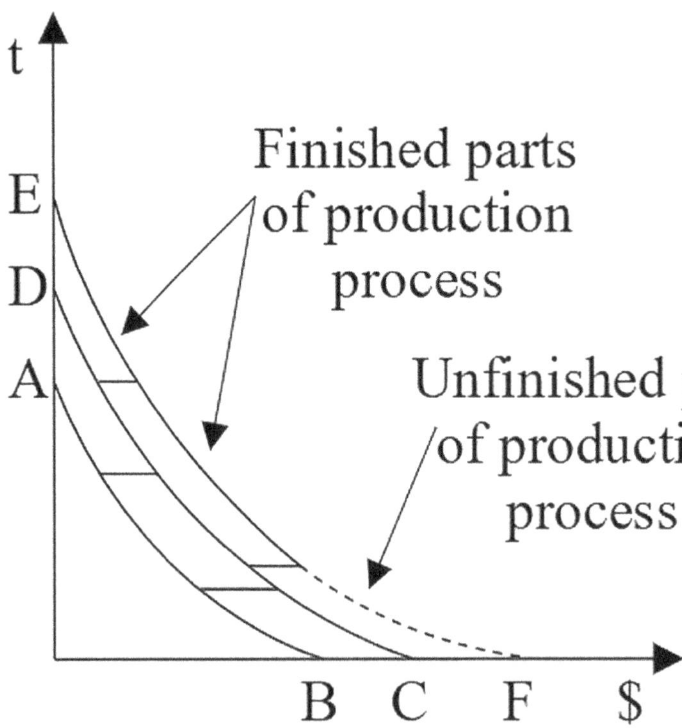


*Source:* Hayek (1935, p. 311).

*Figure 10.2 Parallel production processes in the economy*

Hayek also drew another version of his triangle, shown in Figure 10.2.

Hayek envisioned the production process as a certain sequence of actions that specific firms undertake. ABCDs define a certain production process that occupies three stages. Each stage involves a different firm (or industry) and the area of one tile defines the amount of capital used in that stage of production. Tiles outlined with solid lines represent completed production stages that are ready to be implemented. One tile outlined with a dashed line from the top is an unfinished production stage. ABCD production process[5] is completed and delivering products, as all investments have been completed and implemented at each stage, making the production process profitable.[6]

The DCFE production process is not yet complete and profitable because the final stage of production has not been completed. In order for the production process to be self-sustaining, funding and inputs are needed to enable the company to complete a production process that can, in the end, sustain itself with receipts from sales.

Why is it necessary to complete this DCFE production process?

Because upstream companies produce factors of production. These factors of production are then sold to the next company in the production process. If the process is not completed, the upstream firms will suffer losses. If the downstream firm, which should complete the production process, is unable to complete its investment, it will not demand the factors of production produced by the upstream firm. The production process has been poorly planned and should involve two stages of production instead of three. However, as it consists of three stages, there are not enough factors of production to complete it and firms in the upper stages will suffer losses.

Resources cannot be moved arbitrarily within the production structure because they are diverse and vary in their degree of specificity. Individual goods are adapted for use in specific production processes – for example, automated production lines are adapted to a specific factory and cannot be cheaply and easily adapted to other production processes. This example factory production line is a specific factor, that is, with a small number of alternative uses. This is important because if it cannot be used profitably in its original application, its value will fall significantly, and so will the capital value of the company that owns the production line. Also, if the manufacturer of that line only produces such specific production lines, its income will fall as the value of that production line falls.

When entrepreneurs decide what type of production process they will engage in, they consider the availability of physical capital, funds to finance the business and their prices (factor prices and the interest rate). They also take into account expected consumption in the near and distant future. As long as they correctly determine the availability of factors of production, consumers' consumption plans and changes in the interest rate and factor prices, they create production processes that can be completed and are profitable.

This requires that, at each stage, entrepreneurs are able to obtain the necessary resources to produce products that they can sell, and that there is sufficient demand for their products – consumer demand for finished consumer goods, or demand from other entrepreneurs for manufactured inputs. Misjudgements by entrepreneurs about the availability of resources, financing and prices will cause them to make losses and plans to be revised.

A key role in coordinating the plans of entrepreneurs and consumers is played by time preference and the interest rate. Entrepreneurs formulate different production plans depending on the interest rate – they produce different types of goods and for different periods of time. If the interest rate on the market falls, this means that people are orienting themselves towards consumption further in the future (Hayek 1933, pp. 144–146). This leads entrepreneurs to increase production in more distant periods and to create more durable consumer goods. Greater savings serve consumers, for example, as a greater personal input for a future purchase of a home or a car. At the same time, higher savings due to lower time preference reduce loan repayments, which induces people to increase their purchases of more durable consumer goods.

When the interest rate rises, this implies a fall in savings and an increase in consumption, forcing entrepreneurs to increase production for the current period. Therefore, as the interest rate rises, it limits the ability of entrepreneurs to initiate additional investment in more future-oriented production processes and instead leads them to expand production in response to falling savings and rising consumption for the current period.

Disturbances in the interest rate lead to the misuse and waste of available resources. If the interest rate prevailing in the economy is lower than it should be according to time preference, then, on the one hand, entrepreneurs want to expand the production structure of the economy with an additional, more long-term production process, which requires more resources and more time to deliver goods to the market. At the same time, consumers increase their consumption because they are not satisfied with the percentage offered, which further stimulates the demand for resources coming from companies producing consumer goods. As plans are not properly coordinated, this creates an excessive demand for resources, which will affect economic activity in the future.

## INVESTMENT DYNAMICS IN HAYEKIAN MACROECONOMIC FRAMEWORK

This was an abbreviated description of the consequences of disturbances in the interest rate setting process. According to Hayek, how does the economy respond to changes in interest rates? How do investment and economic activity change under the influence of first a fall and then a rise in interest rates?

## First Changes in Investments due to Lowering of Interest Rate

According to Hayek's statement, "an increase in the quantity of capital goods will necessarily decrease the return to be expected on further investment" (1937, p. 524) isn't correct. As he states in the beginning of his article:

> [T]he effect which the current production of capital goods will have on the future demand for investable funds will depend not so much on the quantity of capital goods produced, as on the kind of capital goods which are produced or on the particular forms which current investment takes, and that an increase in the current output of capital goods will frequently have the effect not of lowering but of raising the future demand for investable funds, and thereby the rate of interest. (Hayek 1937, p. 524)

According to Hayek's theory of the business cycle, new money enters the economy primarily in the form of business loans. In order for additional credit to be granted, banks must offer a lower interest rate than that which is currently set in the economy on the basis of time preference alone. This provides entrepreneurs with additional purchasing power, which they can invest in expanding their production facilities and increasing production for the future. However, according to Hayek, a lower interest rate does not induce every firm to make additional investments. Thanks to the lower interest rate, it is possible to start additional investments that were previously sub-marginal.

However, it is important to understand exactly how Hayek understood marginal investment. In Hayek's terms, marginal investment is investment in adding an additional production process to the production structure. This can be illustrated again in Figure 10.2, where the production process ABCD is the production process in the economy that existed before. When the interest rate falls, entrepreneurs are able to start an additional production process DCFE. Marginal investments are those that create an additional production process that is added to the overall production structure. This is what Hayek said about the effect of the interest rate on investment:

> Only for a very small fraction of the total investments—the marginal investments which represent the beginning of new chains of investment—will the demand for funds promptly react to a change in the rate at which capital can be borrowed. For the rest, the demand for capital will be highly inelastic with respect to changes in the rate of interest. (Hayek 1937, p. 526)

When the interest rate falls, the process of expanding the production structure begins. Firms begin to order additional factors of production, such as machinery, materials or labour. This increases the demand for factors of production and the prices of factors of production relative to the prices of consumer goods. This triggers further changes in the production structure as plans change under the influence of the change in the interest rate.

With a lower interest rate on credit, entrepreneurs will first of all start to order additional durable factors of production, such as factory machinery or vehicles. Increasing the input of non-durable factors of production allows production to increase to a limited extent, as the firm is further limited by its machinery stock – either increasing production is not possible or the firm may find itself on the rising parts of the average and marginal cost curves. This means that, usually at the first moment, a reduction in the interest rate by the central bank will primarily stimulate demand for durable capital goods.

The lowering of interest rates will in the first place stimulate prices and sales of durable capital and consumer goods, since interest is a substantial cost only of durable goods. Because of that, lower interest payments do not substantially affect demand for non-durable goods (Machlup 1932).

Factor prices do not respond uniformly to an increase in demand in the economy. In response to credit expansion, the prices of specific factors of production rise first. Specific factors of production are mainly durable capital goods that are tailored to the needs of a particular firm – machinery or parts that are adapted to very specific production technologies that few firms use. As the prices of these specific factors of production rise, non-specific factors of production are transformed into specific ones. For this reason, the increase in orders for durable capital goods leads to a further increase in the demand for non-specific factors of production – energy, materials, labour. Initially, however, when interest rates are lowered, it is primarily the demand for and production of durable capital goods that will increase.

Once the machinery has been installed, the firms initiating the sub-marginal investments will need additional materials and labour, but also energy. For this reason, some time after firms begin to report demand for additional machinery, the same firms begin to report additional demand for complementary non-durable capital goods and labour needed to increase their own output.

## Influence of Additional Investment on Economic Activity

Certain initial investments, which are initiated under the influence of the interest rate squeeze, entail a series of complementary investments by other firms. A single firm does not entirely produce consumer goods on its own. It either buys factors of production from other firms or produces factors of production itself, which it then sells on the market. In Hayek's view, investment by one firm entails complementary investment by other firms. Higher expenditures by one firm begin to induce other firms offering complementary factors of production to increase their capacity, which is necessary to complete the additional production processes that are added to the structure of economic production. For this reason, firms producing complementary factors of production under the influence of increased income will themselves also increase their orders of durable and non-durable factors of production to increase the scale of economic activity, which is necessary to expand and maintain a larger production structure.

It is worth recalling here that a reduction in the interest rate and the creation of credit causes the money supply and nominal expenditure in the economy to increase, which also causes the nominal profits of firms to increase under the influence of additional orders placed by firms that have started sub-marginal investment. This increased demand for factors of production raises the incomes of firms producing the goods needed to complete and operate the additional investment that has been started. As long as these firms expect the higher demand to continue in the future, they will also decide to expand their production capacity to meet the higher demand. There will be an increase in their demand for durable capital goods and then for the complementary factors of production such as materials, labour and energy needed to expand production. Investment by these firms will be less sensitive to interest rates, as the additional cash flow will improve the creditworthiness of the firms and enable them to finance investment to a greater extent from their own resources.

Some time after the credit expansion begins, the prices of non-specific factors of production begin to rise more rapidly than the prices of specific factors. As noted above, non-specific factors of production, such as materials, energy or part of the labour force, are used to produce specific factors of production, and this demand remains high because non-specific factors of production also need to be maintained and replaced. However, over time, as the construction of durable capital goods is completed, additional demand for non-specific factors arises as firms that have expanded their production capacity wish to use them. Therefore, according to Hayek, the real prices of raw materials, energy and labour will rise in the late stages of the boom phase (Hayek 1939, pp. 29–31). But the demand for factors of production such as semiconductors or microprocessors, which are used to produce more and less durable capital goods as well as more and less durable consumer goods, will also continue to rise.

The initiation of additional investment creates additional demand for the funds needed to finance that investment, as Hayek argued. This does not necessarily mean that interest rates will rise. In the modern financial system, it depends on the monetary policy of the central bank and the credit policy of the commercial banks. If central banks do not expect inflation to rise, they will not raise their own interest rates. On the other hand, in response to an increase in nominal spending and hence profits in the economy, banks are unlikely to tighten credit significantly or increase margins for some time as they compete for customers. The higher incomes induced by lower interest rates and money creation generally improve the creditworthiness of investment projects that companies want to start.[7] Therefore, an increase in the demand for funds will primarily lead to an increase in lending and, to a lesser extent, to an increase in lending rates at the beginning of the boom.

Since credit expansion initially finances the expansion of productive capacity, it is mainly the output and prices of durable capital goods that rise. For this reason, the profit margins of firms engaged in the production of non-specific factors of production increase. However, as the boom progresses, workers' incomes and profits paid out rise, allowing for increased spending on consumer goods. For this reason, in the late phase of the boom, some of the non-specific factors of production are drawn away from the sectors in which they are produced and shifted to sectors closer to the production of consumer goods. This means that first the costs of firms producing consumer goods rise relatively more, and then those of firms producing specific factors of production.[8]

Additional lending means that the money supply in the economy increases further. This causes further increases in profits and income in the economy. It also contributes to further increases in factor prices, including wages, which causes production costs to rise some time after the credit expansion begins and the threat of rising inflation to emerge. Then central banks decide to start a cycle of interest rate rises, which raises banks' funding costs and leads to higher interest rates in the market. But this will not at all result in a rapid stifling of economic activity precisely for the reasons outlined above.

An increase in demand due to the lowering of interest rates below the equilibrium rate and an increase in the money supply weakens companies' financial constraints. Cash flow also matters for companies' investment decisions. An increase in interest rates alone does not mean that firms will immediately decide to reduce the scale of economic activity. Higher flows further encourage the scale-up of production and, even despite higher interest rates, make it possible both to obtain financing from investors and to finance investments to a greater extent from own resources (Campello et al. 2010).

For the reasons mentioned above, the over-expansion of the economy, which is the result of credit expansion and an artificially lowered interest rate, continues some time after the central bank has started the cycle of interest rate increases. Higher nominal spending and the gradual spread of money around the economy create the illusion that the economy is in better shape than it actually is. The gradual rise in prices first gives the impression of stronger economic growth than is actually the case. However, over time, as companies' costs adjust and inflation accelerates, then the economy will begin to weaken as corporate profits and real wages begin to fall. It could be said that it is the Cantillon effect that is responsible for the lag between the rise in interest rates and the weakening of the economy.

However, a rise in interest rates can stimulate activity in certain sectors of the economy in the short term. It has already been said that a fall in interest rates stimulates the production of durable capital goods. When interest rates rise, the production of durable goods becomes less profitable. This is also true for consumer durables – a fall in interest rates stimulates the purchase of consumer durables, such as property or cars, in particular, as interest payments fall. However, when interest rates rise, it becomes less profitable to buy more durable goods. For this reason, people will allocate more money to the purchase of less durable and non-durable consumer goods as well as services.

It is relatively more profitable for companies to increase their production of goods, but also to build up inventories of finished goods, materials or semi-finished products, as interest rates rise. At the same time, this means that while some industries will gradually deteriorate as orders for their goods fall, other sectors of the economy will continue to do well – these will be sectors that produce less durable and non-durable consumer goods, as well as companies that supply less durable and non-durable factors of production.

For this reason, in the late stages of an economic boom, some time after the central bank and commercial banks have raised interest rates, we should see not only a lower dynamic of spending on durable capital goods, but also an increase in business inventories and orders for less durable inputs, which also sustains economic activity for some time. This will be accompanied by a weakening in the performance of sectors such as construction and automobiles. However, other sectors – such as services and retail trade – may continue to perform well.

This is something of a paradox – a rise in interest rates should dampen economic activity, while in the short term it can stimulate certain sectors of the economy by changing the relative profitability of producing different types of goods. Combined with the Cantillon effect and wage growth, this helps to explain the persistent dynamics of economic activity for some time after the start of the monetary tightening cycle.

## SAVINGS AND EXPANSION OF STRUCTURE OF PRODUCTION

In the previous section, I explained how initial investment in expanding the production structure induces other firms in the economy to initiate complementary investment, which is necessary to complete the additional production processes that are added to the macroeconomic production structure. It is explained why an increase in interest rates does not quickly stifle economic activity. Attention is also paid to the relative profitability of producing different types of goods. Finally, the role of savings in completing the expansion of the production structure is considered.

Expanding the production structure (assuming no technological change) requires sufficient savings to maintain the additional production processes introduced into the economy. However, these savings can come from a variety of sources – firms can borrow from external parties or save from current income. Investments and production processes that have already been implemented can pay for themselves out of the revenues they generate. In order to finance new investments, however, entrepreneurs must either attract investors with a sufficient supply of savings or save part of the revenues themselves. This means that a sufficiently high interest rate is needed to induce agents to save. This requires: (1) offering a higher interest rate so that potential or existing investors decide to increase the amount of savings needed to realize the investment accordingly; (2) reducing people's time preference so that, at a given (or lower) interest rate, they are willing to invest a larger proportion of their income.

In the Hayekian view, entrepreneurs assume before investing that they will be able to raise the necessary funds at a certain interest rate. As soon as their expectations turn out to be wrong and the supply of funds is lower than expected, then they have to offer a higher interest rate for the funds in order to complete their investments. The mismatch between the supply of real savings (offered purchasing power allowing them to purchase a certain amount of factors of production) and the demand for them (an amount of money demanded by firms necessary to purchase needed factors of production) is important. An artificial lowering of the interest rate causes people to consume more of their income, resulting in a decline in net savings. However, one has to take into account how much of the additional production process has already been completed when looking at the impact of a fall in the net savings rate on economic stability. According to Hayek, as long as the amount of available net savings does not fall faster than the additional production process is getting closer to being completed, the structure of production will be sustainable, because there will be enough additional real savings to finance the investment that needs to be completed. And when the additional production process is completed, it can finance itself with its receipts (Hayek 1935, pp. 313–316). But it is much harder to provide firms with enough real savings when people consume a higher part of their income due to artificially lowered interest rates, thus moving more resources towards the production of consumer goods.

The increase in investment that has contributed to the increased demand for funds does not necessarily mean that interest rates on funds will remain at an elevated level forever. Once caused by monetary expansion, the increase in the demand for funds may, after a certain period of time, fall, and with it interest rates. This is provided, however, that there is a sufficient amount of real savings to complete the additional production processes and that the savings rate does not fall below the level necessary to meet the replacement demand.

This is one possible scenario. It is necessary to consider cases where the production process has been completed thanks to the funds set aside for depreciation, and where the savings have fallen by more than is necessary to complete the additional production process and depreciate the capital already in place.

The net savings rate does not have to increase permanently to maintain the production structure. As soon as a production process is completed and is profitable, then the companies' revenues are sufficient to maintain the additional production processes that have been implemented to cover depreciation costs. In such a situation, higher depreciation in absolute terms will not necessarily translate into higher interest rates. However, if the funds needed for the replacement of the firm's physical capital are used for additional investments and not for replacing worn-out capital goods, then the demand for funds will remain higher, contributing to keeping interest rates higher. This is because if the funds needed to replace pre-existing capital were used to produce new capital, firms need to raise additional funds in the market to replace capital goods in the future.

As for the third case, with a significant fall in gross real savings, there will not only be a recession in which there will be a lack of demand for the completed part of the additional production process. With the decline in gross real savings, unless the trend is reversed, there will be a decline in the level of economic activity, because the gradual consumption of capital will lead to a decline in the availability of some of the factors of production necessary for the operation of the production processes already implemented. Since the various factors of production are complementary, a decline in the supply of some factors of production will reduce the use of others. To present it with a simple example: too much iron ore is used in the production of cars, and not enough is used to produce factory machines. And when those factory machines fall apart, the factory workers will become unemployed. This will mean a gradual decline in investment demand and economic activity, that is, economic decline. But this is extremely unlikely, since it would require radically irresponsible monetary and fiscal policies aimed at a drastic increase in current consumption at all costs.

## CONCLUSIONS

This chapter presents the theory of macroeconomic investment dynamics found in Hayek's work on business cycles. Although this aspect of the business cycle has been overlooked by Austrian School economists, it is an important part of Hayek's theory of the business cycle and allows us to better understand why an increase in interest rates does not lead to a rapid suppression of economic activity.

If this theory is correct, it has important implications for the study of the business cycle and monetary policy. To determine the state of the economy and where it is in the cycle, we need to look at the types of goods being sold and the relative performance of different sectors of the economy. Observing these changes helps us to determine what might happen in the future and whether the crisis is closer or further away. This can be important information for central banks trying to determine whether the poor performance of parts of the economy is a random economic fluctuation or perhaps caused by the mechanism responsible for the business cycle.

## NOTES

1. The only Austrian School economist known to the author writing on this issue is Michael R. Montgomery (1995a, 1995b, 2006).
2. By production structure I mean the whole set of production processes that take place in the economy – all the activities carried out by firms and workers, involving all the available factors of production. By production process, on the other hand, I mean here a particular set of tasks and factors of production that are intended to produce a certain share of consumer goods.

   Of course, in reality it is very difficult (if at all possible) to specify which activities lead to the production of particular consumer goods. However, it is possible to see analytically what happens to production in the economy when firms produce additional factors of production and organize them to produce additional consumer goods. If this is what firms do – organize additional activities using additional factors of production to produce additional consumer goods – then I say that the structure of production is extended by an additional process of production.
3. This Hayekian triangle assumes that there is only working capital in the economy.
4. For a thorough discussion of the developed version of Hayek's triangle, see Rothbard (2009) and Skousen (2015).
5. To clarify – ABCD and DCFE are two different production processes, which together create a whole structure of production.
6. Although Hayek does not state it explicitly, he assumes that consumption expenditure is high enough to cover the expenses of firms in the final stage of production (Hayek 1935, pp. 310–312).
7. A reduction in interest rates by the central bank can also contribute to lower credit requirements by banks (Altunbas et al. 2010).
8. According to Alvarez et al. (2024), after 2020 in the US, manufacturers' and retailers' margins moved in opposite directions. In the second half of 2020, manufacturers' margins were increasing and retailers' margins were decreasing. In 2021, manufacturers' margins began to fall and retailers' margins began to rise, and the peak in retailers' margins and the peak in manufacturers' margins occurred in 2022, when inflation was highest. This is consistent with

Austrian Business Cycle Theory prediction, where new credit is mainly spent by entrepreneurs, resulting in increased factor expenditure, which allows their manufacturers' margins to rise. Retailers compete for non-specific factors of production with manufacturers, causing the price of these non-specific factors of production to rise and retailers' margins to fall. Over time, as companies' wages and profits rise, spending on consumer goods increases. This allows retailers to raise margins and offer better prices for non-specific inputs, and this leads to a fall in manufacturers' margins.

## REFERENCES

Altunbas Y., Gambacorta L., Marques-Ibanez D. (2010). *Does Monetary Policy Affect Bank Risk-Taking?*, ECB Working Paper No. 1166, 2010.

Alvarez S., Cavallo A., MacKay A., Mengano P. (2024). *Markups and Cost Pass-through Along the Supply Chain*, Working Paper. https://papers.ssrn.com/sol3/papers.cfm?abstract_id=4935032 [Accessed at 21.05.2025].

Baddeley M. (2017). *Investment: Theories and Analyses.* London: Bloomsbury Publishing.

Borio C. (2014). The Financial Cycle and Macroeconomics: What Have we Learnt? *Journal of Banking and Finance*, 45, pp. 182–198.

Caballero R. (2010). Macroeconomics after the Crisis: Time to Deal with the Pretense-of-Knowledge Syndrome. *Journal of Economic Perspectives*, 24(4), pp. 85–102.

Cachanosky N., Lewin P. (2014). Roundaboutness is Not a Mysterious Concept: A Financial Application to Capital Theory. *Review of Political Economy*, 26(4), pp. 648–665.

Calvo G. (2013). Puzzling over the Anatomy of Crises: Liquidity and the Veil of Finance. Background paper for the Mayekawa Lecture at the Institute for Monetary and Economic Studies Conference. *Monetary and Economic Studies*, 31, pp. 39–64.

Campello M., Graham, J, Harvey, C. (2010). The Real Effects of Financial Constraints: Evidence From a Financial Crisis. *Journal of Financial Economics*, 97(3), pp. 470–487.

Cloyne J., Hürtgen, P. (2016). The Macroeconomic Effects of Monetary Policy: A New Measure for the United Kingdom. *American Economic Journal: Macroeconomics*, 8(4), pp. 75–102.

Cloyne J., Ferreira C., Froemel M., Surico P. (2018). Monetary Policy, Corporate Finance and Investment. NBER Working Paper no. 25366.

Coibion O. (2012). Are the Effects of Monetary Policy Shocks Big or Small? *American Economic Journal: Macroeconomics*, 4(2), pp. 1–32.

Durante E., Ferrando A., Vermeulen, P. (2022). Monetary Policy, Investment and Firm Heterogeneity. *European Economic Review*, 148, 104251.

Edwards H., Lane K. (2021). Why are Investment Hurdle Rates So Sticky? *RBA Bulletin,* December. https://www.rba.gov.au/publications/bulletin/2021/dec/why-are-investment-hurdle-rates-so-sticky.html [Accessed at 26.02.2026].

Farooq U., Ahmed J., Khan S. (2021). Do the Macroeconomic Factors Influence the Firm's Investment Decisions? A Generalized Method of Moments (GMM) Approach. *International Journal of Finance & Economics*, 26(1), pp. 790–801.

Givens G., Reed, R. (2018). Monetary Policy and Investment Dynamics: Evidence from Disaggregate Data. *Journal of Money, Credit and Banking*, 50(8), pp. 1851–1878.

Hambur J., La Cava G. (2018). Do Interest Rates affect Business Investment. Evidence from Australian Company-Level Data. *Reserve Bank of Australia Research Discussion Paper RDP,* April.

Hayek F. von (1933). *Price Expectations Monetary Disturbances and Malinvestment,* in Hayek, F. von (ed.), *Profits, Interest and Investment.* Clifton, NJ: Augustus M. Kelley, pp. 135–157.

Hayek F. von (1935). *Prices and Production*, in Hayek, F. von (ed.), *Prices and Production and Other Works.* Auburn, AL: Ludwig von Mises Institute, pp. 189–330.

Hayek F. von (1937). *Investment that raises demand for capital*, in Hayek, F. von (ed.), *Prices and Production and Other Works.* Auburn, AL: Ludwig von Mises Institute, pp. 521–530.

Hayek F. von (1939). *Profits, Interest and Investment*, in Hayek, F. von (ed.), *Profits, Interest and Investment And Other Essays on the Theory of Industrial Fluctuations.* Clifton, NJ: Augustus M. Kelley, pp. 3–72.

Lane K., Rosewall, T. (2015). Firms' Investment Decisions and Interest Rates. *RBA Bulletin*, June.

Leijonhufvud A. (2008). *Keynes and the Crisis*, CEPR Policy Insight no. 23, May. https://www-ceel.economia.unitn.it/staff/leijonhufvud/files/copenhagen2008.pdf [Accessed at 26.02.2026].

Machlup F. (1932). The Liquidity of Short-Term Capital. *Economica*, 37, pp. 271–284.

Montgomery M. (1995a). Capital Complementarity, Time-to-Build, and the Persistence of Investment Starts. *Journal of Macroeconomics*, 17(2), pp. 187–205.

Montgomery M. (1995b). "Time-to-Build" Completion Patterns for Nonresidential Structures, 1961–1991. *Economics Letters*, 48(2), pp. 155–163.

Montgomery M. (2006). Austrian Persistence? Capital-Based Business Cycle Theory and the Dynamics of Investment Spending. *The Review of Austrian Economics*, 19(1), pp. 17–45.

Peersman G., Smets F. (2005). The Industry Effects of Monetary Policy in the Euro Area. *The Economic Journal*, 115(503), pp. 319–342.

Romer D. (2019). *Advanced Macroeconomics.* New York, NY: McGraw Hill.

Rothbard M. (2009). *Man, Economy and State with Power and Market.* Alabama, AL: Ludwig von Mises Institute.

Shackle G. (1946). Interest Rate and the Pace of Investment. *The Economic Journal*, 56(221), pp. 1–17.

Sharpe S., Suarez, G. (2021). Why isn't Business Investment more Sensitive to Interest Rates? Evidence from Surveys. *Management Science*, 67(2), pp. 720–741.

Skousen, M. (2015). *The Structure of Production.* New York and London: New York University Press.

# 11. Hayekian case against nominal spending stabilization policy

**Mateusz Benedyk**

The goal of this chapter is to present Hayek's considerations regarding the problems associated with stabilizing nominal spending in an economy. To achieve this, I will analyze Hayek's texts, where we can find insights into understanding this issue. In the following sections, I will discuss the following themes: (1) the mechanism of the diffusion of changes in economic data; (2) the impact of stabilizing nominal spending in the face of changes in payment habits; (3) the impact of stabilizing nominal spending on the ratio of consumption to investment expenditures; (4) the impact of stabilizing nominal spending in the case of a single country operating within the so-called monetary nationalism system; (5) stabilizing nominal spending in light of the general goals Hayek set for monetary policy. The chapter concludes with findings and suggestions for further research on this topic. Addressing this subject is particularly important because, in the literature—even among respected scholars specializing in Hayek's work—the view that a monetary policy of stabilizing nominal spending in the economy was strongly favored by the Austrian economist has become deeply entrenched (White 2008, Gustavson 2010, Cachanosky 2014, Evans 2015). My analysis in the subsequent sections demonstrates that this view does not stand up to scrutiny when compared with Hayek's own assertions.

## HAYEK'S VISION OF HOW CHANGES DISSEMINATE IN THE ECONOMY

Hayek presented a fairly concrete vision of how a change in one element of the economic puzzle spreads throughout the entire economic system in a modern market economy. He articulated the most complete version of this mechanism in his lectures delivered in Geneva, later published as *Monetary Nationalism and International Stability* (Hayek 2008a). To discuss the issue of monetary nationalism, the Austrian economist chose to illustrate the structural economic changes that a single shift in demand between countries would introduce. He applied this same analysis to three different systems (a point I'll return to in the section on monetary nationalism).

The simplest system to analyze would be a homogeneous international currency—a hypothetical situation where people use a uniform currency, and the banking system doesn't create any substitutes based on it. This would be like a world where only gold coins and bars were used, without bank deposits or banknotes entitling one to withdraw gold.

Hayek analyzes what would happen if there were a shift in demand, and a former client of firm A in one country started purchasing goods from firm B in another country. Standard international economic theory would correctly state that this would lead to a worsening of the trade balance in country A's origin and an improvement in the trade balance of country B's location. According to Hayek, this observation is merely the beginning of the analysis. Equally important is what happens next: adjustments in the structure of incomes and the allocation of productive resources among the suppliers of A and B, and then among their suppliers as well.

In other words, a single change will trigger a chain reaction in the economy, leading to a shift in the structure of relative prices and incomes. These changes will persist until all affected economic entities adjust their actions to the new economic situation. Hayek even writes:

> But whether any particular individual in the country will be affected will depend on whether he is a link in that particular chain, that is, whether he has more or less immediately been serving the individuals whose income has first been affected, and not simply on whether he is in the same country or not. In fact this picture of the chain makes it clear that it is not impossible that most of the people who ultimately suffer a decrease of income in consequence of the initial transfer of demand from A to B may be in B and not in A. This is often overlooked because the whole process is presented as if the chain of effects came to an end as soon as payments between the two countries balance. In fact however each of the two chains—that started by the decrease of somebody's income in A, and that started by the increase of another persons income in B—may continue to run on for a long time after they have passed into the other country, and may have even a greater number of links in that country than in the one where they started. They will come to an end only when they meet, not only in the same country but in the same individual, so finally offsetting each other. This means that the number of reductions of individual incomes and prices (not their aggregate amount) which becomes necessary in consequence of a transfer of money from A to B may actually be greater in B than in A. (Hayek 2008a, p. 356)

According to Hayek, we are therefore dealing with de facto two chains of adjustment: one stemming from an increase in demand and the other from a decrease in demand. The network of economic interconnections determines where the subsequent links in these chains will be located. It's possible that firms experiencing an increase in demand might even be situated in country

A's origin. These adjustments will continue until, for certain specific firms or individuals, the rise in demand from the first chain equals the fall in demand from the second, at which point that entity will no longer need to make further adjustments.

This analysis, though it refers specifically to a "real" change—a demand shift caused, for instance, by a change in buyer preferences— strongly resembles the treatment of monetary changes familiar to all monetary theorists interested in the so-called Cantillon Effect.[1] This effect describes the uneven impact of new money spreading through the economy on individual prices and incomes. New money doesn't raise all prices and incomes to the same extent and at the same time; rather, its effect depends on the channel through which it propagates. It's worth noting that this convergence is no surprise, as Hayek spoke of Cantillon with great esteem and even placed an epigraph from his work at the beginning of the first lecture in *Prices and Production* (Hayek 2008d).

It's also no surprise that Hayek chose this kind of framework as the foundation for the complex analysis of monetary influences on the economy that he undertook in *Monetary Nationalism*. This framework also resonates well with Hayek's general approach to macroeconomic analysis. The Austrian economist wasn't content with merely looking at aggregate changes; he believed that the most interesting things often happen within aggregates and require deeper investigation.

Similarly, Hayek criticized, among other things, the mechanical version of the quantitative theory of money, which completely disregarded the potential impact of monetary changes on the structure of relative prices and, for example, the possibility of triggering a business cycle. Bearing in mind this general framework for how changes, including monetary ones, propagate throughout the economy, let's now turn to Hayek's specific remarks concerning the implementation of policies aimed at stabilizing the flow of nominal spending in the economy.

## STABILIZING NOMINAL SPENDING AND CHANGES IN PAYMENT HABITS

In *Prices and Production*, Hayek introduced the idea of neutral money. As I understand Hayek's approach here, this concept was primarily necessary to fill a theoretical gap he perceived when transitioning from the theory of barter exchange to the theory of exchange in a monetary economy. Neutral money would allow the valuation principles present in a direct exchange system to be applied to the reality of indirect exchange.[2]

A separate task for economic theory (and one in which Hayek, in a way, specialized) was to trace the influences on the economy of various monetary institutions (e.g., fractional-reserve banking or the gold standard) that did not meet the requirement of monetary neutrality. Putting aside the usefulness of such an approach for constructing an economic system, it's worth noting that Hayek identified three conditions for monetary neutrality to exist. The most commonly discussed is maintaining a stable flow of nominal spending in the economy; we'll return to the other two conditions in the section on Hayek's general guidance for monetary policy.

Since the idea of neutral money was, for Hayek, a specific, unrealistic theoretical concept rather than a description of an actual economic state, he openly admitted that money would never be fully neutral for many reasons. The first practical problem the Austrian economist observed in this regard concerned changes in the demand for money that weren't strictly linked to changes in productivity and income structures. As an example of such changes, he pointed to alterations in the structure of firms—their mergers or divisions—which could affect the number of transactions money needs to facilitate and, consequently, the demand for cash balances. For instance, splitting firms into independent units means that more entities now need to hold cash balances, and money must facilitate more transactions. The opposite situation would lead to a decrease in the demand for cash balances.

Is there a simple way for, say, monetary authorities or the banking system to mitigate these changes and, in a sense, "extinguish" the chain of subsequent adjustments in the economy—the structure of prices and monetary incomes—forced by the change in the demand for money? Let's quote Hayek himself here:

> For, in order to eliminate all monetary influences on the formation of prices and the structure of production, it would not be sufficient merely quantitatively to adapt the supply of money to these changes in demand, it would be necessary also to see that it came into the hands of those who actually require it, i.e., to that part of the system where that change in business organization or the habits of payment had taken place. It is conceivable that this could be managed in the case of an increase of demand. It is clear that it would be still more difficult in the case of a reduction. But quite apart from this particular difficulty which, from the point of view of pure theory, may not prove insuperable, it should be clear that only to satisfy the legitimate demand for money in this sense, and otherwise to leave the amount of the circulation unchanged, can never be a practical maxim of currency policy. (Hayek 2008d, p. 297)

Hayek raises several important points here. First, changes in the demand for money emerge in specific parts of the economy. To counteract these changes, and thereby maintain a stable flow of nominal spending, a precise quantity of money must be injected or withdrawn. However, for monetary neutrality to be preserved, the change in the money supply within the economy would need to occur *exactly* where the original change in demand took place.

Without any intervention, this change would trigger a chain of adjustments throughout the economy. For instance, a firm experiencing increased demand for money would have to cut back on purchases to reduce expenditures or make its sales terms more attractive to customers to boost revenue and thus build up cash balances. Such actions by this firm would lead to changes in both supplier and customer incomes and prices. These parties, too, would need to adjust accordingly to the new situation until a new equilibrium is established with new cash balances and a new structure of prices and incomes.

To prevent this chain of events, the cash balance of the firm suddenly demanding more money would need to be increased. Hayek notes that, theoretically, such a firm could be granted credit, thereby avoiding these adjustments. I would add that, in essence, this would only stretch out these adjustments over time, as the firm with the credit would need to generate larger positive cash flows from its operations in the future to repay the loan. If, on the other hand, there's a *decrease* in the demand for money, it's difficult to even imagine how such "sterilization" of additional purchasing power could precisely withdraw the surplus money from the cash balances of the firms whose demand for money has changed.

Why then can't the money supply be increased or decreased anywhere in the economy? According to the vision of how changes propagate in a monetary economy, as presented in the previous section, a change in the money supply at any random point in the economy would trigger a similar chain of adjustments. Someone's cash balance would either increase or decrease, thereby altering the structure of expenditures. Entrepreneurs and owners of factors of production would then have to adapt to the new situation, depending on whether these changes meant higher or lower revenues from their operations or incurred expenses.

Therefore, if the response from the money supply side were to appear at a different point than the change in money demand analyzed by Hayek, the economy would have to undergo two chains of adjustment to the new monetary situation. We have no reason to suspect that the changes induced by adjusting the money supply would appear in the exact same places as the changes caused by the shift in money demand, but operating in the opposite direction. One could even imagine a scenario where a change in the money supply actually amplifies the necessary adjustments for some households or firms.

## STABILIZING NOMINAL SPENDING AND THE INVESTMENT–CONSUMPTION RATIO

The difficulties of conducting a policy of injecting new credit in response to an increased demand for money aren't limited to the problem discussed in the previous section. The second issue, crucial for Hayek, regarding the potential stabilization of nominal spending by banks or monetary authorities, concerns the possible cyclical fluctuations such actions could induce.

At the heart of the business cycle theory developed by the Austrian economist is the observation that additional injections of bank credit can alter the ratio between investment and consumption expenditures, leading to intertemporal discoordination (Hayek 2008b, Hayek 2008d). In this scenario, entrepreneurs embark on ventures that, in the short term, reduce the available supply of consumer goods, aiming to significantly increase it in the more distant future. Simultaneously, consumers expect a faster increase in the flow of consumer goods. This mismatch leads to a lack of profitability for some of the commenced investments and necessitates economic restructuring.

Could such a scenario also occur when credit is expanded to mitigate changes in the demand for money? I haven't found direct statements from Hayek that explicitly answer this question, but I believe the following passage will be useful in this context:

> In theory it is at least possible that, during the acute stage of the crisis when the capitalistic structure of production tends to shrink more than will ultimately prove necessary, an expansion of producers' credits might have a wholesome effect. But this could only be the case if the quantity were so regulated as exactly to compensate for the initial, excessive rise of the relative prices of consumers' goods, and if arrangements could be made to withdraw the additional credits as these prices fall and the proportion between the supply of consumers' goods and the supply of intermediate products adapts.itself to the proportion between the demand for these goods. And even these credits would do more harm than good if they made roundabout processes seem profitable which, even after the acute crisis had subsided, could not be kept up without the help of additional credits. Frankly, I do not see how the banks can ever be in a position to keep credit within these limits. (Hayek 2008d, pp. 274–275)

The scenario Hayek considers here would unfold as follows: during the restructuring phase of the economy, following the discovery of erroneous investments, entrepreneurs react with excessive pessimism. They curtail even those processes that could be sustained given the planned temporal distribution of consumption. Their actions can be interpreted as an increase in the demand for money—investors release factors of production and liquidate inventories and some fixed assets, aiming to accumulate higher cash balances in anticipation of future investment opportunities.

According to the Austrian Nobel laureate, there's a possibility that this increase in demand will be excessive, and entrepreneurs will eventually revert to some of their old processes, repurchase previously sold assets, and re-employ factors of production. In such a situation, a credit injection could theoretically accelerate the return to economic activity by reducing the need for further cash balance accumulation through restructuring actions.

In these deliberations, Hayek did not use terms like "neutral money" or "stabilizing expenditures," but I believe my interpretation of this case as an increase in the money supply in response to increased demand for money has been well justified above. Why, then, did the Austrian economist not explicitly advocate for such actions?

Instead of the problem discussed in the previous section—the precise injection of additional money into the specific places where demand for it has risen—this time, he draws attention to the issue of the adequacy of the expenditure structure relative to the preference structure. Even if we assume that initially, the pendulum swung too far towards consumption and the initial credit injection balances this, a new problem arises: how to withdraw this additional money so that its continued presence in the system doesn't excessively tilt the expenditure structure towards investment relative to consumption.

We can say that the ordinary operation of the price system, even if prolonged and imperfect, would eventually bring the production structure and consumer preferences regarding consumption over time into equilibrium. If entrepreneurs were to remain with an additional credit injection, it would lead to the initiation of another business cycle, even though the economy had just dealt with the effects of the previous one. Hayek sees no cognitive procedure on the part of banks or monetary authorities to dispense credit in such a way as to maintain a state of equilibrium.

Thus, to the previously discussed objection that nominal spending stabilization policy can cause another chain of adjustments in the economy instead of offsetting the effects of the previous one, we can add a further caveat: if this policy relies on credit creation, it can disturb the proportions between consumption and investment expenditures, thereby triggering a business cycle.

## STABILIZING NOMINAL SPENDING UNDER MONETARY NATIONALISM

Hayek's analyses also pose problems for proponents of nominal spending stabilization policy in the realm of international monetary systems. Hayek dedicated his perhaps somewhat underappreciated Geneva lectures at the Graduate Institute of International and Development Studies, later published as *Monetary Nationalism and International Stability*, to this very issue. In the first section, I already referenced a longer excerpt from his preliminary analyses on this topic. The Austrian economist aimed to present the economic functioning of three international monetary systems: homogeneous international currency, national reserve system, independent currencies (monetary nationalism).

We would encounter the first system if different countries used the same commodity as money, and the banking system created no money substitutes based on it. An example of such a system would be the gold standard, where only gold coins and bars served as money, without any involvement from banking products like deposits or banknotes. In today's world, a widely adopted global Bitcoin could also be an example of such a system (where the development of classical fractional-reserve banking, though theoretically possible, isn't currently practiced).

The national reserve system combines an international currency with national substitutes for that money. The historical gold standard operated precisely in this manner. Domestically, people often didn't use the commodity money itself, but various banking products (from central or commercial banks) built upon a precious metal reserve. This reserve was primarily used to settle international transactions and, for example, to finance trade deficits or capital outflows.

Currently, we largely live in a system of monetary nationalism. In this system, there's no international money. At most, you can buy or sell another country's currency in exchange for your domestic currency at current exchange rates.

Hayek's lectures are dedicated to explaining how adaptation to changes in international demand for consumer or capital goods unfolds within each of these three systems. Most relevant to this chapter's purpose is the discussion on monetary nationalism. Here, Hayek based his analysis on the premise that a country's central bank would pursue a policy of stabilizing the nominal flow of expenditures in its domestic currency (Hayek 2008a, p. 368). So, how would this monetary policy rule fare in the current international monetary environment, according to the Austrian economist?

Hayek believed that the combination of the currency system and monetary policy he analyzed would lead to monetary disturbances in the structure of production. These disturbances would eventually become apparent and necessitate correction. In his view, this would represent another type of reversible monetary distortion in the economy, alongside the business cycle. How would these distortions arise?

A shift in international demand would cause a change in exports from the affected country. Let's analyze an example of an increase in exports. This situation would lead to greater purchases of the domestic currency by foreign counterparts, thereby causing its relative appreciation. This appreciation would make imported goods more attractive and export activities less profitable.

In turn, this would mean a decrease in the flow of domestic expenditures. According to the adopted rule of operation, this should lead to an expansionary monetary policy, such as granting additional credit to entrepreneurs.

However, these changes in the price system and the actions of monetary authorities would not correspond to real data changes in the economy. They would send false signals regarding the necessity of increasing or decreasing production. For instance, the appreciation of the domestic currency worsens the position of exporters despite the fact that their production methods haven't become less efficient at all. While firms affected by currency appreciation will face short-term difficulties, as this price impulse spreads throughout the economy, their operating costs will begin to fall because imported factors of production will be cheaper, and there will be less competition for domestic factors of production.

At the same time, there's no basis for an additional credit injection to reflect a permanent change in the proportion of consumption to investment expenditures. Such an action would only trigger a business cycle.

We can, of course, conduct an analogous analysis for a country experiencing a decline in exports. Here too, the exchange rate mechanism and potential actions by monetary authorities will compel temporary adjustments that later prove unnecessary.

Generalizing this analysis, we can say that, according to Hayek, a country's nominal expenditures should adjust to international shifts in money demand. For instance, a country experiencing productivity gains might see increasing demand for its currency as its share of world income grows. Counteracting this process through an active monetary policy that stabilizes nominal expenditures at all costs will result in a multiplication of adjustment processes in the economy, rather than their mitigation.

## HAYEK'S GENERAL GUIDELINES FOR MONETARY POLICY

Hayek relatively rarely offered specific monetary policy recommendations that he believed should stem from his macroeconomic theories. The following quote quite effectively explains this state of affairs:

> It is probably an illusion to suppose that we shall ever be able entirely to eliminate industrial fluctuations by means of monetary policy. The most we may hope for is that the growing information of the public may make it easier for central banks both to follow a cautious policy during the upward swing of the cycle, and so to mitigate the following depression, and to resist the well-meaning but dangerous proposals to fight depression by "a little inflation." (Hayek 2008d, p. 298)

From the preceding quote, we can draw several conclusions. First, Hayek did not believe that business cycles could be entirely eliminated through appropriate monetary policy. Second, in his view, the most crucial task of monetary policy was to prevent excessive credit expansion during the expansionary phase of the cycle, thereby minimizing economic distortions caused by intertemporal discoordination. This would, in turn, reduce the scale of necessary economic restructuring during a crisis. Third, Hayek was skeptical of attempts to alleviate this restructuring through monetary policy tools. As I mentioned in the section regarding the consumption–investment ratio in the economy, Hayek did not dogmatically reject all attempts to provide credit to the economy during a severe crisis; however, in his opinion, the conditions for such an undertaking to succeed are so restrictive that its practical and effective implementation is difficult to imagine.

I bring up this context of Hayek's monetary advice because the policy of stabilizing nominal spending, sometimes even referred to as "Hayek's rule," is often invoked in the context of economic crises—such as the Great Depression of 1929–1933 or the Great Recession of 2007–2009. And it appears not as a warning that this rule was not met during boom years, leading to significant imbalances in the economy, but rather as a remedy for an overly severe recession that could be easily minimized by a more expansionary monetary policy during ongoing economic restructuring.[3] Such a presentation of the issue is, in my opinion, inconsistent with the general guidelines for conducting monetary policy that Hayek left behind.

In the previous three sections, I outlined three specific economic arguments by Hayek that challenge the validity of implementing a policy to stabilize nominal spending in the economy. Here, I point to the inconsistency of such a policy with the goal Hayek ascribed to monetary policy.

So, why the conviction among other researchers that such a policy genuinely fulfills some Hayekian dictum? The quotes from Hayek's works that appear in this context most often refer to the idea of neutral money, not to actual monetary policy. To illustrate the difference between these levels of analysis, we can quote a larger passage from Hayek himself:

> The true relationship between the theoretical concept of neutral money, and the practical ideal of monetary policy is, therefore, that the former provides one criterion for judging the latter; the degree to which a concrete system approaches the condition of neutrality is one and perhaps the most important, but not the only criterion by which one has to judge the appropriateness of a given course of policy. It is quite conceivable that a distortion of relative prices and a misdirection of production by monetary influences could only be avoided if, first, the total money stream remained constant, and second, all prices were completely flexible, and, third, all long term contracts were based on a correct anticipation of future price movements. This would mean that, if the second and third conditions are not given, the ideal could not be realized by any kind of monetary policy. (Hayek 2008d, p. 304)

In the quote above, Hayek indicates that maintaining monetary neutrality can serve as a metric against which monetary policy is evaluated. Though characteristic of his style, he immediately qualifies this by stating it's not the only way to assess monetary policy. He then lists three conditions for monetary neutrality to exist: a stable flow of monetary expenditures, price flexibility, and accurate predictions of changes in the purchasing power of money when entering into long-term contracts.

However, including a stable flow of expenditures among the three conditions for monetary neutrality does not in itself signify support for adopting a direct monetary policy target aimed at stabilizing nominal expenditures in the economy. This is merely intended to be an effect of proper policy. But perhaps—Hayek doesn't specify the precise means here—this goal could be achieved by focusing on some other macroeconomic aggregate (in other Hayekian writings, ideas such as stabilizing the prices of factors of production (Hayek 2008c) or having the central bank observe the profit rate of firms and the long-term interest rate appear (Hayek 1975)), or, for instance, by fundamentally changing the operating conditions of the monetary system (from various phases of Hayek's work, we find proposals for changes in the functioning of the gold standard (Hayek 2008a), proposals for commodity-backed money (Hayek 1958), or the idea of money denationalization (Hayek 1990)).

As I highlighted in the previous three sections, within the very same Hayekian texts that mention monetary neutrality, we find discussions about the practical problems of implementing a policy that seeks to stabilize the flow of nominal expenditures at all costs. These problems arise from: the discrepancy between where changes in money demand occur and where monetary intervention might take place; the potential for shifts in the consumption–investment ratio after monetary intervention; and the failure to account for the international context of monetary changes.

Let's also note that Hayek provided three, not just one, conditions for monetary neutrality to exist. So, by analogous reasoning, would we then conclude from this passage that Hayek advocated for banning unindexed (to inflation/deflation) long-term contracts or for entering only into short-term contracts for acquiring factor services (e.g., labor) to maintain price flexibility?

## CONCLUSION AND FUTURE RESEARCH AREAS

In this chapter, I have sought to demonstrate that Hayek identified serious theoretical problems with the validity of a monetary policy aimed at stabilizing nominal expenditures. These concerns touched on three areas: the localized nature of changes in money demand and the chain effects these changes unleash; the potential for such monetary policy to trigger a business cycle; and the international context of shifts in money demand and the challenges of accommodating this, especially under a regime of flexible exchange rates for local currencies. Based on these considerations, I believe it is incorrect to categorize Hayek among the proponents of nominal spending stabilization policy, despite his view that nominal spending stability was one of the conditions for monetary neutrality to exist.

In the previous section, I suggested further directions for research into monetary policy. I believe that in this context, we should also address questions related to Hayek's work such as: Can we find any guidance in Hayek's writings regarding aggregates or direct monetary policy targets other than stabilizing nominal expenditures? Can Hayek's treatises on the commodity standard and the denationalization of money somehow be integrated into this framework?

From the perspective of current discussions on monetary policy, pertinent questions in this context also include: From today's standpoint, can any of these policies be effectively implemented? Is there a justification for adopting nominal GDP as a proxy for nominal expenditures? Does neutrality ensure stable nominal income or overall monetary expenditures? These, however, are areas for further contemplation.

## NOTES

1. Hayek saw a close relationship between changes in income and changes in the demand for money, although he did not equate these magnitudes (Hayek 2008a, pp. 351–353). He built the entire analytical framework for examining changes in demand precisely to highlight the role of monetary systems and shifts in the flow of monetary expenditures and relative monetary prices.
2. The idea of neutral money has caused considerable arguments among Hayekian scholars. Main points of discussion can be found in Salerno (2002), Caldwell (2002), Hülsmann (2007), Huerta de Soto (2012), and Salerno et al. (2020).
3. Only Cachanosky (2014) underlines this point.

## REFERENCES

Cachanosky N. (2014). Hayek's Rule, NGDP Targeting, and the Productivity Norm: Theory and Application. *Journal of Stock & Forex Trading*, 3(2), pp. 1–9.

Caldwell B. (2002). Wieser, Hayek and Equilibrium Theory. *Journal des Economistes et des Etudes Humaines*, 12(1), pp. 47–66.

Evans A. J. (2015). *Sound Money. An Austrian Proposal for Free Banking, NGDP Targets, and OMO Reforms*. London: Adam Smith Institute.

Gustavson M. (2010). The Hayek Rule: A New Monetary Policy Framework for the 21st Century. *Reason Foundation Policy Study 389*.

Hayek F. von (1958). A commodity reserve currency, in Hayek F. von (ed.), *Individualism and Economic Order*. Chicago, IL: University of Chicago Press, pp. 209–219.

Hayek F. von (1975). Profits, interest and investment, in Hayek F. von (ed.), *Profits, Interest and Investment and Other Essays on the Theory of Industrial Fluctuations*. New York, NY: Augustus M. Kelley, pp. 3–71.

Hayek F. von (1990). *Denationalisation of Money – The Argument Refined*. London: Institute of Economic Affairs.

Hayek F. von (2008a). Monetary nationalism and international stability, in Hayek F. von (ed.), *Prices and Production and Other Works*. Auburn, AL: Ludwig von Mises Institute, pp. 331–422.

Hayek F. von (2008b). Monetary theory and the trade cycle, in Hayek F. von (ed.), *Prices and Production and Other Works*. Auburn, AL: Ludwig von Mises Institute, pp. 1–130.
Hayek F. von (2008c). On "neutral" money, in Hayek F. von (ed.), *Good Money: Part I. The New World*. Indianapolis, IN: Liberty Fund, pp. 228–231.
Hayek F. von (2008d). Prices and production, in Hayek F. von (ed.), *Prices and Production and Other Works*. Auburn, AL: Ludwig von Mises Institute, pp. 189–329.
Huerta de Soto J. (2012). Book review: Jörg Hülsmann Guido, *Mises. The Last Knight of Liberalism*. *Quarterly Journal of Austrian Economics*, 15(4), pp. 469–479.
Hülsmann J. G. (2007). *Mises. The Last Knight of Liberalism*. Auburn, AL: Ludwig von Mises Institute.
Salerno J. (2002). Friedrich von Wieser and Friedrich A. Hayek. The General Equlibrium Tradition in Austrian Economics. *Journal des Economistes et des Etudes Humaines*, 12(2/3), pp. 357–377.
Salerno J., Dorobăţ C., Israel K.-F. (2020), Two Views on Neutral Money: Wieser and Hayek versus Menger and Mises. *The European Journal of the History of Economic Thought*, 27(5), pp. 682–711.
White L. (2008). Did Hayek and Robbins Deepen the Great Depression. *Journal of Money, Credit and Banking*, 40(4), pp. 751–768.

# 12. Bitcoin in light of the Austrian theory of money

**Olga Peniaz and Aliaksandr Kavaliou**

## INTRODUCTION

The world economy in the twenty-first century has shown a new round of searching by economic agents for ways to improve the institution of money. The emergence of new means of payment such as Bitcoin, and then its analogues, questions the current fiat money system. There are also attempts to implement official digital currencies such as Central Bank Digital Currency.

The representatives of the Austrian school of economics pay particular attention to the understanding of the essence of cryptocurrencies. The reasons for such interest lie in the existence of three specific elements of the theory of money in the Austrian tradition: the theory of the origin of money by Carl Menger, the theory of the value of money by Ludwig von Mises, and the concept of competitive currencies of Friedrich August von Hayek. There are many important theoretical questions related to the emergence of cryptocurrencies. We will focus specifically on the most common cryptocurrency, Bitcoin, and attempt to answer the following questions:

- Is the emergence of Bitcoin consistent with the evolutionary theory of the emergence of money?
- Is Bitcoin good? What are the determinants of its value, and does it have intrinsic value?
- Is Bitcoin money?
- Does the emergence of Bitcoin as a medium of exchange contradict Mises' regression theorem?
- Can the proliferation of cryptocurrencies be interpreted as a competition between currencies?

All these questions will be covered in this chapter. The first cryptocurrency, Bitcoin, will be the main subject. The chapter is structured as follows: the first part outlines the principles of Bitcoin's functioning and analyses its correspondence with Menger's evolutionary theory of the origins of money; the second part compares Bitcoin's performance of money functions in comparison to fiat money; in the third part the possibility to apply Mises' regression theorem to Bitcoin and the analyses of Bitcoin in light of Hayek's approach to currency competition are discussed.

## THE EVOLUTION OF THE MONETARY SYSTEM AND BITCOIN

Throughout its history, the institution of money has not been a static phenomenon. Money emerged, like other spontaneous orders, to reduce the fundamental uncertainty of exchange (Kavaliou, 2020). It has constantly evolved, adapting to the changing demands of economic agents. The evolution of forms and types of money took place under the influence of financial and organizational innovations, as well as technology development and state intervention (Kavaliou and Peniaz, 2022).

The selection of goods for the role of money is the result of billions of human actions. Each action improves the condition of an individual, but is not intended to "invent" money or even to select any commodities for the role of money. In the process of evolution, precious metals such as gold and silver, being the most marketable commodities, were selected for the role of money.

Originally, the monetary system was completely decentralized: the holding of a sum of money justified that its owner had previously created a certain good, which received public recognition through its purchase by other persons (we leave aside the non-legal violent-coercive variants of wealth acquisition). The presence of economic interest to obtain the most appropriate payment instrument and the inconvenience of paying with ingots led to the appearance of coins.

The monopolization of coinage by governments and the establishment of legal tender, with all the negative factors associated with the possibility to manipulate the quality of the coin, contributed to the unification of the monetary system between different regions, and thereby conditions for the development of trade were improved.

The choice of one currency via legal tender helps to reduce transaction costs but creates the possibility of abuse in relation to the quality of the coinage. In his analysis, Hülsmann demonstrates that the introduction of legal tender and coinage monopoly could lead to a decrease in the diversity of coins available on the market and lead to the alteration and debasement of the money (Hülsmann, 2008). Moreover, it may spur fractional reserve banking (Hülsmann, 2003).

In addition to the problem of the quality of the money issued by the state, legal tender has a negative influence on money as an institution. The state propagates among the public a dangerous illusion about the essence of money: a coin, which is a certified unit of weight, could be represented as a kind of conventional sign (Menger, 2007). The function of legal tender is emphasized by the state, while distorting the understanding of the essence of money.

The emergence of money substitutes in the form of private banknotes exchanged for coins at the first demand of depositors had a dual effect. It gave elasticity to the money supply and, to some extent, contributed to the stability of the value of the monetary unit: banks expanded the volume of lending during the boom of economic activity and, during the decline, reduced it, thus levelling inflationary and deflationary trends. Such a task could only be accomplished when the reserve ratio on money substitutes was relatively high, that is, when the issue of banknotes and deposits was relatively small compared to precious metal reserves. As soon as the link with the gold reserve was abandoned, the unrestrained bank emission caused prices to rise. The described credit money came in the form of banknotes, bills, or other securities, as well as in the form of records of bank accounts, that is, deposits. Technological progress in the twentieth century, in particular computerization, led to the transformation of accounts and corresponding records into electronic ones, to the use of payment cards. Money increasingly lost its material basis. Private banknotes were replaced by government banknotes, which gained a monopoly on the existence of centralized monetary systems. Finally, technological innovation has led to the emergence of digital currencies in centralized (such as WebMoney) and decentralized (such as Bitcoin) networks.

The first observation concerns the status of cryptocurrencies, like Bitcoin, the best-known and most common cryptocurrency (50% of cryptocurrency market capitalization, see CoinMarketCap, 2024b), based on four key elements: 1) peer-to-peer network; 2) asymmetric cryptography; 3) distributed ledger technology (blockchain); 4) mining based on proof of work.

In various studies, the definition of its role in the economy ranges from money ("Bitcoin is the digital equivalent of gold") to a money laundering tool. Bitcoin, as determined by its creator, is "an electronic coin as a chain of digital signatures. Each owner transfers the coin to the next by digitally signing a hash of the previous transaction and the public key of the next owner and adding these to the end of the coin. A payee can verify the signatures to verify the chain of ownership" (Nakamoto, 2008).

The Bitcoin emission algorithm is as follows. The total supply of Bitcoins to be issued is set at 21 million coins. The first 50 coins became the property of the author for creating the first block of transactions; then the emission took place as a reward for "mining". Transactions create a new block in the blockchain. The first miner who solves the equation receives a reward consisting of a certain number of coins. Every four years, the amount of reward decreases by half – from 50 coins in 2009–2012 to 1 "satoshi" ($10^{8}$ Bitcoin) by 2140, when the emission will be finished. However, today the volume of issues has already exceeded 19.74 million Bitcoins, that is, more than 94% of the maximum amount (CoinMarketCap, 2024a).

Anonymity, transparency, absence of centralized control, the security system, high speed of payments, especially international ones, and absence of difference between cash and non-cash sums determine the advantages of the described system and create a high stable demand to join the Bitcoin network (Sinel'nikova-Muryleva et al., 2019). Bitcoin was followed by a great number of various cryptocurrencies. Their number exceeded 20,000. The cryptocurrency market capitalization is close to $2.10 trillion (CoinMarketCap, 2024b) and Bitcoin represents more than 50% of the total cryptocurrency market capitalization (see Figure 12.1).

The evolutionary theory of the origin of money was formulated by Carl Menger (1985, 2002, 2007, 2009), developed by Ludwig von Mises (1981, 1998). Menger affirms that the emergence of money is an evolutionary process, spontaneous in character, and conditioned by the economic interest of agents, which appears without convention or legislative constraint (Menger, 2007, pp. 261–262). Money arose from the intentions and interests of economic agents, from their actions in finding an instrument to achieve their ends in the

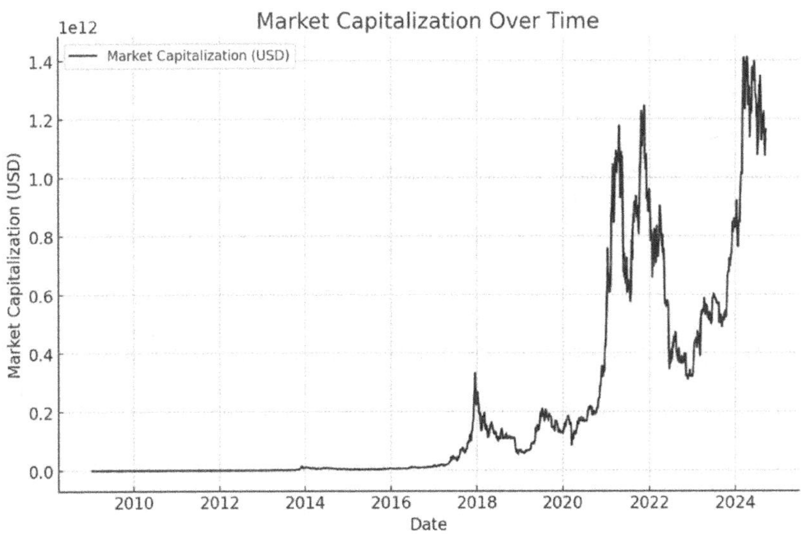


*Source:* https://www.blockchain.com/

*Figure 12.1* *Bitcoin market capitalization*

shortest time possible (in this case: the rapid acquisition of goods to satisfy human needs). The theory of the origin of money is consistent with the theory of human action and the general theory of goods. The final purpose of all economic activity is to satisfy human needs. Both production and exchange operations, which can satisfy human needs only indirectly, are undertaken in the pursuit of this final objective. In Menger's conception, only an economic good can be selected for the role of money.

To analyse the subject of this chapter we will focus on the following aspects of the theory. First, the origin of money was the result of the process of selection of goods for the role of medium of exchange between different economic goods. This indicates that these commodities had the ability to meet some human needs before they started being used as a medium of exchange.

It is important to note that the process of selection was spontaneous, based not on human design, but on human action, determined by the subjective interests of economic agents, with no social contract or any legislative recognition required:

> The origin of the money (as distinct from a coin, which is only one variety of money) is, as we have seen, entirely natural and thus displays legislative influence only in the rarest instances. Money is not an invention of the state. It is not the product of a legislative act. Even the sanction of political authority is not necessary for its existence. (Menger, 2007, pp. 261–262)

Such institutions Menger called organic.[1]

Another substantial point is that the process of selection was competitive with the freedom of economic agents to choose goods with the greatest marketability (goods that are sold and bought the easiest). Furthermore, the process of selection was evolutionary and progressive, and it depended on habits and imitations. Not all individuals understand immediately the benefits of owning a commodity that is more exchangeable than other commodities. As people realize that there is an advantage in using one specific commodity to reduce the cost of exchange, indirect exchange develops and promotes this commodity to the rank of a universal medium of exchange.

It should be emphasized that the spontaneity of the process means not only the absence of an initial design for the institution of money, an "ultimate goal" in the Aristotelian sense, but also the uncertainty of the result to which the development will eventually lead ("ends-independent" in the sense of a multiplicity of possible end states) (Horwitz, 2015).

The Bitcoin payment system cannot be considered an organic institution; it is a product of human invention, but the presence of such an element within the evolution of the monetary system is in line with the idea of the uncertainty of its final state. Bitcoin was designed to perform a role as digital cash, and in this sense, it does not fit the description of evolutionary theory either. Finally, there is no gold or any other commodity or collateral behind Bitcoin; it is a digital currency. At the same time, some similarities allow us to compare Bitcoin's status with gold in light of evolutionary theory. First, there is the absence of any role of the state in its origin. Second, the limited supply of Bitcoins and the direct cost of its production (mining) are distinct from fiat currencies. Similar to gold, the production cost of Bitcoin is currently increasing over time, as its consensus algorithm requires miners to consume massive amounts of electricity. Third, as in the case of gold, Bitcoin's value depends neither on the trust in its emitter nor on the emitter's financial health.

The evolutionary theory of money explains the emergence of money as an institution and the choice of a certain commodity for the role of universal medium of exchange. Bitcoin is compatible with this theory because it can be considered a new candidate for the role of money. Thus, various aspects of the emergence of Bitcoin can be described in terms of the evolutionary approach.

## BITCOIN AS A GOOD AND THE FUNCTION OF MONEY

To answer the question of whether Bitcoin is money, it is necessary to analyze how fully it performs the functions of money. Bitcoin can be used for transactions, and selling/buying goods and services; therefore, it can fulfil the role of medium of exchange that represents a key function of money. Menger considers it in this way: "…in a word, in trade markets certain wares emerge from the sphere of all the others and become means of barter, 'money' in the broadest sense of the word" (1985, p.152). Meanwhile, money is a common, generally accepted, universal medium of exchange. Bitcoin is far from such status; it serves a negligible volume of transactions in the economy.

The duality of the economic nature of cryptocurrencies is emphasized by The Committee on Payments and Market Infrastructures of the Bank for International Settlements, which refers cryptocurrencies to a group of electronic "money", which is a system of monetary settlements using electronic computer technology, for which it is typical to have some properties of money in addition to the properties of goods or an investment asset (Sinel'nikova-Muryleva et al., 2019). The International Monetary Fund does not consider cryptocurrencies to be money, but rather a high-risk investment asset.

We will first answer the question of whether Bitcoin is a good through the prism of the general theory of goods. An object acquires the character of a good under four conditions: 1) the presence of a human need; 2) the presence of a causal link from the object to the satisfaction of this need; 3) human knowledge of this causal link; 4) the possibility of using the object to satisfy the need (Menger, 2007).

The need for a means of payment with a stable value, unaffected by government monetary policies and ensuring rapidity and transparency of transactions, caused the permanent emergence of various kinds of private money covering local communities (Genkin, 2002).

Bitcoin was created as digital cash, and the need for a secure means of payment is arguably satisfied by it, meeting the second to fourth conditions. The volatility of Bitcoin's price is determined by the limited supply and unstable demand for Bitcoin as a digital investment asset from users who do not see it as a means of exchange and do not use it for that purpose. We can state that Bitcoin is a good and, like any good, has a source of value in its utility and rarity. Bitcoin's rarity is due to the maximum stock inherent in the issuance algorithm, and its usefulness relies on its role as a means of payment/investment asset etc. There are two important uses of Bitcoin: 1) Bitcoin as a payment infrastructure: an infrastructure composed of an open-source software protocol and a distributed ledger with unmatched technical robustness, enabling the transfer of funds/values (as used by the startup Strike for fund transfers); 2) Timestamping and data authenticity verification: Bitcoin technology allows for timestamping digital documents and verifying their authenticity.

The following properties are required to perform the function of a medium of exchange. The first property is the recognition by economic agents of it as a payment instrument and the convenience of its use. The Bitcoin payment system was first used in a narrow environment of IT specialists, and later spread to a wider audience. Payments with Bitcoin are robust and fast. With the development of the Lightning Network, the transaction fee is low and is independent of distance and state borders. The Lightning Network allows for Bitcoin transactions to be conducted off the blockchain (off-chain). After an initial escrow of funds on the blockchain (on-chain), only the balance of the aggregated transactions is occasionally recorded on the blockchain. This network functions like an accumulation of clearing houses, aggregating different positions of buying and selling bitcoins (de Mombynes, 2020).

The second property is its relative rarity and inelastic supply. Bitcoin's initial code for limited issuance ensures rarity. Therefore, Bitcoin, like gold money, if it were adopted as money, would result in deflationary growth (an increase in the production of goods and services accompanied by price decreases).

Furthermore, certain technical properties are required, such as durability, a high degree of security, divisibility, and compactness. Bitcoin meets all technical requirements. The minimum unit – satoshi – corresponds to $10^{-8}$ Bitcoin, which allows even small transactions to be serviced. The disadvantage is the necessity to have special equipment and software, but the same disadvantages are inherent to modern electronic money, settlements which are performed through cards or electronic devices (computer, phone).

Another key characteristic is the relative stability of its value. Fiat money is characterized by depreciation, which can cause the loss of its function as a store of value or a measure of value. Bitcoin is characterized by large volatility of its value (Figure 12.1) which undermines the possibility of it playing the role of medium of exchange for the time being. "Commodities whose prices are not well known or subject to considerable fluctuations also do not pass easily from hand to hand" (Menger, 2007, p. 255). It is difficult to implement a transaction with a medium of exchange which is constantly changing price; therefore, it is extremely difficult to plan future sales/purchases. As well, the volatility of the Bitcoin price does not contribute to the quality of its function as a measure of value. The fixing of transactions in Bitcoin, which is very volatile in price, does not help its participants to reduce the uncertainty in the economy. However, financial analysts have noticed a decrease in Bitcoin's volatility over the last 10 years despite some price booms. Based on the current trend, they predict that its volatility will decrease further over time, or at least continue to lessen the fluctuations in its price (Kaiko-research).

The further important trait is low transaction cost, which, in the case of Bitcoin, is achieved through the implementation of the Lightning Network. Money arose from the intentions and interests of economic agents, from their actions in finding an instrument to achieve their ends in the shortest time possible (in this case: the rapid acquisition of goods to satisfy human needs). The Bitcoin network can process no more than seven transactions per second. The average time for a transaction to be confirmed with Bitcoin is 10 minutes, although it can take from a few seconds to a few hours (this point concerns only on-chain transactions). When the Bitcoin network is overloaded, transaction times can increase significantly. This limitation in Bitcoin's transaction processing capacity represents a serious constraint for its use as a medium of exchange. This problem was resolved with the appearance of the Lightning Network in 2018, which allows transactions to be completed off-chain in a short time and at low costs (de Mombynes, 2020).

The debate over whether Bitcoin has intrinsic value is a controversial issue concerning its ability to fulfil the role of money. Some authors consider the presence of the costs of Bitcoin creation to be a factor allowing for intrinsic value, and the presence of consensus among users to be a measure of value (Andryushin, 2020). Others, on the contrary, believe that Bitcoin has no basis and its true value is zero (Kiselev, 2018).

In Austrian tradition, value is not an intrinsic property of an object; it is the judgement of economic agents about the value of a given good, and it has a different value in the eyes of different people. We will discuss not the intrinsic value of Bitcoin, but the presence/absence of its value other than monetary use. Should money have an independent value, or can it be a kind of "certificate" for the purchase of goods? For Menger, the medium of exchange should have a value from non-monetary uses, at least at the initial stages. The lack of such value in fiat money can easily be explained by the attachment of its rate to gold and silver and the process of substitution, which took centuries; today, the value of fiat money is the value derived from the performance of the function of the medium of exchange.

The production costs of money are irrelevant. Fiat money is valuable not because it requires some amount of paper, ink, printing, and human energy. Its value is not based on the existence of costs, but the utility of money as a means of exchange. Bitcoin mining, like many other industries, requires energy. Bitcoin's closest and most referenced real-world analogue is gold: Bitcoin requires 99.71 TWh per year and gold needs 131 TWh per year (see The Cambridge Bitcoin Electricity Consumption Index, https://ccaf.io/cbnsi/cbeci).

Finally, money serves as a measure of value; its value itself can only be measured through the number of goods that can be purchased with a unit of money. When we ask today how much Bitcoin costs, everyone will answer with its price in US dollars or euros or another fiat currency. Bitcoin itself is not a measure of value today.

The higher price volatility (see Figure 12.2) in combination with uncertainty about future value does not allow Bitcoin to fully perform the function of

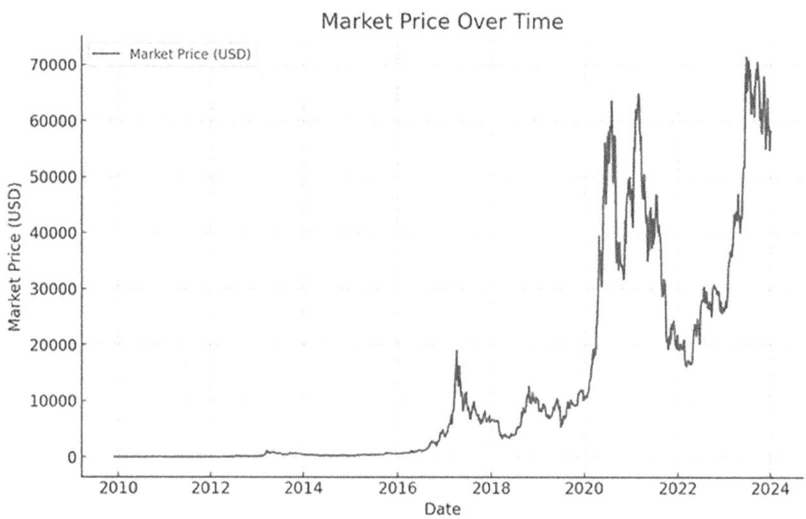


*Source:* https://www.blockchain.com/

*Figure 12.2* *Bitcoin market price*

storing value, although the limited and transparent issuance algorithm gives it credibility.

It is important to note that Bitcoin volatility is the result of fluctuations in speculative demand combined with its limited supply. Additionally, there is a risk that future technological advances could lead to the devaluation of Bitcoin due to the emergence of more attractive, robust, and efficient digital alternatives in the long term.

Term deposits, buying investment assets with money, and so on, are not savings in money, even though the value of those assets is expressed in monetary units. The only case in which money generates income is when commodity prices go down, when those who have been keeping money in their hands can buy more goods. In that sense, Bitcoin is not different from gold in periods of deflation.

As for its function as a means of payment, it requires the conclusion of a transaction with a deferred payment term, the certainty of a future flow of payments in Bitcoins and its existence, and the ability to predict the future value of the currency or to hedge the risk of value change, with hedging instruments already developed and in use. Loans in Bitcoins and other cryptocurrencies are common, with low interest rates and short terms, also due to volatility. (Andryushin, 2020).

The analysis of Bitcoin's performance of money functions does not allow us to conclude that the first of the cryptocurrencies has reached the status of a universal means of exchange. Qualitative performance of the function of means of circulation is limited to a negligibly small area of action. The functions of a means of savings and a means of payment are severely limited by the volatility of Bitcoin prices. Finally, Bitcoin's function as a measure of value is not fulfilled due to the weak spread of Bitcoin, and it is most convenient to measure the value of goods in a universal medium of exchange; the value of Bitcoin itself is usually expressed in fiat currencies.

## BITCOIN THROUGH THE PRISM OF MISES' REGRESSION THEOREM

The emergence of Bitcoin provoked a debate between representatives of the Austrian school of economics about its correspondence to Mises' regression theorem. The theorem was originally applied by Mises to solve the logical problem of explaining the exchange value of money by marginal utility, which, in turn, depends on the exchange value of money (Mises, 1981).

In his analysis, Mises includes a historical component – and explains the present exchange value (purchasing power) of money through its valuation by economic agents based on yesterday's exchange value. Regressing the emergence of money to a commodity and the appearance of corresponding additional demand for this commodity to fulfil the monetary function, Mises shows that at this point the value of future money is based only on its non-monetary utility. This approach is in line with Menger's theory of the origin of money, which claims that a commodity without "non-monetary" value could not be promoted for the role of money.

As soon as one commodity or a number of commodities have become generally used media of exchange for a people, there arises in every individual economic unit that participates in the division of labour, in addition to the demand that may have existed previously for these commodities for purposes of consumption and technical production, a further and different demand for medium of exchange purposes… at first it probably is not separated from the stock intended, for example, for consumption purposes, but subsequently it becomes a separate stock, especially if the part of the commodity that has become money acquires a special form in trade or a special name and even a different look (Menger, 2002, p. 107).

In *Human Action*, Mises extends the requirement of the theorem not only to money, but to any asset that, over time, may become a new medium of exchange: "The regression theorem establishes the fact that no good can be employed for the function of a medium of exchange which at the very beginning of its use for this purpose did not have exchange value on account of other employments" (Mises, 1998, p. 500).

This is why the following arguments do not seem correct. The first one asserts that we should not analyse Bitcoin in light of the regression theorem at all, since it is not money. Murphy (2013) accurately observes that the process of promotion to the role of universal medium of exchange is long and we cannot determine the exact moment when a commodity from non-money turns into money.

The second argument states that Bitcoin should not be analysed in connection with the regression theorem, as it only deals with the initial promotion of money *de novo* from the state of barter and the relative prices formation. It does not apply to the problem of the emergence of new means of payment as long as economic calculations are settled in the current money. "The theory therefore is not an explanation for the origin of all money or all media of exchange" (Davidson and Block, 2015, p. 318). However, Mises points out that "It merely explains how a new kind of media of exchange can come into use and remain in use" (1998, p. 500). New kind does not equal to *de novo*.

There is no contradiction either with Bitcoin's value from alternative uses or with the explanation of its current exchange value.

The "non-monetary" value of Bitcoin could be based on people's desire to participate in testing a new network, engaging in a game, collecting, or simply helping to promote an idea (Graf, 2015). Other motivations might include using a blockchain-based payment system and, more importantly, transferring funds across borders without government control, among other reasons.

The motives for determining Bitcoin as a good are irrelevant to the problem (Šurda, 2014). When the first exchange using Bitcoin was carried out, one of the counterparties to the transaction was its owner, and both counterparties of the exchange evaluated it, so there is no contradiction with the regression theorem. Since Bitcoin was used before the exchange, it had utility for its owner, and the nature of this utility within the framework of methodological individualism is not under dispute.

The question, however, is what was the subject of the first Bitcoin transaction. Hansen (2019) shows that contrary to the popular perception that two pizzas were purchased for 10,000 Bitcoins on 22 May 2010, the pizza acted as a medium of exchange for the agent who wanted to purchase 10,000 Bitcoins and had the information about the person interested in buying the pizza for Bitcoins. He bought two pizzas for fiat money and exchanged them for Bitcoins. This interpretation reveals a different picture. This transaction can be interpreted as well as a rejection of the use of fiat money. The purchase of Bitcoin could well be interpreted as the purchase of a financial asset in anticipation of a rise in its price.

Murphy (2014) argues, if someone decides first to give up some economic good in exchange for an asset that has the potential to be an effective medium of exchange, it may contribute to the actual emergence of that medium of exchange. Murphy says that there is a *loophole* in Mises' argument in such a case. However, if we take into consideration that the commodity given by the participant of the first transaction was a fiat currency, it makes sense. The prohibition of gold money by governments and the unsatisfactory performance of monetary functions by fiat money prompted the first experimenters to try to replace it with Bitcoin. The process of the emergence of money is evolutionary, progressive, and dependent on habits and imitations. Not all individuals understand immediately the benefits of owning a commodity that is more exchangeable than other commodities. As people realize that there is an advantage to using one specific commodity to reduce the cost of exchange, indirect exchange develops and promotes this commodity to the rank of universal medium of exchange. The diffusion of knowledge leads to the formation of a social institution, and this process takes a long time (Menger, 2007, Festré, 2012).

## BITCOIN THROUGH THE PRISM OF HAYEK'S CURRENCY COMPETITION

For many economists, Hayek's *Denationalisation of Money* (1976) is a prediction of the new monetary phenomenon of cryptocurrencies. In his book, the author proposes a way to obtain monetary stability through the private emission of money. The book was set during a period of high inflation, caused by expansionary monetary policy, as a response to the government's monopoly on the issue of money.

The theoretical idea is simple: money should be considered as an ordinary commercial commodity and therefore should be produced through market forces. In the same way that competition between ordinary goods improves their quality and removes low-quality products from the market, competition between private currencies allows the selection of high-quality ones which perform the role of money in the best way (for currency Hayek used the Latin term *valutus*, which means the object with a changing value).

The design of the monetary system proposed by Hayek can be characterized by the following features.

The first one is the government abolishes the legal tender, revokes its monopoly on issuing money, and allows private money producers to issue currency under their own brand name. This system differs from free banking, where all money producers issue the same currency.

The second aspect is that the quality of a currency depends on its quality as a medium of exchange. This requires relative stability of a currency's value over time.

The third point is that money issuers will take various measures to ensure the stability of the value of their currency. In the early stages, for example, they will guarantee the redemption of banknotes in existing national currencies at the exchange rate declared at the time of issue. At the same time, convertibility is not the key point of his idea: "Convertibility is a safeguard necessary to impose upon a monopolist, but unnecessary with competing suppliers who cannot maintain themselves in the business unless they provide money at least as advantageous to the user as anybody else" (Hayek, 1976, p. 84).

Furthermore, as people become familiar with different types of money, they will form a demand for those that best fulfil the function of money. Hayek identifies several uses of money, complementing the medium of exchange function: creation of reserves for the future; fulfilment of contracts with delayed payments; a unit of account – and points out the reliable unit of account function as the primary factor that determines the demand for money. The quality of the last will be an important factor in the demand for currency (Hayek, 1976, pp. 55–57).

Another important feature is that, to test the stability of a currency's value, it is advisable for money issuers to link the currency to a particular set of goods that will help maintain its value (Hayek, 1976, p. 40), and to adjust this set over time according to the revealed preferences of the public.

Finally, once a stable demand for the currency has been established, the money producer can manage its value by regulating the money supply. In a competitive environment, Hayek argued, such a system would best ensure the credibility and stability of the currency.

The value of money, like that of any other commodity, is based on its utility and rarity, with its utility depending on how well it performs its primary function – as a medium of exchange. Therefore, money producers will compete to fulfil this function in the best possible way.

How can Hayek's ideas be applied to the cryptocurrency market? The answer to this question is obscured by the absence of a key condition for currency competition: the state has not relinquished its monopoly on money issuance; therefore, cryptocurrencies primarily play the role of financial instruments. In fact, the share of transactions in which cryptocurrencies serve as a medium of exchange is negligible. The same conclusion is reached by the authors of the article "Cryptocurrency Competition: Empirical Testing of Hayek's Vision of Private Monies" (Mayer and Bofinger, 2024). They notice that competition between cryptocurrencies is not centred on their role as a means of payment, but rather on their role as speculative stores of value.

There are some implications of this position for cryptocurrencies. The first consideration is that the stability of value, as an important demand factor for money, has not yet become a central issue for cryptocurrencies. In fact, their price volatility exceeds that of other financial instruments. Another point is the inability of any of them to serve as a unit of account. And it's not just because of the high volatility of the value of cryptocurrencies. It makes no sense to measure the value of commodities in terms of an asset as long as the asset itself is priced in traditional fiat US dollars or euros.

At the same time, we can observe in the functioning of cryptocurrencies the confirmation of the idea that trust in a currency is a fundamental factor of its demand. And "pure trust" as one of the bases for the value of fiat money has been replaced by a more fundamental factor: cryptographic verification of transactions.

Notably, stablecoins, which are tied to the value of commodities or currency baskets, more closely resemble the private currencies described by Hayek. In this segment of the market, the most stable currencies have been selected, with one of them (Tether) dominating payments, in line with Hayek's reasoning (Kochergin and Ivanova, 2022).

Hayek's idea that different degrees of liquidity entail different degrees of "monetization" of a particular cryptocurrency is confirmed (Sanz Bas, 2020). Bitcoin has higher liquidity than other cryptocurrencies, as it was the first decentralized digital currency and its network is larger than others.

The development of the cryptocurrency market remarkably confirms Hayek's general theoretical framework of evolution. Competition has opened up unknown opportunities for market development due to the market process. Thus, special crypto-exchange markets and other virtual financial platforms were created, accepting different crypto-assets as instruments of payment – and segmentation of the cryptocurrency market appeared rapidly.

## CONCLUSION

For any medium of exchange to be promoted as universal, that is, money, it does not need to be recognized as legal tender by the state. What is important is the spreading of the habit of using this instrument of exchange under free competitive choice among economic agents in the same way that gold and silver were once chosen to play this role.

Contrary to gold and silver, which won the competition for the right to play the role of money from a multitude of alternative goods, Bitcoin has to compete with fiat money (among others), which is controlled by a government monopoly.

Bitcoin was the first and continues to be the most prominent cryptocurrency due to its widespread usage. Its key strengths include decentralization, enhanced security, and incorruptible governance. Fiat money itself is money because its monopoly was imposed by governments through the legal ban on the use of gold money in transactions, first as an instrument of payment and then as a measure of value (the abolition of the "gold clause" in the era of F. Roosevelt's "New Deal").

Bitcoin does not fully perform the functions of money today, is not a universal means of exchange, and therefore is not money. At the same time, it either partially performs or is capable of performing all the basic functions of money, including, in the case of its use spreading widely, the function of a measure of value, that is, it can potentially become money.

According to Menger's evolutionary theory, the selection of goods for the role of money is the result of countless human actions, each of which improves the condition of an individual, but none of which are intended to "invent" money or even to select any commodity for this role. Bitcoin, by its nature and the functions it performs, can be considered one of the candidates for the role of money. Nevertheless, the answer to the question of whether it will become money is outside the scope of theoretical economics: the process of selecting a good for the role of money is spontaneous in the free competition of all alternative instruments of exchange. However, hypothetical speculations about what economic agents would prefer – gold and silver coins, commercial banks' accounts with electronic cards, or a digital record in a distributed ledger – may be relevant and will therefore continue to excite the inquiring minds of those interested in monetary theory.

# NOTE

1. "Social phenomena come about as the unintended result of individual human efforts (pursuing individual interests) without a common will directed toward their establishment" (Menger, 1985, p. 133).

# REFERENCES


Andryushin S. (2020). Cryptocurrencies: Issue, Circulation, and Problems of Regulation. *Actual Problems of Economics and Law*, 14(3), pp. 455–468 (in Russian).

CoinMarketCap. (2024a). Historical Snapshot – 01 September 2024. CoinMarketCap. https://coinmarketcap.com/historical/20240901/ [Accessed 01.10.2024].

CoinMarketCap. (2024b). Live Cryptocurrency Charts & Market Data (Global Market Cap). https://coinmarketcap.com/charts/ [Accessed 01.10.2024].

Davidson L., Block W. (2015). Bitcoin, the Regression Theorem, and the Emergence of a New Medium of Exchange. *Quarterly Journal of Austrian Economics*, 18(3), pp. 311–338.

de Mombynes Y. (2020). *Comprendre le Lightning Network*. Paris, France: Institut Sapiens.

Festré A. (2012). Carl Menger and Friedrich von Wieser on the role of knowledge and beliefs, in Arena R., Festré A., Lazaric N. (eds.), *Handbook of Knowledge and Economics*. Cheltenham, UK: Edward Elgar Publishing, pp. 73–98.

Genkin A. (2002). *Private Money: History and Modernity*. Moscow, Russia: Alpina Publisher.

Graf K. (2015). On The Origins of Bitcoin: Stages of Monetary Evolution – Part I. *MISES: Interdisciplinary Journal of Philosophy, Law and Economics*, 3(2), pp. 427–440.

Hansen K. (2019). The Menger–Mises Theory of the Origin of Money—Conjecture or Economic Law? *Quarterly Journal of Austrian Economics*, 22(1), pp. 26–48.

Hayek F. von. (1976). *Denationalisation of Money: The Argument Refined*. London: Institute of Economic Affairs.

Horwitz S. (2015). *Hayek's Modern Family: Classical Liberalism and the Evolution of Social Institutions*. New York, NY: Palgrave Macmillan.

Hülsmann J. G. (2003). Facts and Counterfactuals in Economic Law. *Journal of Libertarian Studies*, 17(1), pp. 57–102.

Hülsmann J. G. (2008). *Ethics of Money Production*. Auburn, AL: Ludwig von Mises Institute.

Kavaliou A. V. (2020). To the Issue of Carl Menger's Theory of the Origin of Money. *The Bulletin of the Institute of Economics of the Russian Academy of Sciences* 4, pp. 147–151 (in Russian).

Kavaliou A. V., Peniaz O. S. (2022). Mutual Influence of Institutions in the Concept of Carl Menger. *Terra Economicus*, 20(1), pp. 27–37 (in Russian).

Kiselev, A. A. (2018). Reply to Bulikov's Article: "Bitcoin and Fiduciary Money." *Theoretical Economics* 2, pp. 179–187 (in Russian).

Kochergin D. A., Ivanova A. I. (2022). Stablecoins: Classification, Functional Features, and Development Prospects. *Journal of the New Economic Association*, 53(1), pp. 100–120.

Mayer F., Bofinger P. (2024). Cryptocurrency Competition: Empirical Testing of Hayek's Vision of Private Monies. *Financial Innovation*, 10(93), pp. 2–46.
Menger C. (1985). *Investigations into the Method of the Social Sciences, with Special Reference to Economics*. New York, NY: New York University Press.
Menger C. (2002). Money, in Latzer M., Schmitz S. V. (eds.), *Carl Menger and the Evolution of the Payment System: From Barter to Electronic Money*. Cheltenham, UK: Edward Elgar Publishing, pp. 25–110.
Menger C. (2007). *Principles of Economics*. Auburn, AL: Ludwig von Mises Institute.
Menger C. (2009). *On the Origin of Money*. Auburn, AL: Ludwig von Mises Institute.
Mises L. von. (1981). *The Theory of Money and Credit*. Translated by H. E. Batson. Indianapolis, IN: Liberty Fund.
Mises L. von. (1998). *Human Action: A Treatise on Economics. Scholar's Edition*. Auburn, AL: Ludwig von Mises Institute.
Murphy R. (2013). Why Miseseans need to tread cautiously when disparaging Bitcoin. http://consultingbyrpm.com/blog/2013/10/why-misesians-need-to-tread-cautiously-when-disparaging-bitcoin.html [Accessed 21.06.2025].
Murphy R. (2014). On Bitcoin and Mises's regression theorem. http://consultingbyrpm.com/blog/2014/03/on-bitcoin-and-ludwig-von-mises-regression-theorem.html [Accessed 21.06.2025].
Nakamoto S. (2008). Bitcoin: A peer-to-peer electronic cash system. https://bitcoin.org/bitcoin.pdf [Accessed 21.06.2025].
Sanz Bas D. (2020). Hayek and the Cryptocurrency Revolution. *Iberian Journal of the History of Economic Thought*, 7(1), pp. 15–28.
Sinel'nikova-Muryleva E. V., Shilov K. D., Zubarev A. V. (2019). The Essence of Cryptocurrencies: Descriptive and Comparative Analysis. *Finance: Theory and Practice*, 23(6), pp. 36–49.
Šurda P. (2014). *The Origin, Classification, and Utility of Bitcoin*. http://ssrn.com/abstract=2436823 [Accessed 21.06.2025].

# 13. Hayek, egalitarianism, and evolutionary game theory

**Miłosz Ślepowroński**

Friedrich Hayek analyzed how people navigate two systems of norms at once – the micro- and macrocosm, the system of intimate relationships, families, and that of markets. Hayek's insights are especially useful if we want to understand the proper role of both systems and where to draw the line between them. However, when sharing Hayek's approach, one cannot help but be interested in naturalistic theories of justice that were formulated using a tool that Hayek lacked access to.

In this text, I will analyze the issue raised by Hayek using the tools of evolutionary game theory, focusing on the naturalistic theory of fairness of Ken Binmore. The goals here are to marry the two approaches in a way and thus fix the problems each is having. We can understand the difference between the two orders with the help of one of the best theories that explains how the lower-level order arises. I also show the affinity between them and how they issue the same warning that we should not apply the rules outside of the environments in which they evolved. The first section of this text explains Binmore's theory. I ask the reader to forgive me for the length, but given the complexity of Binmore's approach, this is required. The second section explores Hayek's famous *two worlds at once* approach, as well as discusses examples of theorists who do not see a separation between the two systems of rules, including Binmore. The third section focuses on the border between the two Hayekian worlds. I argue that the border between the two cosmoses cannot be defined purely abstractly and is not fixed or impermeable.

## GAME THEORY

Around the same time when *The Fatal Conceit* was published, another discipline that tackles similar issues was being advanced and expanded: game theory, including its evolutionary version and applied to issues of moral and political philosophy. Game theory is an analytical tool used to describe strategic situations, situations where there is more than one decision maker, who pursue some objectives, and their decisions influence one another. If they did not, we could use a simple rational actor model with a person who maximizes their expected utility. This would be an example of a parametric choice, since strategies would include parameters of the world that are kept constant across strategies. When we need to take into account that our decisions may influence the decisions of others, the situation changes from parametric to strategic. Hence, we need a more sophisticated tool. Game theory has been useful for many disciplines, but it had some important limitations, with its static form and requirements of rationality of the players being the main ones. Moreover, its development was hindered by several issues, such as the equilibrium selection problem. This problem refers, in short, to the fact that a Nash equilibrium (or other) equilibrium is never guaranteed to be unique or desirable. We face a situation where there are many competing equilibria with no clear rational way of choosing between them. This leads to hope that evolutionary game theory can fix those problems. Instead of proposing rational actors maximizing their expected utility, we have populations of agents interacting with each other, and the differences in their payoffs becoming the basis for their different rates of reproduction – the higher the payoff relative to others, the higher chance to produce offspring in the next generation. Evolutionary game theory has been fruitfully applied to biological evolution to explain animal behavior or sex ratios. In most of such theories, fitness is assumed to be genetic. However, the theory can also be applied to cultural evolution, where instead of genes, we describe cultural transfer. This approach can help us understand the emergence, transformation, and stabilization of behavior (Gintis 2009). We do not need ultra-rational agents that do costly computation before choosing their strategies, but rather strategies spread across populations of agents utilizing mimetic learning, which nevertheless leads to optimal behavior. Therefore, we can use it to learn about the interactions of individuals when reasoning is costly. On the other hand, analyzing unique events or those in which agents explicitly use their cognitive capacities to their full extent is better dealt with using classical game theory.

## Binmore's Approach

One of the most famous and certainly the most ambitious approaches that uses game theory in political philosophy is that of Ken Binmore. This groundbreaking proposal to explain the evolution of fairness was published in 1994. The British mathematician and economist published his naturalistic theory of justice in his two-part book, *Game Theory and the Social Contract*, later changed into a more popular science style in *Natural Justice* (Binmore 1994, 1998, 2005). It helped in popularizing the approach, but also started a lively discussion, perhaps due to many controversial assumptions.

Binmore suggested that the Rawlsian concept of the original position is not merely a philosophical exercise but reflects a fundamental aspect of how real fairness norms function. It acts as a tool for coordinating social interactions and helps us address key challenges in cooperation. Furthermore, this concept is embedded in our genes, as it helped our ancestors align their behaviors over a long period of time. The following part will describe in detail what Binmore means by a coordination device and why it is needed.

Binmore is a naturalist par excellence, but in a quite idiosyncratic way. In ethical philosophy, he distinguishes between two traditions, that of the science of morals, where he places, among others, Aristotle, Adam Smith, David Hume, and John Mackie, and that of the metaphysics of morals, in which he places Plato, Immanuel Kant, John Rawls, and John Harsanyi. He sees himself following the tradition of the former group rather than the latter. However, what is interesting is that the basic ideas of his theory are taken from the two representatives of the "metaphysical" group, namely Rawls and Harsanyi, although in a very naturalized form. Aside from that, he is fiercely critical of anyone doing ethical philosophy in this way – calling them "moral pundits" and considers all efforts to understand morality in such a way to be utterly wasted. According to Binmore: "Orthodox moral philosophy has gotten nowhere because it asks the wrong question. If morality evolved along with the human race, then asking how we ought to live makes as much sense as asking what animals ought to exist, or which language we ought to speak" (Binmore 2005, 1).

There is a Humean assumption here that the reasons for our actions are not philosophical rules that have their origin in the convention of the Good or the Right, but rather conventions, customs, and instincts that come from evolutionary processes. These are not "simpler" in any meaningful sense, and, in fact, can be more difficult to understand and notice. There is no role for ethical universals and non-natural rules in his theory. Instead, he proposes that we should instead ask what morality is and how it actually evolved. Binmore promotes a naturalistic, scientific, descriptive, and non-normative approach to morality, by focusing our attention on rules that are actually followed (Binmore 2005, 37). It is also a very peculiar kind of descriptive approach, aimed not at describing existing moral rules but only the ultimate causes of the observed moral phenomena, those which brought about certain patterns of behavior, which caused most of humanity to follow the rules of a society to which we are born rather than to break them. However, this approach is not subjectivist in the metaethical sense. For norms to serve their function, they need to be understood and shared by members of the society. There is an element of subjectivism in the normative sense, though, as Binmore admits that any proposals he is making for what ought to happen are only indicative of his preferences. The role of moral theory is to help us understand the mechanisms that shape it and how we can use it to assess the consequences of various plans.

Binmore's main goal is to "seek naturalistic foundations for Rawls' powerful intuitions about the way human fairness norms work" (Binmore 2005, viii). This goal is indeed interesting, as whatever we may think about egalitarian philosophies or behaviors, they are influential and seem to exist in most societies to some extent. Understanding them, their sources, and evolution would help to find out if they are worthy of support, modification, or opposition. Binmore claims that his focus on Rawlsian theory is caused by the fact that it is the best at capturing the idea of fairness. Consequently, nearly everyone who hears about it for the first time recognizes it as something very close to their common thinking about fairness. He refers here to Rawls' *A Theory of Justice*, which proposes that, in short, justifying any rules of justice or fairness is to show that they could be accepted while taking into account truly moral conditions – and only those. Such conditions are fulfilled under the so-called original position, which is a counterfactual heuristic device used to deliberate about the basic rules of society. In the original position, an individual does not know his or her traits, qualities, personal history, place in society, material goods, and so on. All these things are said to be irrelevant to justice and may only cloud a fair view of the world. Under such conditions, self-concerned individuals should come into agreement about the basic rules of justice, which are methods of distribution of primary goods and ways of political organization of the society. Rawls gives such rules in his theory. The first principle of justice would be to provide everyone with an equal system of basic freedoms. After such freedoms are established, and only after that, we can follow up with the second principle, establishing the rules for distribution of goods. Such a distribution should primarily be concerned with the maximization of benefits for the least privileged members of society (Rawls 1999). However complicated the details of the Rawlsian theory might be, it is in general egalitarian, but it does not eliminate all inequalities. Instead, it selects from all possible social contracts the one which is efficient and at the same time gives the least well-off the highest amount of primary goods, while also assuring that all citizens enjoy basic democratic freedoms.

If we start with a bundle of completely descriptive and naturalistic presuppositions, one might be surprised to see John Rawls as the main inspiration, as he was one of the least naturalistic political philosophers of the twentieth century. He did not aim at a mere description of social customs, and more importantly, did not think that political or ethical philosophy depends on any empirical science, but neither did he completely ignore reality. In his method, known as reflective equilibrium, our intuitions about justice are an important starting point, but aside from that, we will not find in *A Theory of Justice* any argument that appeals to empirical facts or history. Binmore's reading of Rawls is somewhat unusual: he does not care about Rawls' philosophical justification of egalitarian political ideas, but takes one very basic idea, that of the original position, and argues that it captures something very important for human morality, which is immediately recognizable by most people (Binmore 2005, vii). He reduces Rawls' heuristic device for solving large-scale political problems to a tool for everyday thinking and coordination on a small scale. Binmore reinterprets Rawls' theory in a Humean fashion, criticizing every bit of Kant's ideas present in it. Now I will turn to showing how exactly he achieved that.

## Game of life

The short summary of Binmore's theory would look as follows: fairness is a coordinating device for the game of life, and its abstract form is best represented by the original position of John Rawls (Binmore 1994, 40). Moreover, the original position is written into our genes, since our hunter-gatherer ancestors have used it to solve social coordination problems for millennia. To explain this, we need several game-theoretic tools, as Binmore extensively relies on them in formulating his ideas, which is not surprising, as before engaging with philosophical topics, he worked as an economist and mathematician and made important contributions to research on bargaining.

The British economist notices that many of our daily interactions, such as road traffic, language, or norms of courtesy, can be represented by coordination games. A coordination game is not a game of pure conflict, and the players in it have incentives to choose the same strategies; however, there are multiple equilibria. One of them is known as the Stag Hunt and is shown in Table 13.1.

The rows in Table 13.1 describe two strategies of player A, whereas the columns describe those of player B. Both can choose to hunt Stag or hunt Hare. Payoffs are shown as pairs (A, B). We see that hunting Stag gives the highest payoff for both (4, 4), but only if both players play it. If one of them chooses the safer option, hunting Hare, they receive a bit lower payoff, but their partner is not able to successfully hunt Stag alone and receives zero. The game has two pure Nash equilibria, with both players hunting Stag or both players hunting Hare. Binmore claims that not just traffic laws and the like

*Table 13.1* *Stag Hunt*

| - | Stag | Hare |
|---|---|---|
| Stag | 4, 4 | 0, 3 |
| Hare | 3, 0 | 2, 2 |

*Source:* Author's own.

have the form of a coordination game – this is also true of private property, political authority, or even the prohibition of murder. Each of these rules is an equilibrium in the game of life (a concept explained later in this section), and there is no qualitative difference between the rule saying which side of the road we should drive on and which item belongs to whom. The differences are only of a degree. The fact that we do not face the games of pure conflict does not help in answering the question – how do we coordinate on them and is it even possible in this framework? To answer that, we would of course need to represent each interaction as an appropriate game, which we would then need to analyze. So, for example, road traffic, namely, the question of which side of the road to drive on, would be a coordination game, while the usage of common pool resources would be a Prisoner's Dilemma-type game. To make matters more difficult, if we are interested in the stability of social norms, we should analyze repeated, not just one-off games. And in those, the situation is more complicated: there are nearly always multiple equilibria, but a successful social interaction demands that multiple people choose one equilibrium and use it consistently.

However, we have a tool to analyze such a situation, namely the Folk Theorem. To see what it can do for us, let us take a look at one of the most famous examples from game theory, the Prisoners Dilemma, which for many reasons has captured the attention of many researchers both on the theoretical and applied sides. Table 13.2 represents the game.

The usual narrative that accompanies the Prisoners Dilemma is about two criminals interrogated by a prosecutor. Each of them separately receives a proposal to admit to a crime they committed (choose "Defect") and, as a reward, will receive a lighter sentence. However, if both confess to guilt, they will both be sentenced. If they choose "Cooperate," that is, keep quiet, they will be charged only on a minor offense. Hence, the best option for each of them is if their partner cooperates and they don't. This leads to a situation where none of them cooperates since it is not in their interest, no matter what their partner does. There are many incorrect interpretations of the game, as at first sight, many see in it a representation of the most basic cooperation problems and the danger of free riding and thus feel that there should be a way to prove

*Table 13.2 Prisoner's Dilemma*

| - | Cooperate | Defect |
|---|---|---|
| Cooperate | 2, 2 | 0, 3 |
| Defect | 3, 0 | 1, 1 |

*Source:* Author's own.

the rationality of cooperation (Binmore 2009, 27). But the introduction of repeated games changes the situation. Formally, the Folk Theorem says that in a repeated n-person game any combination of actions observed in any finite number of repetitions is an equilibrium, provided that:

1. The rate of time preference is sufficiently small;
2. The probability that the game ends at any repetition is sufficiently small;
3. The set of payoff combinations must be individually rational and feasible.

What it tells us is that in a game that is infinitely repeated, or if there is sufficiently small probability of the game ending, when the players are sufficiently patient, any outcome is sustainable in the long term provided that it is better than what can be secured by playing the minimax strategy (which is just minimizing the worst-case potential loss) and the payoff is a convex combination of possible payoffs of the stage game (Rasmusen 2006, 112).

Let us take the example of the Prisoner's Dilemma. The only equilibrium is an uncooperative one where both players betray each other. But if players could communicate and somehow choose the outcome before playing the game, they would undoubtedly choose some more efficient point than mutual defection. Even if it weren't "always cooperate" but some mixture of cooperation and defection, the outcome would still be more favorable. Of course, in a one-shot Prisoner's Dilemma, there is no way to enforce this deal, but in a repeated game, there are many. Players always have a threat available to them, that of non-cooperation, if the conditions of cooperation are broken. Thus, we can choose any point in the set of efficient possible outcomes of our game, and the Folk Theorem says that it can be sustained.

If the interactions are repeated, the set of possible solutions is greatly expanded. We might pick a point in the feasible set of a repeated game and make it an equilibrium by punishing anyone who does not play the strategy associated with this point. Hence, every outcome of some game on which rational players might agree when they assume a presence of some external enforcement is also available as an equilibrium in a repeated version of this game. An application of this theorem to human behavior would say that in communities where rules of behavior are common knowledge and whose members know that they will interact repeatedly, any pattern of behavior that makes the members of a community better off can be sustained by social norms. But it does not mean that anything goes and any practice can be sustained. The equilibrium must be sustained by a system of duties that provides all players with the right incentives to do the right thing. Still, this leaves us with many possible arrangements, yet the important question of feasibility is always important (Binmore 2005, 92).

The Folk Theorem shows that any efficient outcome of a non-repeated game on which the players might agree approximates an equilibrium outcome of the repeated version of this game (Binmore 2005, 8). Although the Prisoner's Dilemma is used in this example, Binmore does not claim that this particular game must represent all social interaction. In fact, the specific game is not very important if we are analyzing long-term repetitions. Binmore even claims that the question of whether cooperation is possible is trivial and the answer, for someone who actually cares about empirical facts, is obvious. The interesting question is what kind of cooperation is possible and which should be chosen.

It looks like our first problem, how is cooperation possible, is solved if we focus on repeated games. However, introducing the Folk Theorem leads to additional problems. The space of possible stable cooperative arrangements becomes so large that even if we limit our choice to Pareto-efficient solutions, pure rationality cannot help us select a unique solution. Figure 13.1 shows the payoffs of Adam and Eve on two axes in a repeated Prisoner's Dilemma.

As can be seen, the worst outcome both can guarantee is (1, 1). The downward sloping curve represents the Pareto frontier, that is, outcomes that cannot

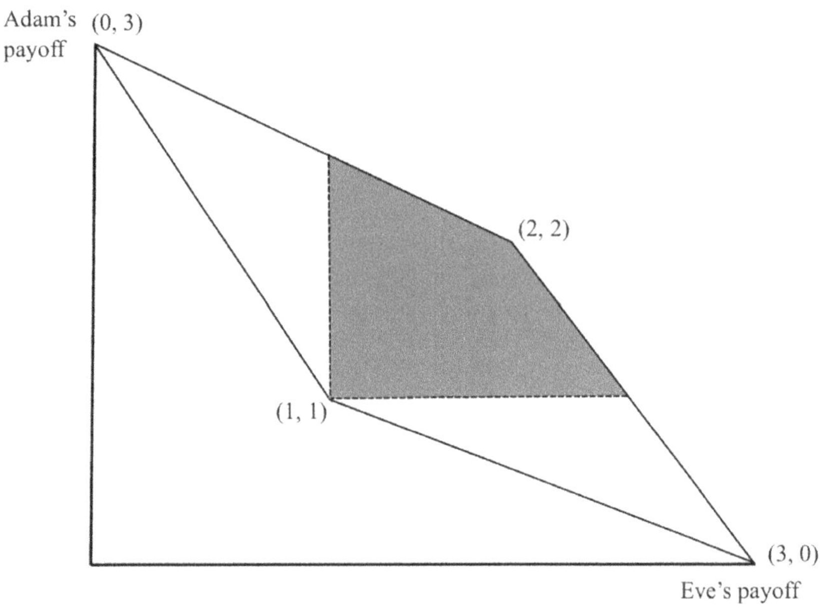


*Source:* Based on Binmore (2005, 80).

*Figure 13.1 Folk Theorem*

be improved without making the other side worse off. The gray-shaded area represents the bargaining set, which means that the outcomes described there are possible to reach and are better than (1, 1). The Folk Theorem can allow us to choose an arbitrary point in that set and "fix" it as a long-term solution. As we can see, there are infinite numbers of these points, even if we focus only on those that lie on the downward sloping curve, which shows the Pareto frontier. This is known as the equilibrium selection problem. We cannot count on social evolution to solve it for us as it may just as well lead to inefficient equilibria. We can also be stuck in an old inefficient equilibrium when a new technology expands the space of possible social contracts. But even if evolutionary processes could be counted on, their work is too slow. Therefore, we should not expect to have a certain equilibrium ready and applicable for every situation. Instead, we need some kind of equilibrium selection device that could work in any situation. Binmore argues that fairness is the tool that solves all these problems, as it can get us quickly out of bad or inefficient equilibria: "When two people use fairness to resolve an everyday coordination problem, I believe they are implicitly calculating the agreement that they would reach if they were to bargain on the assumption that their identities would be reassigned at random after negotiation was over" (Binmore 2005, 21). Hence, we can see how fairness is similar to the Rawlsian original position.

To analyze how we choose in a bargaining scenario if the roles we would end up with are unknown to us, Binmore proposes the notions of the game of moral and the game of life. The infinitely repeated "game of life" is a metaphor for the daily challenges of coordination and competition that we all face, with its primary objective being to establish the rules governing the production and distribution of goods. It is ruled by the same forces as those in the real world: technology, social structure, and the fundamental laws of physics and biology. These rules are equally binding, in contrast to purely social rules, which are only effective if enforcement mechanisms exist. Importantly, individuals do not have the power to change the rules of the game of life.

The "game of morals" is played between rounds of the game of life, and during it, players can appeal to the original position, where they negotiate behind a "veil of ignorance" not knowing who they will end up being (Binmore 1998, 15). The goal of this negotiation is to establish the equilibrium that should govern the game of life. In this sense, the game of morals serves as a coordination mechanism for the game of life (Binmore 1998, 42). However, unlike the natural rules of the game of life, the rules of the game of morals are not truly binding. So why consider them at all? Binmore suggests that, in any game-theoretic model, one should think about how the game of morals would be played if its rules were binding. His work, like that of a novelist, creates a fictional world with imagined characters but takes its rules seriously (Binmore 1998, 41). In reality, only the rules of the game of life, like the laws of physics, are truly binding. Social contracts are obeyed only insofar as following their rules serves the interests of the parties involved. If someone abides by the rules of the game of morals, it is because they choose to. Nevertheless, studying the game of morals is valuable because its rules evolved to align with the game of life. No leaders or external coordination devices are necessary for it to function effectively.

This, however, leaves an important question unanswered: What is the reason behind using this equilibrium selection device, why should we negotiate in the original position, behind a veil of ignorance, rather than directly in the real world? Binmore addresses this through his evolutionary account of fairness, which originated within families. He suggests that fairness began as a mutual insurance mechanism against misfortunes like hunting failures. Individuals, facing genuine uncertainty about their future success in hunting or foraging, insured each other against hunger. This early form of cooperation only required one to imagine himself in different future scenarios. The second evolutionary step introduced the veil of ignorance, where individuals no longer knew who they would be after negotiations, and fairness extended to more distant relatives and eventually nonkin. This expansion occurred because fairness proved to be an effective strategy (Binmore 2005, 140).

However, the bargaining process itself is more a theoretical model. In reality, coordination happens much faster, without the need for formal bargaining or simulations. We don't have time to negotiate every situation, but the possibility of bargaining, even if rare, influences the results of our current social contracts. Fairness evolved to address everyday problems efficiently, acting as a shortcut when there is no time for detailed negotiations. Binmore even suggests that fairness may have evolved before humans developed language (Binmore 2005, 27). In practice, people do not actually bargain; rather, they coordinate the outcomes they would likely agree on if they were bargaining behind the veil of ignorance. For these solutions to be meaningful, whether egalitarian, utilitarian, or Nash-based, the payoffs must be adjusted by social indices. Without these indices, comparing utilities would be impossible. Social change can thus be understood as a process of adjusting these indices, which, in turn, changes the distribution of payoffs.

Can we count on a social order conceived in such a way to be efficient? By efficiency here I mean that it does not waste resources and that no person can be made better off without making anyone else worse off. Unfortunately, not all equilibria are efficient, which is obvious from the previous analysis of the Prisoner's Dilemma. As Binmore asserts, "The invisible hand can be counted on to take a population to an efficient outcome of a game in the exceptional case when all its equilibria happen to be efficient" (Binmore 2005, 8). But there is a mechanism which can bring about efficiency: evolution. Binmore makes an evolutionary claim that, after a long time of interaction and competition of various human ancestral groups, only those societies which operated efficient equilibria could have been successful. The evolutionary processes in his models operate between every game, changing the frequencies with which the players' strategies are played. Thus, high payoffs are identified with increasing frequency and low payoffs with decreasing frequency. In a biological setting, this interpretation is intuitive, as an organism that is more fit has a higher probability of reproducing (tautologically). In a cultural setting, the situation is more complicated. Essentially, the claim is that those with higher payoffs are more imitated and the patterns of behavior spread in this manner. However, Binmore's claims are a mixture of biological and cultural. If a group is to be stable against deviations, it has to operate in an equilibrium. Some of those equilibria will necessarily be better than others, and members of one group will be better on average than members of a different group, especially if they operate an equilibrium which is a Pareto improvement on the equilibrium used by a worse group. Because of that, we can expect that evolution will eliminate all groups operating equilibria that are Pareto-inferior (Binmore 1998, 130).

Here, two caveats are needed. First, this type of argumentation is not a group selection argumentation, which Binmore, together with some other scientists (Pinker 2015) considers to be a fallacy. Group selection would mean that individual fitness is sacrificed in order to increase the average fitness of group members when an individual acts not in order to maximize his fitness but altruistically. Binmore thinks that this is implausible, but his theory avoids that, as selection is being made among multiple equilibria and individuals do not need to sacrifice anything in the interest of the group. Acting according to equilibrium is, by definition, optimal. Second, fairness is not the same thing as efficiency, although efficiency is a necessary prerequisite for a fair equilibrium. There are many more unfair but efficient equilibria.

## The deep structure

So far, the theory looks purely conceptual. However, Binmore does not want to restrict himself to a conceptual analysis, as he calls himself an empiricist. So what is the empirical content of his theory? Let us take a look at the best known problem of public goods, the Tragedy of the Commons. There is a grassland capable of sustaining 100 goats and 10 families want their goats to graze it. The classical problem with this situation is that of enforcement, because although it is in the interest of everyone not to overgraze the land, each family also has an incentive to graze more goats than their share. But even assuming some enforcement mechanism, there are multiple equilibria in this situation. It is equally rational to have one family grazing 90 goats and nine families one goat each, as it is for every family to graze the same number of goats. However, as Binmore asserts, the solution with every family grazing 10 goats "shrieks to our attention" and is considered fair. This is the equilibrium selection mechanism at work and a clue that evolution endowed us with a preference for this particular mechanism. This outcome, if we know nothing else about the families in question, would probably be viewed as fair by most human societies, and that is because it is supposedly caused by a "deep structure" of human morality, which would unite at the deeper level all different observed moralities. One proof of the existence of such a deep structure is that all primitive societies that survived to modern times share a strikingly similar social contract.

This pattern holds even in diverse environments such as Greenland, the Kalahari Desert, or the Amazon rainforest. Despite their differences, all of these societies are profoundly egalitarian, with relationships based on sharing and a lack of long-term dependencies (Woodburn 1982). Wealth, power, and status distinctions are systematically eliminated. Although some individuals may seek power, these societies resist through what Christopher Boehm called a "reverse dominance hierarchy." Unlike most primates, humans do not tolerate control by an alpha male (Boehm 1999). When someone tries to accumulate power, they are warned, mocked, ostracized, and, if necessary, punished, even killed. As a result, these small-scale societies do not have single chiefs or decision makers who could impose a particular coordination method or establish a dominant equilibrium. Binmore argues that fairness evolved alongside these antidominance mechanisms, eliminating the need for chiefs by serving as a natural means of coordination. More controversially, he suggests that this antidominance mechanism is part of human biology and remains relevant today (Binmore 2005, 131). The fact that every hunter-gatherer society follows a similar social structure, despite their environmental differences and lack of contact, suggests a genetically determined human tendency toward this type of social contract. Our hunter-gatherer ancestors likely shared this arrangement, and over time it became ingrained in our genes. While modern societies differ in their social contracts, Binmore reconciles this with the idea of an underlying unity by proposing that what varies are the standards of interpersonal utility comparisons, which serve as input to the original position. These standards are shaped by specific cultures and evolve over time. Thus, while societies differ in how they compare utility, they share a common deep structure rooted in fairness and egalitarian principles.

Fairness is ingrained in our biology, functioning similarly to Rawls' concept of the original position. Binmore suggests that the original position is a modern version of the Golden Rule: treat others as you want to be treated, but adjusted for varying preferences. Moral behavior likely began within families, where a fairness approach similar to the original position helped individuals thrive. Over time, evolution extended this principle beyond kinship, allowing cooperation with nonrelatives. This shift happened by chance, as we unknowingly applied rules from more restrictive family-based interactions to broader social contexts, leading to cooperative outcomes. What initially occurred by accident and largely for nonbiological reasons eventually became ingrained in our genetics and solidified biologically over time (Binmore 2005, 171).

This highlights a key difference between Binmore's and Rawls' conceptions of the original position. In Rawls' theory, individuals are imagined behind a veil of ignorance, without any knowledge of their place in society or their abilities. In contrast, Binmore's original position allows individuals to know who they are, but asks them to imagine that they don't know which specific person they will be in a particular situation. Rawls' approach leads to the use of the difference principle and the selection of primary goods, while Binmore focuses on using the original position to solve everyday coordination problems, not for designing institutions.

Rawls' theory has a clear normative framework, whereas Binmore's is more ambiguous in this regard. In particular, Binmore's theory permits highly unequal outcomes, since payoffs are adjusted using social indices. In Rawls' framework, all individuals behind the veil of ignorance are essentially equal, so assigning them unequal outcomes would be arbitrary. However, in Binmore's view, different tastes and relative power are considered, which requires interpersonal utility comparisons as input. His approach is not normatively justified; rather, he claims that it is descriptive, reflecting how people actually behave. To use the original position in Binmore's model, we must consider how it would feel to emerge with someone else's preferences. This requires us to empathize with others, taking into account their tastes and perspectives when making decisions. These standards of comparison are not independent of the power structure of a particular society, and therefore Binmore's theory of fairness is not a replacement for power. Indeed, fairness is shown to have evolved as a means of balancing power, not its substitute: "To behave morally is not to transcend the need for compromise. On the contrary, morality evolved in our species because a successful human society needs to institutionalize the compromises that allow it to operate" (Binmore 1994, 4). This shows careful respect for morality as a coordination device, rather than something that can replace all other considerations.

## Empathy

Empathy is crucial in Binmore's theory, as it allows us to make interpersonal utility comparisons, which are needed as data to properly use the device of the original position. The notion of utility began its career in social philosophy with Jeremy Bentham, but, as it was an intangible unit of happiness or its expectation affecting human decision making, almost anything could be said about it without any fear of empirical refutation. To make it more useful, it had to be related to something measurable. It can be done thanks to the work of John von Neumann and Oskar Morgenstern. Von Neumann–Morgenstern lotteries also have the advantage of allowing one to describe the utility function in cardinal terms, not just ordinal (Binmore 1994, 194). But this approach does not help us if we want to compare the utilities of different persons, and the orthodox position in economics would say that there is no way of doing so. Binmore, however, thinks that the problem lies in finding a meaningful way to compare the utilities of different people – anything can be compared to anything else with regard to some specific quality. The task is to find the right way of comparison. Therefore, the utility scales of two different persons are compared to two different temperature scales, such as Fahrenheit and Celsius (Binmore 1994, 54). In this way, the problem is reduced to finding the zero point and the rate of trade-off of preferences of one person to preferences of another.

We must find this rate of trade-off, as we cannot compare utilities of some events happening to two persons without it. Even if we could do a direct comparison, in case the gains were commensurate – like monetary gains – the experimental results suggest that this is not how human fairness works. To do such a comparison, Binmore focuses on empathy as part of his broader view that game theory serves as a tool to operationalize Hume's philosophical ideas, particularly with regard to empathy (Binmore 1994, 285). In addition to empathy, Binmore highlights the concept of "empathetic preferences." These are expressed when we state that we would prefer to be one person in a certain set of circumstances rather than another in a different set (Binmore 1994, 59). Unlike personal preferences, which reflect individual tastes, there are empathetic preferences to account for the different preferences of others.

When we empathize, we don't abandon our own identity or preferences but rather engage with the perspectives of others. For instance, expressing empathetic preferences might involve saying that we would prefer to be a modest Eve wearing a fig leaf rather than immodest Adam eating an apple, knowing that he likes apples (Binmore 2005). If a person has a consistent set of empathetic preferences in different possible situations, they can compare the utility of Adam and Eve using von Neumann and Morgenstern's utility scales, which are based on personal preferences. This process enables us to determine the rate at which Adam's utilities can be traded for Eve's. However, Binmore notes that this is still an intrapersonal comparison, meaning it compares the utilities of different individuals as perceived by a single person, rather than making true interpersonal utility comparisons.

Empathy and empathetic preferences bring us closer to utility comparisons. However, the problem still exists, as they all are intrapersonal rather than interpersonal. As Binmore does not want to rely on any non-natural and a priori theory of an objective way of comparing utilities, like many utilitarian "*ideal observer*" theories, he could be forced to abandon this way of reasoning. However, there is a naturalistic way of interpreting it, started by Harsanyi.

He asserts that at some deep level people are similar and that when the effects of our upbringing and other individual distortions are eliminated, our empathetic preferences are supposed to be essentially the same (Harsanyi 1977, 59). But while Harsanyi could ignore these differences on the basis of his moral theory, Binmore, who actually wants to build his moral theory on the basis of empathetic preferences, cannot do so. In this point, he rescues his theory by posing that, in actuality, interpersonal comparisons of utility conducted by people with similar cultural backgrounds, social statuses, and personalities are very similar (Binmore 1994, 62).

The important point here is to understand what empathetic preferences are really. The orthodox way of describing preferences is to construct them after the choices of a person are made; they are not mental constructs according to which people are supposed to act, but a posteriori descriptions of choices that have been made. Empathetic preferences are not choices, but they are inputs that we use in the original position, and we can describe them after observing how people behave and coordinate their actions. Binmore claims that they are cultural memes which are common knowledge (Binmore 2005, 126). We do not acquire them as some mathematical functions, but as behavior patterns: children observe how others coordinate and "divide the cake" and imitate these behaviors, thus acquiring empathetic preferences. Binmore here subscribes to the "memetic" version of a theory of social evolution based on imitation, where the payoffs in the game are determined by whatever makes the bearer of a meme a locus for the replication of the meme to other bearers. The most obvious interpretation of this mechanism is social status, where person A imitates the behavior of person B, because she has high status, which is defined by a large number of persons imitating her (Binmore 1998, 260).

Evolutionary arguments are crucial to Binmore's theory, for several reasons. First, the games our species is playing must have been around for some time for us to adjust to them: "The best that one hopes for is a theory that would predict human behavior in games in which players have had enough time for their behavior to adjust to their incentives through trial-and-error learning" (Binmore 2005, 75). On one level, this might be read as an assertion that, when describing social behavior, we cannot use one-shot games, but repeated games instead, so that agents can have some time to learn how to play. But there also is a second meaning here – as most of the processes of learning are supposed to happen on a cultural or even biological level, it will always take some time for this to happen. Second, it is due to evolution that our social contract is in place, as it has helped us reach complex social arrangements that are difficult to police. In many cases, policing the deal can be detrimental to the immediate concerns of the individual. An example would be a situation where someone betrays us in a game instead of following a cooperative strategy, but punishment would put some cost on us. As rational agents are not likely to pay that cost, the option of punishing someone for not following the rules of the game will not be a successful deterrent. But in such a situation, emotions might change the game itself: anger or desire for vengeance will decrease the cost of punishment or increase the payoff from punishing.

## Binmore's Social Contract

The concept of the original position in Binmore's theory is similar to the Golden Rule: treat others as you would like to be treated. The Golden Rule likely originated within mutual insurance contracts, first established among family members and later extended to others. In evolutionary terms, when two animals are able to monitor each other's behavior, they can achieve outcomes similar to those obtained through legally binding contracts with external enforcement (Binmore 2005, 139). Mutual insurance works like bargaining behind a veil of ignorance, where individuals don't know if they will be lucky or unlucky. To engage in this, one must imagine themselves in the shoes of their future selves. Evolution favored individuals capable of this kind of imagination if mutual insurance proved adaptive. As a result, the neural mechanisms necessary for insurance and future self-imagination evolved into what directs the original position. However, insurance contracts against hunger were probably not common among strangers, as trust and long-term cooperation were easier to maintain within families. The next evolutionary step was a fortunate error – mistaking a stranger for a family member, which led to the application of cooperative behaviors to nonkin. Although this did not always succeed, it occasionally resulted in effective equilibrium solutions.

In summary, the evolutionary development of the original position followed three steps. Initially, individuals behind a "veil of uncertainty" insured each other against hunger, using only sympathy for themselves and the ability to imagine future scenarios. The second step involved the "veil of ignorance," where empathy toward others was necessary as individuals did not know who they would become after negotiations. Finally, the third step led to a utilitarian or egalitarian social contract, depending on the presence of external enforcement mechanisms. Binmore's version of egalitarianism is unusual and differs from what most philosophers would describe. It does not specify any particular social institutions, rights, or liberties, nor does it detail any social practices. Instead, it focuses on the abstract form of the distribution of goods. Even so, the results would likely surprise many traditional egalitarians or utilitarians.

Binmore's theory goes beyond merely describing the social contract and its origins. A recurring theme in his work is the call to apply the concept of the original position on a broader scale than it is currently utilized. He advocates the use of this device not just for small-scale negotiations or personal interactions, but as a tool to address larger social and coordination issues:

> I would like to see the original position used as Rawls envisaged to focus the reforming zeal of those among us who think our children's children would lead more satisfying lives in a more fair society. But I differ from most people with similar aspirations in believing that its potential for solving social problems will evaporate if we fail to use it for large-scale purposes in the same way we currently use it when settling picayune fairness questions. (Binmore 2005, 21)

Binmore argues that applying fairness on a larger scale is compatible with human nature, as fairness is already a familiar tool for individuals. Expanding its use to broader social contexts is, in his view, not difficult. However, he does not offer a normative justification for this, as he rejects the idea of objective moral truths or normative principles, viewing them merely as expressions of personal preference. Despite this, he promotes his approach as both feasible and optimal for addressing social coordination and fairness on a wider scale. He calls his proposal "whiggery," an apt name for planned decentralization, which means an increase in the scope of the use of fairness to solve the issues of distribution of goods in society.

## TWO WORLDS AT ONCE

Hayek embraced an evolutionary theory of ethics similar to that of Binmore. Ethical rules are not invented rationally but are a product of evolution. Some behaviors, according to Hayek, support the development and persistence of what he termed "the Great Society" or "extended order," while other behaviors hinder it. Historically, the rise of the Great Society occurred because people engaged in behaviors that encouraged social and cultural survival while avoiding those that did not. These successful behavioral patterns became widespread over time. Hayek's ethics trace the evolution of human societies from small hunter-gatherer tribes to the Great Society. In early human history, survival depended on group cohesion. Deviation from established practices could threaten the group's survival, fostering deep-rooted ethical norms that persist today. Human civilization, being a relatively recent phenomenon, has not entirely replaced this biological-cultural heritage. Thus, the key ethical principles of the extended order were not deliberately created but gradually discovered through centuries or even millennia of social evolution (Hayek 1988). Hayek's evolutionary history of ethics is simpler than modern ones that use game theory or other similar tools, but the core of the argument is not too dissimilar. Hayek views institutions such as money, language, law, and markets as spontaneous orders, emerging naturally without design. Similarly, modern industrial society arises from people following evolved rules of justice. However, since these rules conflict with our long-evolved instincts and are not products of reason, the challenge is to ensure adherence to them despite rationalism and our inherited moral tendencies.

## Hayek's Two Worlds

Hayek proposed that we face the difficulty of navigating between two systems of norms: the macrocosm, the wider society and the market, where formal, impersonal rules are in place, and the microcosm, intimate relationships, where small-scale ethics is appropriate. The micro world does not only mean families, but also groups such as sports clubs, friendships, companies, and music bands. Hayek argues that the values essential for the extended order of liberty, such as respect for rights, or the Golden Rule, are generated within smaller social units or microcosms. These ideas allow the larger system of contracts, consumer interactions, and the rule of law to function smoothly. This extended order reduces the barriers to interacting with strangers. In contrast to the state of nature, where strangers were met with violence, in the modern world, we engage with them through trade, turning potential conflict into economic exchange (Horwitz 2005). But we always need to be wary of applying the logic of the macrocosm to the microcosm, as it may destroy it and with it, also the source of the values that enable the extended order:

> Part of our present difficulty is that we must constantly adjust our lives, our thoughts and our emotions, in order to live simultaneously within the different kinds of orders according to different rules. If we were to apply the unmodified, uncurbed, rules of the microcosmos (i.e. of the small band or troop, or of, say, our families) to the macro-cosmos (our wider civilization), as our instincts and sentimental yearnings often make us wish to do, we would destroy it. Yet if we were always to apply the rules of the extended order to our more intimate groupings, we would crush them. So we must learn to live in two sorts of worlds at once. (Hayek 1988, 18)

We can understand this quote in several ways. Insisting on a strict separation to keep both in balance is one. But we can also focus on what it means to "apply the *unmodified*, uncurbed, rules of the microcosmos," that is, to see that some of the rules of the microcosm could be applied in the wider world, but only after the proper modification and while being curbed by other rules. However, we need to note that both types of rules are not really capable of being articulated and explicitly transmitted, but are learned through observation and imitation. Additionally, Hayek notices that some of the small-scale rules are actually "hardwired" by our evolutionary past and we are guided by our instincts rather than by learned behavior. They are also in conflict with the rules that enable prosperity and peace of the Great Society.

The reason is in Hayek's theory of the origin of abstract rules. In Hayek's theory of mind, people are guided by abstract rules, which they often cannot articulate or are even unaware of following. Such rules constitute the majority of the laws and morality that underpin every civilization. Most of its principles, and certainly all the fundamental ones, did not arise from rational reflection but from an accidental process of adopting rules that regulate the behavior of individuals. Those that proved effective survived, without any philosophical justification (Hayek 1960, 46). The rules were followed because of the effects they had on the group that adhered to them. Thanks to these rules, the group could be more effective; its members lived in relatively greater prosperity, attracted members of other groups, or otherwise grew and displaced others. This did not need to be a process understood by the members of the groups, who, if asked, probably would not have been able to articulate the principles that contributed to their success (Hayek 2012, 11). The understanding that they were guided by certain principles came much later than their adherence to them.

By recognizing the imperfections of the cognitive process, one can still discover some of the principles that govern societies that have survived under their influence, precisely through understanding their evolutionary character. This requires that the principles we uncover contribute to the success of given communities, even if only by facilitating coordination. Coordination, in fact, is the fundamental problem society must face because, apart from small, primitive communities with shared goals and individuals who know each other well, all societies face the diversity of goals and the differing knowledge and skills of individuals. Rules are needed that allow people to form probable expectations about the actions of others and to establish cooperation, knowing in advance how its fruits will be distributed. None of these elements need to be centrally coordinated; moreover, for the process to be effective, they should not.

Civilization, in this sense, is an order through which individuals can predict and rely on their predictions, contributing to increased stability. It is also an entity that serves as a transmitter of knowledge, allowing one to benefit from knowledge they do not possess, not necessarily through contact with the person who holds that knowledge. This is achieved through the ability to use dispersed knowledge, embodied in institutions, rules, ethical codes, the market, etc. (Hayek 2012).

The extended order enables the coordination of human actions and the resolution of cooperation problems without any formal agreement – it is the source of peace, not rational consent as in contractual theories. Hayek recalls two categories used by the Greeks to describe the world: *taxis* and *cosmos*. *Taxis* refers to an order deliberately established, simple, and possessing a designer. *Cosmos*, on the other hand, is complex, not easily perceived in a simple way, arising unintentionally and spontaneously. It can only be described through abstract relations between the defined properties of its elements (Kuniński 1999, 112). Spontaneous order belongs to the category of *cosmos*. As we can see, this order had no designer assigning it a purpose, but its individual elements, that is, individuals, act purposefully, thus maintaining it. In the long run, the coordinating function of this order optimizes the actions of individuals, which is why one can rely on the effectiveness of the principles it develops.

The creation of order did not require the actions of individuals to be united by a common goal – it was sufficient that they were similar to some extent. This extent influenced the character of the order and its effectiveness in coordinating individuals' actions and enabling them to benefit from dispersed knowledge (Hayek 1960). Hayek refers to a special kind of order, not necessarily existing in every civilization, as *catallaxy,* the market order, best suited for coordinating the actions of individuals who do not know each other and do not share common goals. For successfully navigating this order, the most important skill is the ability to follow abstract rules of conduct, which are necessary due to the imperfection of our knowledge of the world. However, this imperfection is not a problem – one does not need to know exact facts or always, for example, perform a utilitarian calculus of pleasures, but rather must know what behaviors are considered appropriate in a given situation. In this way, we do not destroy the order that created us and gave us the ability to survive. Most of these rules are passed down through the process of socialization, without conscious awareness, allowing us access to the knowledge of previous generations. Moreover, since these principles constitute our system of thinking, there is more wisdom within them than we could create on our own.

An example of a successful spontaneous order is, of course, Western civilization, which Hayek also calls the Great Society. It is based, as mentioned earlier, on principles and patterns of behavior not fully understood by the individuals who follow them, yet they are neither imposed nor designed. Spontaneous order is another illustration of the rationality embedded in institutions, as a result of customs and habits, rather than an understanding of all cause-and-effect relationships.

However, we need to note that, despite underlining the role of imitation in learning, Hayek does not advocate mindless subjection to the rules of the macrocosm. If we want to understand and justify the extended order, our rational faculty is here to help:

> Only a mental reconstruction of the overall order of the Great Society enables us to comprehend that the deliberate aim at concrete common purposes, which to most people still appear as more meritorious and superior to blind obedience to abstract rules, would destroy that larger order in which all human beings count alike. (Hayek 2012, 301)

It is trivial, of course, to conform to the rules by reacting to incentives or by imitation. What is meant here is not understanding how an individual is to act but rather how to justify the rules. A justification of the system lies not in its conformity to instinctual desires, but in the consequences it produces, peace and plenty. This Hayekian insight about the two types of worlds is an important one, and a political philosophy that ignores it does so at its own peril, and a full example of that we can see in the egalitarian philosophy of Binmore.

## Who Doesn't Want to Live in Two Worlds?

Certainly, we can find philosophers that do not want to listen to Hayek's warning and readily apply the rules of the microcosm to the macrocosm or the other way around. Horwitz even argues that:

> (…) every kind of totalitarian regime or authoritarian regime is trying to take the values of the microcosm and apply them to the macrocosm. Nazism is tribalism for one race; fascism is tribalism for one country; communism is tribalism for one class. It's trying to take those notions of social solidarity and intimacy from the microcosm and apply them to the macrocosm, and when you do that, you destroy liberty and the rule of law. (Gillespie 2018)

But there can be many ways of applying the rules of one level to the other. As an illustration, I will briefly mention how this is done in both ways in some respects by Michael Huemer and Ayn Rand. Later, I return to the theory of Ken Binmore as an illustration of many egalitarian theories.

Huemer provides a fascinating argumentation where he uses common sense logic to justify libertarian philosophy and show that the government does not have political authority. Including Huemer in a list of philosophers who mix the Hayekian two worlds might be considered surprising. Huemer does not advocate structuring large-scale institutions according to how families or clubs work. But there is an element of applying the logic that we use in resolving small-scale problems to how a legal system should be organized. Huemer proposes that all comprehensive moral and political doctrines are controversial and cannot be used in a convincing argumentation (Huemer 2012). Therefore, to analyze the issues, he only uses very concrete, low-level moral premises, instead of abstract moral theories. When deciding whether the state has a right to tax or imprison someone, he advises us to consider under what circumstances an individual would have that right. If we conclude that neither a hypothetical contract, consequences, nor democratic voting would lead to an individual or a group of individuals acquiring political authority, this shows that the state also does not have such authority. We will not analyze in detail the argument that Huemer provides, just show that there is an assumption here that the same system of rules is in place for individuals and the governments, and we can use the small-scale, individual-level considerations to draw conclusions about the desired shape of the extended order. Hayek's insights about two systems of rules cast doubt on the suitability of Huemer's procedure.

We can use the philosophy of Ayn Rand as a striking example of a reverse process, applying the rules of the extended order to govern that of family. Rand famously advocated for rational egoism, where all an individual owes to others is that he has to avoid the use of force and fraud and keep their contracts (Badhwar and Long, 2023). However, she did not stop at applying this thinking to political or economic issues. In fact, she was fiercely insistent on applying her ideas comprehensively, even to family life: "Devotion to the family was a con game in Rand's view, in which the weaker and irresponsible family members are dependent on those who are stronger. Frequently, the relations within the family mirror those of master and slave. Just as the stronger members are exploited, they are also obeyed" (Sciabarra 2013, 249). We can see here what Hayek meant by "crushing" the intimate grouping with the rules of the macrocosm.

Finally, returning to game theory and Binmore's proposal, the system he is arguing for, "whiggery," is basically a decentralized expansion of the usage of the original position in the wider society. However, while Binmore advocates for applying fairness on a broader scale, he does not clearly define what that entails. Compulsory sharing common in hunter-gatherer societies and their tightly knit social contract would likely be intolerable for most people in modern societies. He might be suggesting a form of large-scale redistribution and higher taxation for the wealthy, but this is not clearly specified. Given the complexity of his fairness model, one might expect him to connect it to some more concrete features of economic systems or practical implications. This framework could be used to analyze aspects of modern society and design practical solutions such as social security or public healthcare. However, Binmore does not really do this; neither is he trying to show that his favored solution, expanding the scope of fairness, is actually stable or feasible to be used in modern societies.

This is even more perplexing due to the fact that Binmore is fond of criticizing philosophers he calls "traditional moralists" for not analyzing whether the solutions they propose are usable on a large scale. Particularly, he issues warnings that one would think are taken from Hayek: "I have repeatedly emphasized that I think it highly misleading to generalize from the social arrangements of small close-knit groups to society as a whole" (Binmore 1994, 287). He cautions against applying norms and behavior patterns outside the contexts for which they evolved. Binmore acknowledges that fairness itself is one such pattern and that people struggle to extend it beyond the environment in which it developed (Binmore 1998, 36). This aligns with modern evolutionary psychology and its "mismatch theory," suggesting that our moral psychology evolved for small group living and does not provide the proper incentives or constraints to function effectively in modern societies (Li, van Vugt and Colarelli 2017). We might suspect that equal sharing has been an effective survival strategy in the past, and genetic predispositions may still lead us to favor it, but the question remains: Why should it continue to be relevant today? Here we find that he agrees with the Hayekian point about the atavistic instincts manifesting in the large-scale society: "We are predisposed toward a kind of social behavior appropriate to a hunter-gatherer society, but these behavioral predispositions have been overwritten by cultural imperatives without which we couldn't [have] been so productive" (Binmore 2005, 137). Yet, expanding the scope of fairness like Binmore proposes would overturn some of those key imperatives. To support this point, Binmore criticizes behavioral studies and claims that they show that people understand and cooperate in Prisoner's Dilemma games: "My own view is that the result simply reflects our confusion over the concept of fairness when it is applied outside the domain for which it evolved" (Binmore 1998, 37). The claim here is that if cooperation in such games is observed, it is because people mistakenly apply the norms from outside the laboratory and they do not understand the rules of the game. However, applying fairness norms at different scales than they evolved in can also be considered as changing the domain for which they evolved. It is interesting that we can find this very Hayekian warning in Binmore's own work that aims to argue for a wider usage of fairness norms.

My goal here is not to dismiss Binmore's theory. I think it is a formidable work and provides an understanding of the evolution of fairness. The difference between the interpretation provided here is that Binmore seems to be showing how and why fairness has a tendency to seem to be a justified and optimal choice, not why it actually is. Thanks to him, however, we can understand that fairness is a part of our evolutionary baggage; it served us in the past and is unlikely to go away. Philosophies based on it are powerful and have emotional force. At the same time, armed with Hayekian insights, we can more accurately apply the warning that Binmore himself is issuing: do not use norms outside the environment to which they are adapted.

## BORDER BETWEEN THE WORLDS

After proposing a Hayekian understanding of two orders and seeing examples of breaking those barriers, like Rand, Huemer, and Binmore do, we may then try to find how exactly we should place the barrier so that we do not either crush the small-scale order or destroy the Great Society. Here I want to disappoint the reader and not provide the precise placement of such a wall, but I will give reasons for this disappointment. Then I want to show that this is what we would expect and how the two orders should not be really thought of as entirely separate.

## Abstract Barrier

If I were a modern analytical moral theorist I would try to find a way to define the precise place for the border between the microcosm and macrocosm, possibly by introducing some necessary conditions for the rules that govern both worlds. We could start from some widely shared moral considerations or from the logical structure of moral ideas in order to find a supreme principle from which we can deduce the rest of morality. So to answer our issue of delineation, we would find out some crucial difference between the rules of the macrocosm and microcosm. We could then state which level of organizations is large enough that the rules of the microcosm cannot apply beyond it, and we should not use them at all. This is a procedure that would be familiar to what many modern moral theorists do, as discussed by Heath (2023). Many analytical anarchists or austro-libertarians would also probably proceed in such a way, defining the border in a priori fashion, with some important differences between them and a more mainstream Kantian or utilitarian approach. It could also be tempting for a liberal theorist to use such an approach to exclude any possibilities for collectivistic thought, as many agree with Hayek that it is the expansion of small-scale ethics into large-scale society that underlies many nonliberal approaches: "I believe that an atavistic longing after the life of the noble savage is the main source of the collectivist tradition" (Hayek 1988, 19).

However, if we share the naturalistic and evolutionary approaches of Binmore and Hayek, we should be skeptical of the usefulness of such admittedly popular abstract theorizing. We first focus on understanding the sources of normative claims, how they evolved, and what problems they solve. If morality lives rather in our actions and practices rather than abstract concepts and is transmitted culturally, when using the approach of purely analytical moral theory, we only craft expressive vocabulary of the underlying moral concepts, but we do not discover deep facts about morality that would let us decide where to put the border between the two worlds. These doubts are strengthened by Schaefer, who argues that the very idea of finding one fixed point of justice is a misguided attempt and that we should be rather concerned with the processes of dynamic adjustment (Schaefer 2023). The same can be said about delimitation between the two worlds. In short, I don't think there is a unique place that can be announced as "the" border between macrocosm and microcosm that would be binding for every society.

## Mutual Influence

The delineation of the border between the worlds is all the more difficult due to the fact that they are not independent of each other. First, we can note that Hayek proposes that the very existence of the Great Society depends on and consists of the lower-level order, as it enables cooperation: "Moreover, the structures of the extended order are made up not only of individuals but also of many, often overlapping, sub-orders within which old instinctual responses, such as solidarity and altruism, continue to retain some importance by assisting voluntary collaboration, even though they are incapable, by themselves, of creating a basis for the more extended order" (Hayek 1988, 18). But we can add to that framework several points, showing how the two systems of rules shape each other and also that the intimate microcosm, despite our positive associations with it, can be a pretty severe place without the macrocosm.

Experiments in behavioral economics done by the team led by Joseph Henrich (Henrich et al. 2005) show that market integration is the best predictor of the propensity to cooperate and altruism towards the nonkin. During studies on three hunter-gatherers, six horticulturalists, four nomadic herders, and four small-scale sedentary farmers in Africa, Latin America, and Asia, members played standard ultimatum, public goods, and trust games. In all these societies, as well as advanced industrial societies, most humans exhibit a high degree of moral motivation and sacrifice some monetary gains to achieve fair results. This also happens in one-shot situations, when perfectly rational agents should not do that. But there are differences in the degree of moral behavior, and these differences coincide with the level of market exposure. The higher the market integration of these societies, the higher the level of empathetic and fair behavior. Markets indeed produced more inequality, but at the same time were not responsible for generating what they are commonly accused of causing – selfish behavior, on the contrary. Some might associate Hayekian microcosm with empathy and contrast it with the uncaring market of the macrocosm. But as we can see, this study shows that while people may be empathetic toward their family, the greater their participation in wider markets, the greater their empathy for strangers. We should not understand the original microcosm as a paradise of noble savages. While we might have innate yearnings to use the solutions that Binmore describes in his theory, as Boehm shows, the tribe is not a place of empathy, freeloading, and openness. It is full of vigilant monitoring and finding out what you can get away with (Boehm 1999). Cooperation sustained by the Folk Theorem is actually a good approximation of how this works, and the level of mutual policing required in it would probably be deemed unacceptable by a member of any modern society.

To further complicate the mutual relationship between the two worlds in which we live, Horwitz (2015) urges us to look at the history of family. Similarly to the microcosm of the tribe, historically family was not an institution that was in stark opposition to the prudential considerations of the markets. In fact, Horwitz shows how children were viewed in much more explicit economic terms, as a resource. They could be used for labor in the field, as pension for the future, or as means to secure an alliance. The Great Society both removed the economic necessity of child labor and displaced intra-family responsibility for retirement. As a result, family relationships became less instrumental and more oriented toward care. Fulfilling the psychological needs of all the members of the household and self-actualization became possible thanks to the extended order.

So, it looks like the two systems are quite interdependent and shape each other, rather than exist in a clean separation. It would be strange to accuse the extended order of being an uncaring, unempathetic place if we owe the origins of empathetic behavior to its very existence. But due to this and the fact that the process of mutual shaping between the two worlds still occurs, it seems impossible to permanently divide them according to some rule. It would be much more sensible to see the division between these two systems constantly change and be renegotiated, and finding solutions here is a practical issue rather than theoretical.

However, the practical matter is not only finding the right place of delineation, which may differ in societies, but also finding the strategy to use both endowments. We do have an evolutionary baggage of inclinations for both microcosm and macrocosm, as our ancestors were not only living in tribes for the last thousands of years but also traded. Many market-friendly theorists have often ignored the microcosm, to their own peril, only for its rules to be used by tyrants and demagogues in promoting the more "natural" ways of living.

## CONCLUSION

There is some affinity between the approaches of Binmore and Hayek, and it is a bit surprising that game theory has not been more widely used in analyses that are influenced by Hayek. More bizarrely, anything remotely associated with libertarian approaches is dismissed by Binmore as having "no relevance to genuine human concerns" (Binmore 1998, 164). This text is an attempt at remedying that and showing that in terms of focus on the history of our moral and political orders, their theories can be used together. Both thinkers agree on what is the source of ethical rules; it is not reason, nor pure instinct, but evolution: "Ethics is the last fortress in which human pride must now bow in recognition of its origins. Such an evolutionary theory of morality is indeed emerging, and its essential insight is that our morals [are] neither instinctual nor a creation of reason but constitute a separate tradition – between instinct and reason" (Hayek 1988, 10). Both thinkers are concerned with understanding how morality can serve as a decentralized coordination device and that ethical principles depend on the institutional context. Indeed, fairness is shown to have evolved as a means of balancing power, not its substitute: "To behave morally is not to transcend the need for compromise. On the contrary, morality evolved in our species because a successful human society needs to institutionalize the compromises that allow it to operate" (Binmore 1994, 4). This shows careful respect for morality as a coordination device, rather than something that can replace all other considerations. Their evolutionary approach is similar, and even if both have opposite preferences when it comes to public policy, both also seem to be much more interested in explanations of why we arrived at what we have rather than on moral criticism.

One of the goals of Binmore is to promote the use of fairness in solving large-scale coordination issues. The argumentation described here shows why this might be a misguided attempt. Hayekian insights show that we need to appreciate the role of both macrocosm and microcosm, and Binmore's proposal threatens to break their balance. Despite their differences, the theories can intersect in fruitful ways. Through both, we can understand why applying the rules of the microcosm to the macrocosm is often misguided, yet why it happens so frequently. Binmore's theory, in particular, helps explain why fairness captures our attention so powerfully.

## REFERENCES

Badhwar N., Long. R. (2023). Ayn Rand, in Zalta E., Nodelman U. (eds.), *The Stanford Encyclopedia of Philosophy*. https://plato.stanford.edu/archives/win2023/entries/ayn-rand/ [Accessed at 21.06.2025].

Binmore K. (1994). *Game Theory and the Social Contract. Volume 1: Playing Fair.* Boston, MA: MIT Press.

Binmore K. (1998). *Game Theory and the Social Contract. Volume 2: Just Playing.* Boston, MA: MIT Press.

Binmore K. (2005). *Natural Justice.* Oxford, UK: Oxford University Press.

Binmore K. (2009). *Rational Decisions.* Princeton, NJ: Princeton University Press.

Boehm C. (1999). *Hierarchy in the Forest : The Evolution of Egalitarian Behavior.* Cambridge, MA: Harvard University Press.

Gillespie N. (2018). The Tribe of Liberty. *Reason.* https://reason.com/2018/09/24/the-tribe-of-liberty/ [Accessed at 26.12.2025].

Gintis H. (2009). *The Bounds of Reason: Game Theory and the Unification of the Behavioral Sciences.* Princeton, NJ: Princeton University Press.

Harsanyi J. (1977). *Rational Behaviour and Bargaining Equilibrium in Games and Social Situations.* Cambridge, UK: Cambridge University Press.

Hayek F. von (1960). *The Constitution of Liberty.* London: Routledge and Kegan Paul.

Hayek F. von (1988). *The Fatal Conceit: The Errors of Socialism.* London: Routledge and Chicago: University of Chicago Press.

Hayek F. von (2012). *Law, Legislation and Liberty.* London: Routledge.

Heath J. (2023). An explicitative conception of moral theory, in Weinstock D., Levy J., Maclure J. (eds.), *Interpreting Modernity.* Montreal: McGill-Queen's University Press, pp. 160–181.

Henrich J., Boyd R., Bowles S., Camerer C., Fehr E., Gintis H. (2005). *Foundations of Human Sociality: Economic Experiments and Ethnographic Evidence from Fifteen Small-Scale Societies.* Oxford, UK: Oxford University Press.

Horwitz S. (2015). *Hayek's Modern Family: Classical Liberalism and the Evolution of Social Institutions.* New York, NY: Palgrave Macmillan.

Huemer M. (2012). *The Problem of Political Authority: An Examination of the Right to Coerce and the Duty to Obey.* New York, NY: Palgrave Macmillan.

Kuniński M. (1999). *Wiedza, etyka i polityka w myśli F.A. von Hayeka.* Kraków: Księgarnia Akademicka (in Polish).

Li N., van Vugt M., Colarelli S. (2017). The Evolutionary Mismatch Hypothesis: Implications for Psychological Science. *Current Directions in Psychological Science*, 27(1), pp. 38–44.

Pinker S. (2015). The false allure of group selection, in Buss D. (ed.), *The Handbook of Evolutionary Psychology*, Hoboken, NJ: John Wiley & Sons, pp. 867–880.

Rasmusen E. (2006). *Games and Information: An Introduction to Game Theory.* Oxford, UK: Basil Blackwell.

Rawls J. (1999). *A Theory Of Justice.* Revised edition. Cambridge, MA: The Belknap Press of Harvard University Press.

Schaefer, A. (2023). Is Justice a Fixed Point? *American Journal of Political Science*, 67(2), pp. 277–90.

Sciabarra C. (2013). *Ayn Rand : The Russian Radical.* University Park, PA: The Pennsylvania State University Press.

Woodburn, J. (1982). Egalitarian Societies. *Man*, 17(3), pp. 431–451.

# Index